Shakespeare Stories II

Also by Leon Garfield and Michael Foreman
SHAKESPEARE STORIES

SHAKESPEARE STORIES II

Leon Garfield

illustrated by

MICHAEL FOREMAN

VICTOR GOLLANCZ

LONDON

To the Editors, past and present

First published in Great Britain 1994
by Victor Gollancz
A Cassell imprint
Villiers House, 41/47 Strand, London WC2N 5JE

Text © Leon Garfield 1994
Illustrations © Michael Foreman 1994

The right of Leon Garfield and Michael Foreman
to be identified as authors of this work has
been asserted by them in accordance with the
Copyright, Designs and Patents Act 1988.

A catalogue record for this book
is available from the British Library

ISBN 0 575 05049 7

Photoset in Great Britain by
Rowland Phototypesetting Ltd,
Bury St Edmunds, Suffolk
Printed in Singapore by
Imago Publishing Limited

Contents

Colour Plates

Much Ado About Nothing

Signior Benedick of Padua was a man's man, and he cared not who knew it! While his master, Don Pedro, Prince of Arragon, had perfumed and barbered himself like a smirking bridegroom for his visit to old Leonato, the Governor of Messina, and all the Prince's officers were polished like brass candlesticks, he, Benedick, had scorned to change his soldier's attire, and he wore a beard as fierce as a bush.

They were in Leonato's clipped and trellised garden which seemed, to his soldier's eye, absolutely infested with all the taffeta ladies of Messina, flouncing and fluttering their fans like monstrous butterflies. Most heartily he wished himself back on the battlefield. However, he was gentleman enough not to say so, and to stifle his yawns as Don Pedro and Leonato exchanged interminable compliments.

"I think this is your daughter," said Don Pedro, bowing to a simpering miss by name of Hero, who peeped out from under her cap like a mouse in an attic.

"Her mother hath many times told me so," said Leonato with a little laugh, and laid a fond arm about his daughter's shoulders.

This was too much! "Were you in doubt, sir, that you asked her?" said Benedick, who could not endure affectation. At once, he was taken to task by Don Pedro. He defended himself vigorously; when a sharp, cold voice interrupted:

9

"I wonder that you will still be talking, Signior Benedick, nobody marks you."

It was, of course, Beatrice, Leonato's niece, who'd spoken. He'd seen her from the first, in her daffodil gown, spying him out with her cat's eyes, and, as usual, biding her time to pounce. He'd hoped that, for once, she'd hold her tongue; but no!

"What, my dear Lady Disdain," said he, as if surprised that a person of such insignificance should address him, "are you yet living?"

She flew at him like a fury, with insults that a fish-wife might have shrunk from. He parried as best he could, and delivered some sharp thrusts of his own, which, he was pleased to see, brought fire into the lady's cheeks and smiles to the faces of the eager audience. Nonetheless, he was not sorry when Leonato laughingly interposed to invite the company into his mansion.

Two remained behind: Benedick, who needed time to compose himself after his brisk encounter with that harpy, Beatrice, and his friend young Claudio the Florentine, who had been making sheep's eyes at the Governor's meek daughter.

"In mine eye, she is the sweetest lady that ever I looked on!" sighed Claudio.

Benedick shrugged his shoulders. "I can see yet without spectacles," said he, "and I see no such matter. There's her cousin, and she were not possessed of a fury, exceeds her as much in beauty as the first of May doth the last of December." This was true. Though he disliked her heartily, he had to admit that Beatrice was indeed beautiful. He looked at Claudio sharply. "But I hope you have no intent to turn husband, have you?"

Alas! that was Claudio's intention. Benedick threw up his hands in disgust. "Is't come to this?" he cried, outraged that any man, in full possession of his senses, should thrust his neck into the yoke of matrimony and lose his glorious freedom. "Shall I never see a bachelor of threescore again?" he mourned, and was about to depart when Don Pedro came out of the Governor's mansion to see what had detained his two officers.

Benedick lost no time in telling him. "He is in love," he said contemptuously, and pointed to Claudio. "With who? Mark how short his answer is. With Hero, Leonato's short daughter."

But Don Pedro did not share Benedick's scorn. He respected Claudio's feelings, and, turning to Benedick, prophesied, "I shall see thee, ere I die, look pale with love."

Benedick shook his head. "With anger, with sickness, or with hunger, my lord," he promised, "not with love."

"Well, if ever thou dost fall—"

"If I do, hang me in a bottle like a cat, and shoot at me!" cried Benedick; and off he went, laughing.

Don Pedro shook his head. He turned to Claudio. He felt a fatherly concern for the young man. The innocence of young love touched him deeply.

"My liege, your highness may now do me good," murmured Claudio, with an anxious look in his eyes. Don Pedro smiled encouragingly; and the lover put the question that was troubling him. "Hath Leonato any son, my lord?"

Don Pedro was a little taken aback. Young love, it seemed, had a practical turn of mind. "No child but Hero," he told Claudio, "she is his only heir."

Claudio's brow cleared; till another doubt struck him. Would not his love seem too sudden to be believed? But Don Pedro reassured him. He himself would undertake the campaign to win fair Hero's heart for his young friend. That night, there was to be music and dancing in Leonato's house. The gentlemen would be masked, so that he, Don Pedro, would be able to present himself as Claudio, and, with his superior skill, woo the innocent Hero in Claudio's name. "And the conclusion is," said he, with an all-conquering smile, "she shall be thine!"

While young Claudio's heart overflowed with gratitude to his kindly master, there was one who wished that princely gentleman to the devil: his bastard brother, the grim-faced, black-suited, black-hearted Don John. In the late war, Don John had fought against him; and, in the happy flush of victory, Don Pedro had forgiven him. For this gracious act, Don John hated him the more. "I had rather be a canker in a hedge, than a rose in his grace," he muttered to his smooth-faced follower, Conrade; then he scowled heavily as sounds of revelry from Leonato's supper-table drifted faintly into his apartment as the door was opened.

"What news, Borachio?" he demanded, as another of his followers appeared.

The news was of a betrothal. Borachio, a slippery lurker behind curtains, hedges and doors, had overheard Don Pedro and Claudio. Don John's thin lips grew tight as a miser's purse. "That young start-up," he remembered, with savage anger, "hath all the glory of my overthrow. If I can cross him any way, I bless myself every way. You are both sure, and will assist me?" His companions nodded. "Let us to the great supper," said Don John; and, with poison in his thoughts, led the way. "Would the cook were o' my mind!"

The supper was over, and the music for dancing about to begin. Leonato, with the ladies of his household, awaited the arrival of the masked gentlemen. "By my troth, niece," warned Leonato, as Beatrice set about demolishing all mankind with her sharp wit, "thou wilt never get thee a husband, if thou be so shrewd of thy tongue!" But Beatrice was unrepentant, and continued with her abuse until the musicians struck up a lively measure, and the maskers appeared.

Benedick, perspiring behind his mask, watched the pairing-off of the dancers with high contempt. There went the courtly Don Pedro, invisible behind a fantastical monkey face, leading off the timid Hero, and already murmuring Claudio's love in her trembling pink ear. And there, with a golden countenance of youth (with all its teeth) hitched over his waggling old head, went Leonato's brother Antonio, happy in the possession of a pretty young woman.

Suddenly Benedick became aware that he was alone. All the maskers and all the ladies, save one, had joined the dance. Beatrice awaited him. He cursed his ill-luck, and made a hideous face behind his mask. She smiled. Plainly, she had not recognized him. He offered his arm. She took it, and away they went, warily.

After a little while, he took the opportunity, in a skilfully disguised voice, of relating some witty abuse of Beatrice that he said he'd over-heard, but declined to reveal who'd uttered it.

"Well, this was Signior Benedick that said so," she said contemptuously.

"What's he?" inquired Benedick, in as off-hand a manner as he could manage.

"I am sure you know him well enough," said Beatrice, staring sharply into the slits that were his eyes. "He is the Prince's jester, a very dull fool."

Benedick burned with indignation; but thereafter thought it wisest to hold his tongue. At last, the dancing was ended, the company dispersed about the room, and the gentlemen unmasked. Benedick found himself addressed by his master, Don Pedro.

"The Lady Beatrice hath a quarrel to you," said he, wagging a reproachful finger. "The gentleman that danced with her told her she is much wronged by you."

"O, she misused me past the endurance of a block!" cried Benedick, outraged. "She speaks poniards, and every word stabs!"

"Look, here she comes," said Don Pedro, warningly.

"Will your Grace command me any service to the world's end?" begged Benedick. "I will go on the slightest errand, rather than hold three words' conference with this harpy!" and off he went.

Don Pedro laughed to see his valiant officer scuttle from the field before a blow had been struck; then he turned to Claudio, who, together with Hero and her father, accompanied the Lady Beatrice. He had good news for the young man. "Here, Claudio," said he with an air of modest pride, "I have woo'd in thy name, and fair Hero is won. I have broke with her father, and his good will obtained."

Leonato nodded in vigorous confirmation, and Claudio was speechless with delight.

"Speak, Count, 'tis your cue," prompted Beatrice.

"Silence is the perfectest herald of joy," sighed Claudio, gazing at the blushing Hero. "Lady, as you are mine, I am yours. I give away myself for you."

"Good Lord, for alliance!" cried Beatrice. "Thus goes everyone to the world but I. I may sit in a corner and cry 'Heigh-ho for a husband!'" and she laughed.

"Lady Beatrice," offered Don Pedro, "I will get you one."

"I would rather have one of your father's getting," said she, with a smile.

"Will you have me, lady?" proposed Don Pedro, gallantly.

"No, my lord, unless I might have another for working-days. Your Grace is too costly to wear every day."

Don Pedro laughed. "You were born in a merry hour!" he declared.

"No, sure, my lord, my mother cried," returned Beatrice gravely, "but then there was a star danced, and under that was I born." She turned to Claudio and Hero, and, with a cheerful, "Cousins, God give you joy!" she departed.

Don Pedro gazed after her. "By my troth, a pleasant-spirited lady," he observed with some admiration. Then he smiled, and murmured softly, "She were an excellent wife for Benedick."

Stark amazement greeted his proposal; but Don Pedro was not to be put off. Having made one match by means of false appearances, he was determined to try his hand at another. "I will," said he, "undertake one of Hercules' labours, which is, to bring Signior Benedick and the Lady Beatrice into a mountain of affection th' one with th' other."

Eagerly he begged the others to assist him, and, when they agreed, he beckoned them close, and explained his plan . . .

★

Even as Don Pedro and his friends plotted to bring two haters into love by means of false appearances, Don John and his confederate, Borachio, were plotting to bring two lovers into hate; and by the same means. "Go you to the Prince, your brother," Borachio advised his scowling master, "tell him that he has wronged his honour in marrying the renowned Claudio to a contaminated stale, such a one as Hero."

"What proof shall I make of that?" asked Don John, wondering how so innocent a lady might be satisfactorily maligned.

"Proof enough to misuse the Prince," promised Borachio, "to vex Claudio, to undo Hero, and kill Leonato. Look you for any other issue?"

At the prospect of such widespread misery, Don John's gloomy face brightened into a smile, and he listened keenly as his companion continued.

It turned out that Borachio, that practised slipper into shadows and corners, had slipped his slithery way into the affections of Margaret, the Lady Hero's waiting gentlewoman. "I can, at any unseasonable instant of the night," he murmured, with a knowing look, "appoint her to look out at her lady's chamber-window."

"What life is in that, to be the death of this marriage?" demanded Don John, mightily puzzled.

"Go then," Borachio bade his master, "draw Don Pedro and Claudio alone. Tell them that Hero loves me. They will scarcely believe this without trial. Offer them instances, to see me at her chamber-window, hear me call Margaret Hero; and bring them to see this the very night before the intended wedding—for in the meantime I will so fashion the matter that Hero shall be absent—and there shall appear such seeming truth of Hero's disloyalty that jealousy shall be called assurance, and all the preparation overthrown."

As he listened, Don John's smile grew broader and broader. His cup was full to overflowing as he foresaw the ruin of his enemies' happiness.

The day was warm and sunny, but Benedick's mood was overcast as he walked in Leonato's garden, brooding on the fall of that fine soldier Claudio into the unmanly folly of love. Suddenly he spied his sadly altered friend, all quilted and flounced like a lady's cushion, approaching with Don Pedro and Leonato, his future father-in-law. Doubtless their talk was all of weddings. With a mutter of disgust, Benedick vanished inside a leafy arbour, and prayed to God he'd not been seen.

"See you where Benedick hath hid himself?" whispered Don Pedro.

"O, very well, my lord," came the soft reply; and the three friends halted.

"Leonato," said Don Pedro loudly, "what was it you told me of today, that your niece Beatrice was in love with Signior Benedick?"

In the arbour, a twig cracked, convulsively; then silence.

"I did never think that lady would have loved any man," said Claudio.

"Maybe she doth but counterfeit?" suggested Don Pedro.

"O God! Counterfeit?" exclaimed Leonato. "There was never counterfeit of passion, came so near the life of passion as she discovers it!"

All marvelled at this secret love for so strange an object. "You amaze me," declared Don Pedro, with his back to the arbour, "I would have thought her spirit had been invincible against all assaults of affection. Hath she made her affection known to Benedick?"

"No," sighed Leonato, "and swears she never will. That's her torment."

"'Tis true indeed," confirmed Claudio, "so your daughter says. 'Shall I,' says she, 'that have so oft encountered him with scorn, write to him that I love him?'"

"She'll be up twenty times a night," said Leonato, his white beard wagging vigorously, "and there will she sit in her smock till she hath writ a sheet of paper. My daughter tells us all."

"Then down upon her knees she falls," cried Claudio, taking up the tale and, with broad strokes, enriching it most wonderfully, "weeps, sobs, beats her heart, tears her hair, prays, curses: 'O sweet Benedick! God give me patience!'"

The three sighed together, as if overcome by the pitiable picture that Claudio had painted. Said Don Pedro, gravely, "It were good that Benedick knew of it by some other, if she will not discover it."

"To what end?" said Claudio sadly. "He would make but a sport of it, and torment the poor lady worse."

The three gentlemen sighed again. It seemed a hopeless case. The

"See you where Benedick hath hid himself?"

poor lady dared not reveal her love, for fear of its being spurned; and so must always wear her mask of cold disdain to hide her aching heart.

Don Pedro made a last effort. "Shall we go seek Benedick," he pleaded, "and tell him of her love?"

Claudio shook his head. "Never tell him, my lord. Let her wear it out with good counsel."

"Nay, that's impossible," said Leonato, "she may wear her heart out first," and the three gentlemen, with faces as long as sermons, went in to dinner.

The arbour trembled, and out came Benedick; but a very different Benedick from the one who'd gone in. "This can be no trick," he whispered, gazing after the three whose words had struck him to the very heart. "They have the truth of this from Hero." Gently, he plucked off a beetle that had been holidaying on his neck and set it tenderly upon its way to join, on uncounted hurrying feet, its lady in the green.

As if by a thunderbolt, all his notions had been overthrown, and he was consumed with love and tenderness for the pining Beatrice, and shame for himself. "I have railed so long against marriage," he remembered uncomfortably, "but doth not the appetite alter? A man loves the meat in his youth that he cannot endure in his age. When I said I would die a bachelor, I did not think I should live till I were married."

As he stood, conversing with his newly-awakened heart, the lady herself came out of the mansion and approached him briskly. "I do spy some marks of love in her," he whispered, seeing her, for the first time, with a lover's eye, which was unsupported by any evidence.

"Against my will," said she, coldly, "I am sent to bid you come in to dinner."

"Fair Beatrice, I thank you for your pains," said he, gazing at her with warmth enough to melt a stone.

But Beatrice was not stone, and was not melted. "I took no more pains for those thanks than you take pains to thank me," said she disdainfully. "If it had been painful, I would not have come," and away she went.

Benedick gazed after her, frowningly. Then his brow cleared. "Ha!"

he cried, in a sudden flash of understanding. "'Against my will I am sent to bid you come in to dinner'—there's a double meaning in that. 'I took no more pains for those thanks than you took pains to thank me'—that's as much as to say, 'Any pains that I take for you is as easy as thanks'. If I do not take pity of her, I am a villain!"

He smiled happily, as his lover's wit, like his lover's eye, divined meanings unsupported by the evidence.

Beatrice was in the devil of a hurry. She had heard from Margaret, Hero's gentlewoman, that Hero and Ursula, another of her women, were in the garden, talking about her; and such was the nature of their talk that Margaret had felt it to be her womanly duty to tell Beatrice of it.

Scornfully, Beatrice had declared that she was not interested in idle gossip; but no sooner had Margaret gone, than she'd rushed out into the garden, fearful of losing a single word. Bending low, she sped behind hedge and bush, until, with a flurry of taffeta and a flash of eager eyes, she vanished inside the very arbour that was still warm from Benedick. And only just in time. Even as she hid herself in leafy obscurity, Hero and Ursula approached, deep in conversation.

At first they were murmuring, almost whispering, and she could hear nothing; then, as if by Providence, their idle feet led them close enough to the arbour for every word to be plainly overheard. And what words they were! As she crouched in breathless silence, with every insect in creation making her its park, she heard the impossible, the unbelievable, the undreamed-of-truth! Benedick loved her!

"But are you sure?" asked Ursula; and Hero, whose innocent heart would never have entertained a lie, nodded her head. "So says the Prince and my new-trothed lord."

"And did they bid you tell her of it, madam?" asked Ursula.

They did indeed, but Hero, that interfering minx, had advised against it.

"Why did you so? Doth not the gentleman deserve as full as fortunate a bed as ever Beatrice shall couch upon?"

There was a certain measure of truth in this, which Hero readily conceded; it was Beatrice herself who was to blame. "Nature never

framed a woman's heart," said the wretched girl, "of prouder stuff than that of Beatrice. She cannot love, she is so self-endeared."

"Sure I think so," said Ursula, feebly agreeing with her mistress.

It seemed that the idle, gossiping pair of mischief-makers were acting only to spare Benedick the pain of mockery and scorn. "Therefore let Benedick, like covered fire, consume away in sighs, waste inwardly. It were a better death than die with mocks," said Hero solemnly, and added, with horrible aptness as Beatrice suffered under the delicate legs of an inquisitive spider, "which is as bad as die with tickling!" It were best that she went to Benedick and told him some harmless lies about her cousin. "One doth not know," said she, "how much an ill word may empoison liking."

"O, do not do your cousin such a wrong," pleaded Ursula. "She cannot be so much without true judgement as to refuse so rare a gentleman as Signior Benedick!"

"He is the only man of Italy," admitted Hero, then showed her own lack of judgement by adding, "always excepted my dear Claudio."

But Ursula had the better eye. "Signior Benedick," said she, "for shape, for bearing, argument and valour, goes foremost in report through Italy!"

Beatrice, in her concealment, agreed with all her heart; and when the talkers had wandered away, she came out of the arbour in a leafy, crumpled dream. "What fire is in mine ears?" she marvelled. "Can this be true? Stand I condemned for pride and scorn so much? Contempt, farewell, and maiden pride, adieu! Benedick, love on, I will requite thee!"

As Beatrice stood, dazed with the sudden onslaught of love, Hero and Ursula cautiously observed her from afar. "We have caught her, madam," whispered Ursula.

"If it prove so," whispered back Hero, "then loving goes by haps: some Cupid kills with arrows, some with traps!"

It was the day before the wedding of Claudio and Hero, and all was cheerfulness in Leonato's house. There was a strong smell of perfume in the air. It was coming from Benedick. He was a changed man. Gone was his warlike leather: the lilies of the field were not arrayed with half his glory. Gone was his beard, and it was as if an angel, not a ram, had been caught in that thicket, as a smooth young face gazed out with all a lover's melancholy.

"Gallants," he sighed to his friends, "I am not as I have been."

"Methinks you are sadder," agreed Leonato; and Claudio said, "I hope he be in love." But Don Pedro shook his head. "If he be sad," said he, "he wants money."

"I have the toothache," said Benedick, casting a bitter look at his unfeeling companions. He approached Leonato. "Old signior, walk aside with me," he murmured, "I have studied eight or nine wise words to speak to you, which these hobby-horses must not hear." And with a lofty glance at the others, he drew Leonato into another room.

"For my life," declared Don Pedro, "to break with him about Beatrice!" The Prince had accomplished his labour of Hercules; he had indeed brought Beatrice and Benedick into a mountain of affection, the one with the other.

As Don Pedro and Claudio were congratulating themselves on the success of their stratagem, a dark and gloomy presence entered the room. It was Don John.

"My lord and brother," said he, "I would speak with you."

Don Pedro frowned. "In private?"

"If it please you, yet Count Claudio may hear, for what I would speak of concerns him."

"What's the matter?"

For answer, Don John turned his grim face to Claudio. "Means your lordship to be married tomorrow?"

"You know he does," said Don Pedro impatiently.

"If there be any impediment," said Claudio, "I pray you discover it."

"I came hither to tell you," said Don John, as if what he was about to reveal was causing him great distress, "the lady is disloyal."

Claudio stared. "Who, Hero?" he said incredulously, and was prepared to laugh. The notion was preposterous.

"Even she—Leonato's Hero, your Hero, every man's Hero," said Don John, his distress increasing.

Claudio grew pale. Don John was not the man for jesting. He was not a man who talked idly. "Disloyal?" whispered Claudio, his new-found happiness trembling.

"The word is too good to paint out her wickedness," said Don John, harshly. "Go but with me tonight, you shall see her chamber-window entered, even the night before her wedding day."

Claudio turned to Don Pedro. "May this be so?" he pleaded.

"I will not think it," said Don Pedro; but the voice lacked its old assurance.

"If you will follow me," murmured Don John, "I will show you enough."

With that, he left the room. Claudio and Don Pedro stared at one another. They were suddenly filled with uncertainty. Don Pedro's plots had ended; Don John's was just beginning.

While Messina slept, the lives, the property and good name of its citizens reposed, for safe keeping, in the capable hands of its sagacious constable, Dogberry. A fine man, a large man, portly and solemn, who, when he gazed in his mirror, perceived a man of importance, a man to be admired. He had a companion in office, one Verges, a worthy enough fellow, but alas! a little past his prime. In a word, he was old; but in matters of intellect, he was a mere child beside Dogberry.

"Are you good men and true?" demanded Dogberry, peering severely at the line of watchmen, whose eyes, ears, and very noses were weeping in the drizzling dark.

They were indeed, so Constable Dogberry gave them their instructions for guarding the peace of Messina's night. They were to go about their business quietly, to wake no one, and to meddle with no vileness, such as thieves . . .

"If we know him to be a thief," asked one, timidly, "shall we not lay hands on him?"

This was a hard one; and Verges saw Dogberry's noble brow furrowed in thought. Then it cleared. "Truly by your office you may," he pronounced, "but I think they that touch pitch will be defiled. The most peaceable way for you, if you do take a thief, is to let him show himself what he is, and steal out of your company."

There was no putting Dogberry down. "One word more, honest neighbours," said he, most earnestly. "I pray you watch about Signior Leonato's door, for the wedding being there tomorrow, there is a great coil tonight." Then, bestowing the lantern on the worthiest of the men before him, warned, "Be vigitant, I beseech you!" Vigitant! He was a rare one with words, was Dogberry. Had the world been kinder to him, he might have been a lawyer, or a politician . . .

"Well, masters," said the lantern-bearer to his comrades when the two constables had departed, "we hear our charge. Let us go sit here upon the church-bench till two, and then all to bed."

Accordingly, they seated themselves upon the long bench that was protected from the teeming rain by the church porch. There, with but a single lantern that served to illuminate no more than their own solemn faces, they watched over the pitchy night. In obedience to their instructions, they were as quiet as mice . . .

"What, Conrade?" called out Borachio.

"Here, man, I am at thy elbow," answered Conrade, wearily. It was a foul night, a night to be warm and dry indoors, and not following the drunken Borachio as he blundered about in the streaming dark.

Borachio had been celebrating. It seemed that their master, Don John, had bestowed a small fortune on him; and most of the money was

still jingling in his pockets. Conrade was mighty curious to discover the reason why. A dozen times, Borachio had begun to explain; but each time, his drunken tongue, like his drunken feet, had wandered away. "Now forward with thy tale," pleaded Conrade, for he was determined to get at the truth.

"Stand thee close then under this penthouse, for it drizzles rain," hiccuped Borachio, clutching at a post and embracing it like a lover, "and I will, like a true drunkard, utter all to thee."

Thankfully, Conrade sheltered under a low roof that projected from the side of a church, while Borachio, with heavy winks and foolish laughter, went forward with his tale.

"I have tonight wooed Margaret, the Lady Hero's gentlewoman, by the name of Hero," he explained; and then, jerking his elbow familiarly into Conrade's ribs, confided, "She leans me out at her mistress's chamber-window, bids me a thousand times good night—" He stopped, shook his head. He had forgotten something. "I tell this tale vilely, I should first tell thee how the Prince, Claudio, and my master, saw afar off in the orchard this amiable encounter."

"And thought they Margaret was Hero?" murmured Conrade, beginning to smile as he foresaw what might become of this villainy.

23

"Two of them did," answered Borachio, with satisfaction, "the Prince and Claudio, but the devil my master knew she was Margaret. Away went Claudio enraged; swore he would meet her as he was appointed next morning in the temple, and there, before the whole congregation, shame her with what he saw o'ernight, and send her home again without a husband!"

His tale done, he collapsed into laughter. Conrade tried to help him to his feet, when a terrible voice shouted in their very ears,

"We charge you, in the Prince's name, stand!"

In an instant, they were surrounded and seized by huge, burly fellows, armed with enormous cudgels!

Dogberry's watchmen, sitting in breathless silence on their bench round the corner of the church, had overheard every single word! They were simple men. They looked for no double meanings to muddle them. They knew plain villainy when they heard it, and they knew a pair of villains when they saw them. And they knew what to do with them.

It was the morning of the wedding, and Leonato's house was in a cheerful uproar. Everywhere servants were running, cooks were shouting and ladies were rushing hither and thither in a commotion of silks, pursued by attendants with their mouths full of pins. And Leonato himself, his head in a whirl, bustled to and fro in his efforts to bring everything to a happy conclusion. The last thing he needed, at the present frantic time, was two idiots from the town, come to chatter in his ear. But he'd got them, in the persons of that fat pompous fool Dogberry, and his skinny companion Verges, who was no better.

"What would you with me, honest neighbour?" asked Leonato, striving to hide his impatience.

"Marry, sir, I would have some confidence with you that decerns you nearly," confided Dogberry, making his usual mincemeat of the language and garnishing it with the onions on his breath.

"Brief, I pray you," urged Leonato, watching with agony as a servant tottered by, bearing a toppling tower of plates, "for you see it is a busy time with me."

It seemed that a pair of villains had been seized during the night; and the two constables, in accordance with their duty, had come to ask Leonato to examine them that very morning.

It was plainly impossible. "Take the examination yourself," cried Leonato desperately, "and bring it to me. I am now in great haste, as it must appear unto you!"

"It shall be suffigance," said Dogberry solemnly. Leonato blinked; then, remembering it was a happy day, and that the two before him were worthy fellows, bade them courteously, "Drink some wine ere you go; fare you well."

Once out of their sight, he shook his head and marvelled that even Dogberry should be so thick-witted as to trouble him, on the morning of his daughter's wedding, with his tale of two villains in the night. How could their examination matter to him at such a time?

Everyone loves a wedding. The church was stuffed to overflowing with gorgeous rustling silks and quilted velvets, and a host of eager, sparkling eyes. Then, as Hero appeared, blessed with the happy radiance of a bride, up went a universal sigh.

"Come, Friar Francis, be brief," begged Leonato, anxious to have done with ceremony and eager to get on with the feasting and music and dancing for which he'd prepared.

"You come hither, my lord, to marry this lady?" asked the friar of Claudio. How pale the young man looked! Perhaps he'd been celebrating too much the night before?

Claudio's pallor increased as he answered the priest. "No," he said.

Leonato frowned. What the devil did Claudio think he was doing? Then Leonato's brow cleared. Of course! The foolish friar had made a mistake. "To be married to her!" Leonato corrected. "Friar, you come to marry her!"

There was a murmur of amusement from the congregation. The friar grew red. He had not made a mistake. The young man's expression confirmed it. However, he put the question to Hero, who answered, sensibly and modestly, "I do."

"If either of you know any inward impediment why you should not be conjoined," said the friar to the two before him, "I charge you on your souls to utter it."

"Know you any, Hero?" the young man asked; and his voice was strangely harsh.

"None, my lord," said she.

"Know you any, Count?" asked the priest.

"I dare make his answer, none!" put in the impatient Leonato, dreading some long, poetical utterance from Claudio; and besides, he knew his daughter's honour was above reproach.

"Father," said Claudio quietly, "will you with free and unconstrained soul give me this maid, your daughter?"

"As freely, son, as God did give her me."

"And what have I to give you back whose worth may counterpoise this rich and precious gift?" asked Claudio.

"Nothing, unless you render her again."

The speaker was Don Pedro. He stepped forward and stood beside Claudio. His countenance was grave. The church was silent.

"Sweet Prince," said Claudio, turning to his master, "you learn me noble thankfulness." He raised his voice; and in tones that shook with anger and bitterness declared, "Give not this rotten orange to your friend! She's but the sign and semblance of her honour. She knows the heat of a luxurious bed; her blush is guiltiness, not modesty!" He took Hero by the arm and thrust her, so fiercely that she stumbled, into her father's arms.

Amazed, the congregation held its breath as the fair wedding crumbled into dust. Frantically Leonato protested, while Hero stood, like one half-dead, staring from her accusing lover to his grim-faced, princely friend.

"What man was he talked with you yesternight out at your window betwixt twelve and one?" demanded Claudio.

"I talked with no man at that hour, my lord," answered Hero, but so faintly that the congregation could scarcely hear her.

But Don Pedro bore witness against her. "Upon mine honour," he swore, "myself, my brother, and this grieved count did see her, hear her, at that hour last night talk with a ruffian at her chamber-window, who hath confessed the vile encounters they have had a thousand times in secret!"

None could doubt the word of the Prince. Once, Hero herself had proposed, in jest, that she should slander her cousin Beatrice. Now it was she who had been slandered, and in deadly earnest. One doth not know, she'd said, how much an ill word may empoison liking. The world had been poisoned, and she had been destroyed.

"Hath no man's dagger here a point for me?" cried her father, tottering amid the wreckage of his hopes; while Hero, with a frightened sigh, sank lifeless to the ground!

Claudio stared down at the still figure lying on the altar steps; then Don Pedro gently touched his arm and led him away. Don John followed, and after him, the shaken congregation. Only her father, the priest, and Beatrice and Benedick remained with the ruined bride.

She lay with her head cradled in Beatrice's lap. At first, it was feared she was dead; but in a little while, her eyelids began to quiver, as life returned.

"O Fate! take not away thy heavy hand, death is the fairest cover

for her shame that may be wished for!" groaned the distracted Leonato; but the others, perhaps because they were not so nearly touched as a father by his daughter's fall, took a kinder view. Beatrice's belief in her cousin's honour was unshaken, and Benedick shrewdly judged that the villainous Don John was somehow to blame; but it was the steady faith of Friar Francis that was of the greatest comfort.

All his long and deep experience of the ways of men, all his knowledge of guilt and innocence, and the masks they wore, had convinced him that Hero was blameless. Therefore he proposed a strange and daring plan that would bring Claudio to his senses. Let it be given out that Hero was dead. Then surely Claudio, learning what his cruel words had brought about, if he truly loved Hero, would be overcome with shame and remorse. "Then shall he mourn," said the friar, "and wish he had not so accused her."

"Signior Leonato, let the friar advise you," gently urged Benedick; and the father, shaking his poor bewildered head, submitted.

"Being that I flow in grief," he sighed, "the smallest twine may lead me."

Gently, Hero was helped to her feet, and, supported by the friar and her father (though he was as much in need of support as she) left the church for her seeming death.

Beatrice and Benedick were alone. Strange meeting for the lovers who had so newly discovered themselves. Beatrice was weeping, and Benedick was serious and pale. The tragedy of Hero had clouded their sunshine, and hung heavy in the air.

"Surely I do believe your fair cousin is wronged," said Benedick, gently.

"Ah, how much might the man deserve of me that would right her!" said Beatrice, her eyes all fiery with tears.

"Is there any way to show such friendship?" murmured Benedick. "I do love nothing in the world so well as you—is not that strange?"

She smiled. "You have stayed me in a happy hour, I was about to protest I loved you."

"And do it with all thy heart!" cried Benedick, joyfully. "Come, bid me do anything for thee!"

For a moment, she did not answer. She stared at him strangely. Then she uttered the most terrible words in the world. "Kill Claudio!"

Benedick fell back in horror. "Ha, not for the wide world!" Claudio was his friend.

"You kill me to deny it. Farewell," cried Beatrice, bitterly.

"Tarry, sweet Beatrice!" pleaded Benedick, seizing her by the hand.

"There is no love in you. I pray you let me go."

"We'll be friends first."

"You dare easier be friends with me than fight with mine enemy."

"Is Claudio thine enemy?"

"Oh God that I were a man!" she cried, wild with grief and anger. "I would eat his heart in the market-place!"

She stood like an avenging fury; yet he loved her, better than his friendship, better, even, than his reason and his honour. "Enough," he said, "I will challenge him," and away he went, to keep his word.

Hero was dead. Everybody knew of it. Don John, fearing discovery and retribution, fled from Messina. But those who had obeyed his orders, remained behind. Conrade and Borachio were in prison, and their fate reposed in the large, important hands of Constable Dogberry.

With Verges to second him, and the Town Clerk to record the proceedings, Dogberry began upon his examination of the prisoners before him. The Town Clerk frowned, he sighed, he shook his head. The constable seemed a little too fond of the sound of his own loud voice. He kept wandering from the point; and unless he was stopped, the proceedings would last all day.

"Master Constable," he said wearily, as Dogberry became more and more involved in a fruitless argument with the prisoners as to whether or not they were villains, "you go not the way to examine; you must call forth the watch that are their accusers."

The constable looked surprised. Plainly, the trifling matter of evidence had escaped him. Nonetheless, he took the Town Clerk's advice. He summoned the watch, who proceeded to give their evidence.

The Town Clerk's eyes widened, his face grew grave, and his pen scratched and scratched like a thousand frantic mice, as he wrote down what the watch had overheard—the villainy of Don John, the vile deception by Borachio, and the wicked slandering of the Lady Hero!

"Master Constable," he cried, finishing his writing in the utmost haste, "let these men be bound, and brought to Leonato's! I will go before and show him their examination!" and away he rushed to the bereaved father with the proof of his daughter's innocence!

Leonato stood outside his stricken house like a statue advertising grief. In vain, his brother Antonio tried to comfort him. He would have none of it. Only a father who had suffered as he had suffered had the right to preach patience at him. "Therefore give me no counsel," he said, shaking off his brother's comforting arm. "I will be flesh and blood, for there was never yet a philosopher who would endure the toothache patiently."

Antonio sighed and shook his head. "Yet bend not all the harm upon yourself," he begged; "make those that do offend you suffer too." Even as he uttered the words, the two chief offenders came walking by.

Although they felt themselves to be guiltless in the affair, Don Pedro and Claudio felt ill at ease when they saw the two old gentlemen, and made to hurry by.

"We have some haste, Leonato," muttered Don Pedro uncomfortably, as the old gentleman sought to detain them.

"Some haste, my lord?" repeated Leonato, with bitter scorn. "Well, fare you well, my lord! Are you so hasty now? well, all is one."

"Nay, do not quarrel with us, good old man—"

"If he could right himself with quarrelling," said Antonio, coming forward and standing by his brother with a threatening air, "some of us would lie low!"

"Who wrongs him?" asked Claudio, trying not to smile at the sight of the two warlike old men. He wished he'd held his tongue, for Leonato turned upon him in a fury.

"Thou dost wrong me," he shouted, "thou dissembler, thou— Nay, never lay thy hand upon thy sword, I fear thee not."

Guiltily, Claudio took away his hand that had gone instinctively to his weapon. But the old man was not to be stopped. "Thou hast so wronged mine innocent child and me that I am forced to lay my reverence by and challenge thee to trial of a man! Thou hast killed my child.

If thou kill'st me, boy, thou shalt kill a man!"

"Away," cried Claudio, angry and alarmed at the turn events had taken, "I will not have to do with you!" Although he was deeply offended that his honour had been questioned, he had no wish to harm the old gentleman.

But his words served only to add fuel to the old man's fire; and they set his brother Antonio alight into the bargain. And he was ten times worse. "God knows I loved my niece," he shouted in his quavering voice, "and she is dead, slandered to death by villains! Boys, apes, braggarts, Jacks, milksops!"

God knew how it all would have ended had not Don Pedro come to the rescue. "Gentlemen both," he said, with princely courtesy and great forbearance—for he had been insulted no less than Claudio, "my heart is sorry for your daughter's death; but on my honour she was charged with nothing but what was true, and very full of proof."

No man could have uttered more; and, though it was plain that Leonato was far from satisfied, he had the good sense to draw his brother away, and back into their house.

Don Pedro and Claudio looked at one another. They smiled. The old gentlemen's fury had certainly had its comical side. Their smiles broadened. Benedick was coming towards them. The very man to laugh with them over their encounter!

"Welcome, signior," greeted Don Pedro, "you are almost come to part almost a fray."

"We had liked to have had our two noses snapped off with two old men without teeth," said Claudio, cheerfully.

"Leonato and his brother," explained Don Pedro. "What thinkst thou? Had we fought, I doubt we should have been too young for them!"

Benedick stared at them. "In a false quarrel there is no true valour," he said coldly. "I came to seek you both."

What was this? Was this pale and stern gentleman their ever-mocking Benedick?

"Art thou sick, or angry?" wondered Don Pedro.

Benedick ignored him. He turned to Claudio. He spoke quietly. "You are a villain. I jest not; I will make it good how you dare, with what you dare, and when you dare. Do me right, or I will protest your cowardice. You have killed a sweet lady, and her death shall fall heavy on you. Let me hear from you." He turned to Don Pedro. "My lord, for your many courtesies I thank you. I must discontinue your company. Your brother the bastard is fled from Messina. You have among you killed a sweet and innocent lady. For my Lord Lackbeard there," he nodded towards Claudio, "he and I shall meet, and till then peace be with him."

With a cold, precise bow, he left them, and walked rapidly away.

"He is in earnest," murmured Don Pedro.

"In most profound earnest," said Claudio, "and I'll warrant you, for the love of Beatrice." He frowned. He was deeply troubled. This second challenge he had received was not one to be laughed away . . .

"How now?" cried Don Pedro suddenly, "two of my brother's men bound?"

Claudio looked up. An extraordinary procession was approaching Leonato's house. It was headed by two constables, one large and fat, the other, ancient and thin. Behind them, surrounded by armed men of the watch, walked Conrade and Borachio in chains.

"Officers," demanded Don Pedro of the constables, "what offence have these men done?"

Dogberry, addressed by the Prince, was more than equal to the occasion. Swelling with pride and importance, he embarked upon a flood of legal eloquence that left his hearers dazed with admiration. The Prince was baffled. Helplessly he appealed to Borachio: "This learned constable is too cunning to be understood. What's your offence?"

Borachio looked wretched. Having no corner to lurk in, no curtain to hide him, and no Don John to protect him, he was exposed for the miserable villain that he was. "Sweet Prince," he answered abjectly, "let me go no farther to mine answer: do you hear me, and let this count kill me. I have deceived even your very eyes." Then he confessed to Don John's wicked plot, of his own guilty part in it, and of how he had tricked the innocent Margaret into becoming his accomplice.

As they listened, Don Pedro and Claudio began to tremble. They grew pale as death. What had they done? What had they done! Between them all, they had killed the blameless Hero.

32

An extraordinary procession was approaching

"Runs not this speech like iron through your blood?" whispered Don Pedro; and Claudio replied, "I have drunk poison whiles he uttered it."

But worse was to come. Out of the house came the two old gentlemen, accompanied by the Town Clerk. It was plain they knew all. Claudio and Don Pedro were now brought face to face with the father who, in all good faith, they had ruined.

"Which is the villain?" cried Leonato. "Let me see his eyes, that when I note another man like him I may avoid him. Which of these is he?"

"If you would know your wronger, look on me," moaned Borachio.

"Art thou the slave that with thy breath hast killed mine innocent child?"

"Yea, even I alone."

Leonato looked carefully at the miserable wretch in chains. He shook his head. "No, not so, villain, thou beliest thyself." He turned to Claudio and Don Pedro. He gazed upon them with contempt. "Here stand a pair of honourable men, a third is fled that had a hand in it. I thank you, princes, for my daughter's death; record it with your high and worthy deeds. 'Twas bravely done, if you bethink you of it."

Claudio and Don Pedro hung their heads in shame as they were brought face to face with themselves. They had dishonoured honour: to guard their own, they had destroyed another's.

"I cannot bid you bid my daughter live," said Leonato sadly, as the pair begged to know how they could make amends, "that were impossible." Then he proposed a strange penance that they should undergo. First, they should publicly proclaim Hero's innocence, then they should visit her tomb that night, and pay the respects of mourning that were her due. "Tomorrow morning," concluded Leonato, solemnly, "come you to my house, and since you could not be my son-in-law, be yet my nephew. My brother hath a daughter, almost the copy of my child that's dead, and she alone is heir to both of us. Give her the right you should have given her cousin, and so dies my revenge."

"We will not fail," said Don Pedro humbly; and Claudio, with tears in his eyes, promised, "Tonight I'll mourn with Hero."

★

33

The heavy clouds that had lowered over Leonato's house were lifting. It was morning, and everyone awaited the arrival of Claudio and Don Pedro. They had performed the penance laid upon them to the very letter. They had publicly proclaimed Hero's innocence, and had knelt, and mourned, and wept at her supposed tomb.

"Did I not tell you she was innocent?" said Friar Francis, with satisfaction.

"So are the Prince and Claudio, who accused her upon the error you heard debated," said Leonato, anxious to restore the honour of his future son-in-law.

"Well, I am glad that all things sort so well," said Antonio.

"And so am I," agreed Benedick, mightily relieved, "being else by faith enforced to call young Claudio to a reckoning for it."

"Well, daughter, and you gentlewomen all," said Leonato, turning to the ladies and bustling them away, "withdraw into a chamber by yourselves, and when I send for you, come hither masked. You know your office, brother," he reminded Antonio when the ladies had gone: "you must be father to your brother's daughter, and give her to young Claudio." He laughed and rubbed his hands together. There had been suffering and remorse enough. Now was the time for forgiveness, even if it was to be concealed under a last comedy of masks.

"Friar, I must entreat your pains, I think," murmured Benedick.

"To do what, signior?"

"To bind me, or undo me—one of them. Signior Leonato, truth it is, good signior, your niece regards me with an eye of favour."

Benedick spoke the truth. He had indeed wrenched from Beatrice an admission—albeit a grudging one—that she loved him.

"What's your will?" asked Leonato.

"My will is your good will may stand with ours," answered Benedick, "this day to be conjoined in the state of honourable marriage."

"My heart is with your liking!" responded Leonato, and clasped Benedick warmly by the hand.

"Here comes the Prince and Claudio!" warned Friar Francis. At once, all joyful smiles were wiped away, and every face wore a look of stern solemnity, to greet the humbled Prince and penitent bridegroom as they entered the room.

"Good morrow, Benedick," greeted Don Pedro, searching in vain for a welcoming look. "Why, what's the matter that you have such a February face, so full of frost, of storm, and cloudiness?"

But before there could be an answer, Leonato clapped his hands and the ladies appeared—so many rustling secrets behind their masks. Claudio stared from one to another; and glittering eyes watched his every move. "Which is the lady I must seize upon?" he asked at length.

"This same is she," said Antonio, taking a mysterious lady by the hand and bringing her forward, "and I do give you her."

"Why then she's mine!" cried Claudio, with all the gallantry he could muster in the face of his faceless bride.

Beatrice, watching her cousin anxiously, marvelled that she could still hold up her mask, for she was trembling violently. Poor Hero! Her love for Claudio had never faltered: she loved him in spite of all his faults. Beatrice smiled ruefully. Her own case was very different. She loved Benedick almost because of his faults.

"Sweet, let me see your face," begged Claudio; and it was as much as Leonato could do to prevent Hero revealing herself too soon.

"No," he cried, seizing her by the wrist that was about to lower her mask, "that you shall not till you take her hand, before this friar, and swear to marry her!"

So Claudio took her hand, and before Friar Francis, declared, "I am your husband if you like of me."

Only then did Leonato allow Hero to reveal her radiant face. Claudio fell back, amazed! He stood, with his mouth open, not daring to speak, lest she vanish like a dream.

"And when I lived," Hero murmured softly, "I was your other wife, and when you loved, you were my other husband."

At last, Claudio spoke. "Another Hero!" he whispered; and Don Pedro, overcome with thankfulness that he'd killed no one, cried, "The former Hero! Hero that is dead!"

"She died, my lord," said Leonato, all smiles at last, "but whiles her slander lived."

Deception on deception; was nothing real? "Which is Beatrice?" demanded Benedick, approaching the masked ladies.

"I answer to that name," said she, taking off her mask. "What is your will?"

"Do not you love me?" demanded Benedick, without more ado.

"Why, no," said she, finding the triumph in Benedick's air too much and too soon, "no more than reason."

"Why then your uncle and the Prince and Claudio have been deceived. They swore you did."

"Do not you love me?" countered Beatrice, unable to deny the evidence.

"Troth, no, no more than reason," said Benedick.

"Why then my cousin, Margaret, and Ursula are much deceived, for they did swear you did."

"They swore that you were almost sick for me."

"They swore that you were well-nigh dead for me."

"'Tis no such matter," protested Benedick indignantly. "Then you do not love me?"

"No, truly, but in friendly recompense," said Beatrice; and their bickering was only put a stop to when Hero and Claudio produced letters that each had written to the other but never sent, protesting undying love.

"A miracle!" cried Benedick, "here's our own hands against our hearts! Come, I will have thee, but by this light, I take thee for pity."

"I yield upon great persuasion," said Beatrice, with dignity, "and partly to save your life, for I was told you were in a consumption."

"Peace," cried Benedick, "I will stop your mouth," and he kissed her not unwilling lips.

Now at a sign from Leonato, the musicians struck up a stately measure, and the dancing began. Don Pedro looked on, like a victorious general, at the success of his campaign, as Claudio and Hero, and Beatrice and Benedick joined together in the harmony of the dance. Then he remembered how nearly all had come to grief, through the campaign of his darker self, his black-browed, bastard brother, John . . .

"Prince, thou art sad," called out Benedick, observing him, "get thee a wife, get thee a wife!"

Don Pedro looked up. He smiled, and nodded, and feeling suddenly lonely, looked about him for some lady to join him in the dance.

Julius Caesar

All Rome was wild with joy! The bright morning streamed with flying caps and pennants, and the very stones danced to the applause of ten thousand feet! Julius Caesar had won a glorious victory over the traitor Pompey, and all the carpenters, cobblers, tradesmen and their wives, shut up shop, put on their best attire, and rushed out of doors to welcome him and crown his statues with garlands, as if he was a king!

"Hence! Home, you idle creatures—"

Two officers of state, high up on the steps of a monument, were shouting furiously to make themselves heard as the noisy crowd came flooding into the market-place, like a filthy, stinking tide, wanting only to lap and lick the feet of Caesar.

"Get you home!"

They drew their swords. The crowd faltered—

"You blocks, you stones, you worse than senseless things!"

Filled with anger and contempt for the common people who, not so long before, had welcomed Pompey even as they now welcomed Caesar, they rushed down and drove them from the market-place, like a frightened flock of sheep. Then, hearing a distant shout of trumpets, they hastened away to clear the streets and uncrown all the stone Caesars they could find.

They were men of the republic. Like the stern marble Romans on their lofty pedestals, who stood on every corner and in every public place, clutching their scrolls of hard-won liberty, they wanted no more crownings and no more kings.

But their task was hopeless. No sooner had they gone, than through a hundred different channels and alleys, the crowd came streaming back, as if the world had tilted Caesar's way. They flowed up steps, they climbed on columns, they clung from windows, as the long brazen trumpets approached, flashing like shooting stars and blasting the air with majesty!

Then came Caesar himself, and suddenly all Rome was one huge adoring eye! Robed in gold and purple, and wearing the laurel wreath of victory, he walked slowly, inclining his head from side to side as he acknowledged the cheering of the people; and the marble Romans on their pedestals seemed to clutch their scrolls more tightly, as if they feared they'd be snatched away.

Following after, like faithful dogs, walked all the great ones of Rome: eager Casca, the noble Brutus with slight Cassius by his side; dry, learned old Cicero, hobbling as if his new sandals pinched, and Mark Antony, stripped and ready to run the course—for it was the Feast of Lupercal when it was the custom for young noblemen to run naked through the streets, striking childless women with leather thongs, to cure them of barrenness.

"Calpurnia!"

The procession halted. The trumpets were stilled. Caesar had spoken. He had summoned his wife. At once she left her place and, almost stumbling over her heavy purple gown in her haste, she came to her husband's side. He bade her stand in Antony's path when he ran the magic course. She was childless and Caesar had need of a son. Humbly, she bowed her head and, accompanied by knowing smiles that made her blush with shame, she returned to her place.

"Set on," commanded Caesar. He raised his hand—

"Caesar!"

He paused, and the trumpets, half-way to lips, stayed motionless. Who had called his name? A silence fell on the market-place. Then there was a stirring among the crowd. An old man shuffled forward, a gaunt old man with wild white hair. He was a soothsayer who, it

was said, looked into tomorrow as clearly as if it was yesterday. He spoke again.

"Beware the Ides of March."

"Set him before me," ordered Caesar; but the old man needed no assistance. Leaning heavily on his staff, he approached and stood before Caesar, his ragged black gown flapping in the gusty air.

"What sayest thou to me now? Speak once again."

"Beware the Ides of March," said the soothsayer, and his words struck a chill into every heart. The Ides of March were close at hand. But Caesar was unmoved. He stared hard into the man's pale blue eyes that blazed either with madness or the harmless folly of age. He smiled.

"He is a dreamer. Let us leave him. Pass." And, with a shrug of his shoulders, as if the warning had been of no more consequence than a pebble cast against the sun, he set on.

Two remained behind: Brutus and Cassius. Wearied of walking in Caesar's shadow, they had no wish to watch him presiding over the

Festival games. They leaned against a wall and stared after the swirling clouds of dust that had been raised by the multitude that had streamed after Caesar. Although they were friends they were, at that moment, separate islands of thought. Then Cassius, the quicker and more passionate of the two, broke the silence. Shrewdly observing the direction of Brutus's gaze, he wondered if his friend was troubled with the same thought that was troubling himself and certain other gentlemen of Rome? Was it possible, he went on, choosing his words with care, that the noble Brutus, whose great ancestor had driven out the last of Rome's bad kings, was growing uneasy over Caesar's ever-increasing power?

Before Brutus could answer, there came a roar from the distant multitude. "What means this shouting?" he muttered. "I do fear the people choose Caesar for their king!"

"Ay, do you fear it?" asked Cassius quickly. "Then must I think you would not have it so!"

Brutus hesitated; then slowly answered, "I would not . . ." and Cassius's heart beat rapidly. Thus far Brutus was with him!

A cloud passed across the sun. Shadows invaded the market-place. The pale Romans on their pedestals seemed to tremble and sway, as if their ghostly world had begun to shake. They glared down in stony dismay on the two men who murmured together: the one tall and upright, the other, slighter and fiercely restless, like a darting flame striving to set a mighty tree ablaze.

Cassius hated Caesar. He hated him for the huge and arrogant thing he had become.

"Why, man," cried Cassius, seizing his friend by the arm, "he doth bestride the narrow world like a Colossus, and we petty men walk under his huge legs and peep about to find ourselves dishonourable graves!"

At the word 'dishonourable' Brutus flushed angrily. Honour was dearer to him than life itself, and Cassius knew it. Indeed, he loved and admired his friend for it, but such was his hatred for Caesar that he did not scruple to play upon Brutus's honour as if it was an instrument, as he led him further and further along the dangerous path that he himself was treading. And Brutus, to the noble tune of honour, followed the skilful piper willingly.

Caesar was returning. Guiltily, the friends drew apart as the procession entered the market-place. They watched curiously. Plainly, something was amiss. The trumpets hung down like broken daffodils and the crowd had drained away to a ragged trickle. Caesar himself looked angry, and those near him were shaken and pale. They halted. Caesar looked about him, as if for someone on whom he might vent his spleen. His eye fell upon Cassius. He beckoned Mark Antony to his side.

"Let me have men about me that are fat," he said loudly, "sleek-headed men and such as sleep a-nights. Yond Cassius has a lean and hungry look. Such men are dangerous."

"Fear him not, Caesar; he's not dangerous," said Antony with a smile; but Caesar, never taking his eyes from the suddenly white-faced Cassius, slowly shook his head.

"Such men as he be never at heart's ease whiles they behold a greater than themselves," he said thoughtfully, "and therefore are they very dangerous." Then, as if remembering who he was, his hand went to his laurel wreath, which he wore as much to hide his thinning hair as to mark his victory, and settled it more firmly on his head. Others might fear, but never Caesar. "Come to my right hand," he said to Antony, "for this ear is deaf, and tell me truly what thou thinkst of him," and, with a last long look at Cassius, he led the way from the market-place.

As the procession passed, Brutus plucked Casca by the sleeve. Casca, careful not to be observed, lingered behind. Brutus asked him what had happened. Casca looked about him, and, seeing there was none else by, smiled broadly and related what had taken place.

He was full of lively mockery, sparing neither Caesar, nor his friends, nor the people from the sharpness of his tongue; for Casca, though he bowed low before Caesar, was never afraid to speak his mind—behind Caesar's back.

The scene had been so comical and ridiculous that it had been as much as he could do to stop himself laughing aloud. Antony had offered Caesar a crown. Caesar had refused it and the rabble had hooted and shouted for joy. Antony offered it a second time. Again Caesar refused, and again the people cheered him for it. But when it was offered for a third time, and for a third time Caesar pushed it aside, the sweaty crowd yelled and shouted so much that Caesar fell down in a fit and foamed at the mouth—as much from the people's bad breath as from his bitter disappointment that they did not want him to be a king.

"What, did Caesar swoon?" asked Cassius softly.

"'Tis very like," said Brutus; "he hath the falling sickness."

Cassius shook his head. "No, Caesar hath it not; but you, and I, and honest Casca, we have the falling sickness."

Casca looked at him sharply. "I know not what you mean by that," he said; but Cassius had seen in his eyes the very image of his own dark thoughts.

"Will you sup with me tonight, Casca?"

"No, I am promised forth."

"Will you dine with me tomorrow?"

"Ay, if I be alive, and your mind hold, and your dinner worth the eating."

With that, they parted, all three agreeing to meet—tomorrow.

A heap of rags stirred in a dusty corner of the market-place, and, with little groanings and cracklings of the joints, raised itself up to the height of a man. It was the soothsayer. He stared after the three who had just gone; and his pale blue eyes, that looked into tomorrow as clearly as if it was yesterday, widened with dread. Tomorrow was the Ides of March. The sky darkened and a wind sprang up. Frightened rubbish flew across the market-place, and the old man, his gown stretched out like a black flag, stumbled away.

Then the storm broke, and all Rome shook. It was a strange storm, of sudden enormous glares and enormous blacknesses, and unnatural roarings as if huge lions were rending the sky. Some said blood drizzled on the Capitol, others saw men, all in flames, walking the streets, and dead men shrieking down alleys with their stained winding-sheets streaming out in the dark wind.

"Who's there?"

"A Roman."

Two muffled figures, meeting in a narrow way, drew close together.
One was Casca, white with fear at the supernatural violence of the
night; the other was Cassius, exulting in it, for he had a storm within
as wild as the one above. Fearfully, Casca spoke of monsters in the
sky; fiercely Cassius spoke of a monster in Rome—

"'Tis Caesar that you mean, is it not, Cassius?"

"Let it be who it is," muttered Cassius; and, while the earth shook
and glaring terrors piled up in the sky, he led the trembling Casca into
the darker terror of his own design: the murder of Caesar!

He was not alone, he promised Casca. Even now there were others
who had no love for Caesar, waiting in the night. But first they must
win Brutus to the cause. The plot had need of him. His noble name
would make the deed seem just and honourable in all men's eyes.

"Three parts of him is ours already," whispered Cassius, "and the
man entire upon the next encounter . . ." He drew a scroll of paper
from his sleeve. It was to be thrown in at Brutus's window. In fiery
words it urged him, in the name of the people, to rise up like his great

ancestor and rid Rome of the tyrant! Cassius had written it himself. Once more he was playing upon his friend's honour; and this time the tune would lead Brutus to take the final step.

Lightning flashed. The muffled figures shrank back, and their monstrous double shadow was flung across the street like a pall. Then blackness engulfed them . . .

Brutus walked alone in his orchard. The worst of the storm's violence was over, but not its weirdness. Mad shooting stars whizzed across the black sky, breaking up the darkness into a patchwork of flickering sights. At one moment all was hidden and secret; at the next, the clustering trees threw up their thin arms in despair.

"It must be by his death," he whispered as, with an anguished heart, he contemplated the terrible deed that Cassius had put into his thoughts: the killing of a friend, for Caesar *was* his friend. But Caesar's spirit, that huge, ambitious thing that stretched its arm across the world, was the enemy of all free men. "It must be by his death . . ." not because of what he was, but because of what he might become . . .

Someone was coming. It was Lucius, his servant. The boy was puzzled. He'd found a scroll of paper inside the window of his master's room. It had not been there before. Brutus took it, and, when the boy had gone, broke the seal and read:

"Brutus, thou sleep'st. Awake and see thyself! Speak, strike, redress!"

He breathed deeply. It was not the first such letter to reach him. There had been others that had been put in his way. It seemed that all Rome was begging him to act. He clenched up the paper in his fist. Rome should not beg in vain! "*It must be by his death!*"

There was a knocking at the gate. Lucius came to tell him that Cassius was waiting.

"Is he alone?"

"No, sir, there are more with him."

"Do you know them?"

Lucius shook his head. They had all been hidden in their cloaks.

"Let 'em enter," said Brutus, and frowned. Unlike Cassius, he was not a man of plots and conspiracy. He despised concealment and felt ashamed to be a part of it.

Presently, quiet, faceless figures approached from among the trees. One by one, they made themselves known: Casca, Decius, Cinna, Metellus Cimber, Trebonius . . . By the light of day, they were men of substance, worthy Romans; but by night, they were something different . . . Softly, they talked together while Cassius and Brutus whispered apart. Then Cassius smiled and nodded, and they knew that Brutus was theirs!

He stepped forward and shook each man firmly by the hand, and the bond was sealed. At once, all constraint vanished and they began talking eagerly of what must be done. Brutus was ever in the forefront; his doubts resolved, he embraced the cause with all his heart, and took it upon himself to lead. Should Cicero be approached? His age and dignity would gain all men's respect. But Brutus was against it, and Brutus had his way. Should no one else but Caesar be killed?

"Let Antony and Caesar fall together," said Cassius; but Brutus was against it, and Brutus had his way.

The death of Caesar was to be the sacrifice of a single man for the good of all. "And for Mark Antony," he said, "think not of him, for he can do no more than Caesar's arm when Caesar's head is off."

"Yet I fear him," muttered Cassius; but he was overruled.

The hour was late. It was three o'clock in the morning, and the heavy blackness was already wearing thin.

"Good gentlemen," urged Brutus, as his companions, with pale and desperate looks, took their leave, "look fresh and merrily . . ." but when they had gone, the show of ease he had put on, left him, and once more he was the lonely brooding figure among the trees. "It must be by his death . . ." They were to meet at Caesar's house at eight o'clock to bring him to the Capitol, and there to kill him—

"Brutus, my lord."

He started. Portia, his wife, stood beside him, like a good spirit in the ugly dark. She was troubled. She had seen the secret men in the orchard, and she knew her husband was distressed. Gently, she begged him to tell her the cause.

He turned away. He dared not tell her. He feared her honesty too much.

45

"I am not well in health," he said, "and that is all."

Angered at being put off with thin excuses, as if she had no more understanding than a child, she reproached him for his lack of trust. Were he and she not one? Why, then, should she not share in his griefs as well as in his joys?

"Am I your self," she demanded, confronting him wherever he turned, "in sort or limitation, to keep with you at meals, comfort your bed, and talk to you sometimes? Dwell I but in the suburbs of your good pleasure? If it were no more, then Portia is Brutus' harlot, not his wife!" In despair, she knelt. "Tell me your counsels," she pleaded, "I will not disclose 'em!"

Eagerly, she dragged up her gown and displayed a deep and bloody wound in her white thigh. She herself had done it and endured the pain in silence as a proof of her fortitude.

"Can I bear that with patience, and not my husband's secrets?"

"O ye gods," wept Brutus, shamed by Portia's courage, "render me worthy of this noble wife!" and, with a warm embrace, promised that she should share in the terrible secret he carried in his heart.

"Help, ho, they murder Caesar!"

But it was only in the dreams of Caesar's wife. She awoke with a cry. She left her bed and rushed in search of her husband. She found him already preparing himself to go to the Capitol. Urgently, she begged him to stay at home that day. Not only had her dreams been full of blood, but all night the sky had roared and glared with fiery doom. But Caesar only smiled and shook his head.

"These predictions are to the world in general as to Caesar."

"When beggars die there are no comets seen," cried Calpurnia, "the heavens themselves blaze forth the death of princes!"

Caesar was unmoved. Neither the savage sights in the streets nor the dreadful portents in the sky could shake him. He was always Caesar.

"Alas, my lord," pleaded Calpurnia, her fears increasing a thousand-fold as a troubled servant came to tell that the morning's sacrifice had been unlucky: no heart had been found in the slaughtered beast, "do not go forth today!"

She knelt and, weeping, implored him to send Mark Antony to say he was not well and would not come to the Capitol today.

Caesar gazed down. A single word from him would turn Calpurnia's trembling fear to boundless joy. He raised her to her feet.

"Mark Antony shall say I am not well," he said; but even as Calpurnia burst into sunshine smiles, a gentleman arrived, a gentleman whose looks were fresh and merry. It was Decius. It was eight o'clock and he had come to take Caesar to the Capitol.

"Bear my greeting to the senators," said Caesar, "and tell them I will not come today."

Decius stared, and the freshness seemed to wither on his cheeks.

"Say he is sick," said Calpurnia quickly.

Caesar frowned. "Shall Caesar send a lie? Go tell them Caesar will not come."

"Most mighty Caesar," pleaded Decius, plainly distressed, "let me know some cause—"

"The cause is in my will. I will not come. That is enough to satisfy the Senate." Then, taking pity on the bewildered Decius, he explained that Calpurnia had begged him, on her knees, to stay at home. She had had bad dreams. She had dreamed that Caesar's statue had spouted blood, and that smiling Romans had come to bathe their hands in it.

Decius, clever Decius, listened carefully. He shook his head. Calpurnia had interpreted her dream quite wrongly. Its true meaning was life, not death. The spouting blood plainly signified the nourishment that Caesar was to give to Rome. Caesar nodded thoughtfully. He picked up his laurel wreath and absently fingered the leaves as Decius went on to say that he'd heard the Senate meant to offer Caesar the crown that very day; but if Caesar did not come, Decius feared they'd change their minds and even whisper that Caesar had been frightened by his wife's dreams.

Caesar's brow grew dark. "Give me my robe," he commanded, outraged that a pack of feeble old men should dare to think Caesar afraid. "I will go!"

Calpurnia cried out in dismay; but her voice was lost and she was brushed aside and forgotten as the room was suddenly filled with smiling friends who had come to drink wine with Caesar, and then to take him to the Capitol and his death.

★

They were betrayed! A man stood in the crowd outside the Capitol, with a letter for Caesar in his hand. In it, the conspiracy was revealed and every guilty name written down! There was a sound of cheering from afar. Caesar was coming! Trembling with excitement, the man began to push his way towards the front . . .

Portia in her house also heard the cheering, but to her distracted ears it sounded ragged and dismayed. Every noise from the Capitol excited her, every silence drove her mad. A dozen times she'd bade Lucius run to the Senate House; but still he stayed, for she could think of no likely reason for his errand. Her husband's secret struggled in her breast, and it needed all her strength to keep it confined.

"O Brutus," she whispered, "the heavens speed thee in thine enterprise!" and once more she bade Lucius run to her husband, for no better purpose than to tell him she was merry!

The sun glared down after the night's storm, as if to see where all the monsters had gone. It was past nine o'clock and Caesar, walking in the midst of his friends, approached the Capitol. He paused. He had spied a face that he remembered among the waiting crowds. It was the mad old man who had spoken to him yesterday. He beckoned and the old man came forward, leaning on his staff.

"The Ides of March are come," said Caesar mockingly.

"Ay, Caesar," answered the soothsayer, "but not gone."

Caesar laughed, and passed on.

"Hail, Caesar! Read this—"

A man had rushed out of the crowd and, before anyone could stop him, had thrust a letter into Caesar's hand! Swiftly Decius interposed with a letter of his own for Caesar to read.

"O Caesar, read mine first," begged the man, "for mine's a suit that touches Caesar nearer!"

"What touches us ourself shall be last served," said Caesar royally; and thrust the fatal letter into the oblivion of his sleeve.

"Delay not, Caesar," cried the man, "read it instantly!"

"What, is the fellow mad?" demanded Caesar; and Cassius bustled him back into the crowd.

Then, with a last smile and wave to the people of Rome, Caesar

"Et tu, Brute?"

mounted up the steps of the Capitol and disappeared within. 'Caesar, beware of Brutus. Take heed of Cassius. Come not near Casca . . .' warned the letter in his sleeve; but in vain.

Trebonius was deep in talk with Mark Antony, and was gently leading him away. It had been agreed. Caesar's was the only blood to be shed. There was to be no frantic butchery. It was to be done swiftly and sternly, in a spirit of justice, not revenge.

Casca was to strike the first blow. With his right hand hidden in his gown, he walked as if on egg-shells, and sweated like an actor fearful of mangling his part. Every sight, every sound was betrayal—the echoing footsteps on the huge marble floor, the murmuring of senators as they moved among the tall shadowy columns to take their places in the solemn circle of chairs; the quick glances, the sudden silences . . . Cassius was pale, anxious; his eyes were burning as if his brain was on fire. But Brutus, as always, was upright and calm . . .

Suddenly there was a stirring. The senators were standing. What had happened? What had they seen? But it was for Caesar. He had taken his place in the chair of state. He motioned graciously with his hand and the senators seated themselves again. They leaned forward, like an expectant audience at the beginning of a play.

It was to begin with Metellus Cimber. Casca moved quietly to the back of Caesar's chair. He waited. Metellus had not moved. He had been forestalled. Someone else was addressing Caesar, and speaking at length. Metellus was rubbing his hands together, as if to wipe off the skin. At last it was his turn. Quickly he came forward and knelt before Caesar and began to plead for the pardon of his banished brother. Coldly, Caesar denied him. Then Brutus came forward, then Cassius, then Cinna . . . until all were kneeling, pleading:

"Most high, most mighty . . . Pardon, Caesar, pardon . . . O Caesar . . ."

But Caesar was unmoved.

Casca stood directly behind. His heart was knocking violently. Of a sudden, the man seated in the chair seemed immense! He towered above the crouching figures before him like a god! Cinna had clutched the hem of his robe, in abject supplication. Caesar spurned him.

49

"Great Caesar—" cried Decius; and Casca's hidden hand was out!

"Speak," he screamed, "hands for me!" and, reaching forward, plunged his dagger into Caesar's neck!

Caesar cried out! He clapped his hand to his wound as if an insect had stung him. He rose to his feet, turned, seized Casca by the wrist— But Casca's cry had been answered! The kneeling figures were up, their arms were lifted, and in every hand was a weapon!

Amazed, Caesar stared from face to terrible face. He knew them all. They were his friends . . .

Then they fell upon him. With gasps and cries and savage grunts, they stabbed and slashed and hacked where they could, driving him this way and that, until Caesar was no more than a swaying, staggering remnant, everywhere spouting blood. But still he would not die; until Brutus, with a sad look, struck the last blow.

"Et tu, Brute?" he sighed as his friend's dagger pierced him through. "Then fall Caesar!" and with his ruined face muffled in his slashed gown, he fell at the base of Pompey's statue. Caesar was dead.

There was silence. It was as if the heart of the world had been torn out, leaving an emptiness. Then Cinna cried out:

"Liberty! Freedom! Tyranny is dead!" and the world awoke!

There was an uproar of overturned chairs and stumbling feet as terrified senators, squealing like chickens rushing from the axe, fled from the men of blood.

"Fly not, stand still!" shouted Brutus. "Ambition's debt is paid!" but the senators, seeing only wild-eyed murderers and streaming knives, stumbled out of doors, leaving behind one old man, grey-faced and trembling, who had been too frightened to move.

"There's no harm intended to your person," Brutus assured him; and Cassius led him gently away.

The conspirators were alone. They stared down at the fallen Caesar. The hugeness of their deed filled them with awe and robbed them of all thought and action. Then Brutus proposed they should stoop and bathe their hands, ceremonially, in Caesar's blood, to sanctify what they had done.

"How many ages hence," murmured Cassius, as his kneeling friends, some boldly, some fearfully, fumbled in the dead man's wounds, "shall this our lofty scene be acted over in states unborn and accents yet unknown?" and he gazed round at the wrenched and broken circle of empty chairs, as if the countless generations to come were already crowding in and looking on.

"How many times shall Caesar bleed in sport?" wondered Brutus.

"So oft as that shall be," said Cassius proudly, "so often shall the knot of us be called the men that gave their country liberty!"

A shadow fell across them. There was a figure standing in the open doorway. It was a servant of Mark Antony. He came quickly forward and knelt to Brutus. His master had sent him. Antony asked for no more than safe conduct to come before Brutus; and, if Brutus should satisfy him that Caesar's death had been necessary, he would be content to follow where the noble Brutus led.

"He shall be satisfied," said Brutus, and sent the servant back. It would be well to have Mark Antony for a friend.

"I wish we may," said Cassius quietly. "But yet I have a mind that fears him much."

Mark Antony came directly. His eyes were still looped with shadows from a long night's drinking and his step was unsteady; for he was a lover of wine and good company. Then he saw Caesar, huddled in his torn and bloody gown, like a dead beast roughly covered over, to keep the flies away. He stopped, and tears filled his eyes.

"O mighty Caesar! Dost thou lie so low?" he wept helplessly. "Fare thee well!"

He was a young man of quick, strong feelings which, try as he might, he could not hide. His heart was breaking, for he had loved and admired Caesar above all other men. He turned to Brutus and his friends and begged them, if they bore him any ill-will, to kill him there and then, with the very weapons with which they had killed Caesar.

"O Antony," protested Brutus, much moved by the young man's grief, "beg not your death of us!" and he promised that, when the frightened people had been calmed, he would satisfy him with good reasons for Caesar's death.

Antony nodded; and, on a sudden impulse that was the mark of his nature, he shook each man by his bloody hand, as if to enrol himself among the givers of liberty. Brutus's wish was gratified. Mark Antony

51

was their friend. All he asked in return, was leave to speak at Caesar's funeral. A small request.

"You shall, Mark Antony," said Brutus warmly.

"Brutus, a word with you!"

It was Cassius. He beckoned Brutus away.

"You know not what you do," he warned. "Do not consent!"

He did not trust Mark Antony and feared what he might say. But Brutus brushed his fears aside. He had foreseen that danger and was prepared. Antony would speak only after he himself had addressed the people and given them the reason for Caesar's death. He was not to blame Brutus and his companions, nor was he to say more in praise of Caesar than was proper for a friend. If Antony did not agree to these conditions, he was not to speak at all.

"Be it so," murmured Antony when Brutus told him. "I do desire no more."

"Prepare the body, then, and follow us," said Brutus; and, with a reassuring smile at the still troubled Cassius, led the way outside to face the people of Rome.

Antony was alone in the silent building. Around him, the pale columns

grew upward, losing themselves in shadows; and on the floor, like the track of a hunted deer, were smears and spots and puddles of blood.

Antony knelt. With trembling hands he uncovered Caesar's face. He stared at it long and hard, as if to engrave each savage wound upon his memory for ever. Then he looked up; and with eyes that blazed with grief and rage, he vowed so terrible a revenge for the foul crime that all Italy would bleed for it!

The news of Caesar's death rushed through the city like a wind, whipping up excitement, fear and bewilderment. The great man, the fixed star that had held all in place, was gone! The world was in darkness, even at noon!

But to Brutus, the world was already a brighter and a nobler place now that the danger of Caesar's ambition had been cut off. He stood on the steps of the Capitol with all Rome crowding to hear him.

"Romans, countrymen, and lovers," he shouted, striving to calm the huge tide of people that rose and fell before him like an unruly sea, "hear me for my cause!"

He told them why Caesar had been killed; and they cheered. He told them they were free; and they cheered. He told them they were proud Romans, and they cheered till the very air was dazed; not for what he said, but because he was the noble Brutus who would tell them what to do. Then, when Mark Antony appeared, with two servants bearing Caesar's sheeted body, which they laid upon a hastily prepared bier, he waved his dagger, still bright with Caesar's blood, over his head and cried that even as he had killed Caesar for the good of Rome, he would kill himself if Rome should ever need his death!

"Live, Brutus, live, live!" roared the crowd. "Let him be Caesar!"

Brutus stared at them, amazed. Was it possible that they wanted another tyrant so soon after they had been saved from one?

"My countrymen—" he pleaded, but they would not listen; and he was compelled to beg them, over and over again, to stay and hear Mark Antony before they let him depart, with "Let him be Caesar!" still ringing in his ears.

Brutus and the conspirators had gone. Antony was alone before the people of Rome. He came forward. The crowd stirred impatiently. After the success of Brutus, Antony was a slight figure on the steps. He began to speak, humbly. He said he spoke by permission of Brutus and his friends; but the crowd, catching only the name, angrily warned him to speak no ill of the noble Brutus. Antony bowed his head.

"You gentle Romans—" he began again; but the crowd was still restless. Suddenly he took a step towards Caesar's bier. The dead man's arm had slipped from the shroud and was hanging down, like butcher's meat. Quickly, Antony took it up, and, kissing the half-clenched hand, laid it across Caesar's breast. It was simply done, and with perfect naturalness; but, like the artless gesture of a skilful actor, it caught every eye.

"Friends, Romans, countrymen," he shouted, in a voice that shook the very stones of Rome, "lend me your ears!"

But there was no need. He had already seized attention by the throat; and he held it fast! The vast crowd stood motionless; wives turned from their husbands, young men from their loves, and even the ever-running children stopped, stared, and listened as Mark Antony spoke of the dead.

Cautiously at first, and ever-mindful of the need to please his hearers with praise for Brutus, he began to conjure up the Caesar they had lost: a Caesar men might weep for, a Caesar who was good and just; a Caesar whose only ambition was for his country, and in whose mighty heart there was room enough for love of every soul in Rome.

He spoke as a simple, honest man to simple, honest men. As Cassius had feared, he spoke not to their reason, but to their feelings—

"Bear with me," he cried, his eyes fiery with tears, "my heart is in the coffin there with Caesar, and I must pause till it come back to me!"

A murmuring of pity sprang up, ruffling through the crowd and shivering it, like a sudden change of wind. Swiftly, he began to work upon it, until the shivering became a heaving and swelling, like the breathing of a giant beast. He showed the people a parchment. It was Caesar's will. The crowd pressed forward. Antony drew back. It was wrong for the people to know that their Caesar had loved them so well that he had made them all his heirs. It might turn them against the 'honourable men' who had stabbed Caesar to death!

"They were villains, murderers!" shouted the crowd, enraged with grief and greed. "The will! Read the will!"

But still Antony held off, knowing that each time he dammed the ever-increasing tide it would gather in strength.

"If you have tears, prepare to shed them now!" he cried, and held up, for all to see, Caesar's robe, torn and bloody from dagger-thrusts, as if wild beasts had been rending it; and then, with one fierce movement, he snatched away the shroud and showed the people Caesar himself, the man who had loved them, hacked and mangled by his friends!

Only then, when the people's fury had mounted to its utmost pitch, did he read the will. For every man, a sum of money, and Caesar's orchards and gardens and walks had been left to the people for them to enjoy for ever!

"Here was a Caesar!" shouted Antony, as the crowd roared and howled for vengeance on the cruel murderers. "When comes such another?"

"Never, never!" came the huge reply; and there was scarcely time for Antony to cover the body for decency's sake, before, like a bloody banner, it was borne triumphantly aloft!

"Mischief, thou art afoot," whispered Antony as he hastened away. "Take thou what course thou wilt!" and the maddened multitude, like a monstrously swollen river, burst its banks!

It rushed through the city, smashing windows, tearing out the frames and sweeping all to destruction in its path, with the dead Caesar, like a piece of wreckage on a raging tide, tossed this way and that, now down, now bolt-upright and grinning horribly at his revenge!

There was a man walking peaceably in a street. He was a quiet, humble fellow, a poet, a dreamer of sweet dreams, who had never done the world any harm. Suddenly the crowd came upon him. Fiercely, they demanded his name. By ill-luck, it was Cinna—

"Tear him to pieces!" screamed the crowd. "He's a conspirator!"

"I am Cinna the poet! I am Cinna the poet!" pleaded the poor wretch; but his name was still Cinna so they tore him, shrieking, limb from limb. Tyranny was dead; and so was Cinna the poet.

Then with howls and yells and blazing brands, the crowd, more terrible by far than the wild apparitions that had stalked the streets in the prophetic storm, rushed away to wreak its vengeance on the conspirators!

In Mark Antony's house, three men sat at a table that was coldly laid for death. One was Antony himself; another was Lepidus, a sturdy soldier with valuable legions at his command; the third was a pale, precise young man, younger, even, than Antony, who glanced with thin-lipped disapproval at the empty bottles and faded remembrances of ladies that littered the room. He was Octavius, grand-nephew of Caesar and heir to his mighty name.

"Prick him down, Antony," he murmured, nodding towards a list of names that lay upon the table between them.

Antony looked down and, with a careless stroke of his pen, condemned yet another man to death. Not for such men as these was there the foolish magnanimity of a Brutus who had once spared Antony's life! It needed but the faintest shadow cast on a man's loyalty for him to be dragged from his bed, his throat cut, and his possessions seized.

It was a dangerous time. The murder of Caesar had split the land and unleashed the terror of war. Brutus and Cassius had fled from the wrath of the people and were, even now, gathering armies beyond Rome. More and more money was wanted for soldiers to march against them. With a wave of his hand, Antony despatched Lepidus to Caesar's house to fetch his will. The promised legacies would have to be cut off. Everything was needed to pay for the war.

"This is a slight unmeritable man," said Antony contemptuously, when Lepidus had gone; and he proposed that, once the fellow had served his turn, he and Octavius should rid themselves of him.

"But he's a tried and valiant soldier," protested Octavius.

"So is my horse," said Antony.

Octavius let it pass. He had no wish to quarrel with Antony. Young as he was, he was already politician enough to know better than to mingle feelings with policy. Nothing must be allowed to deflect them from their chief purpose, which was the destruction of Brutus and Cassius and all who had inclined to them. He stood up, and, looking over Antony's shoulder, observed with cold satisfaction that the list of names was black with spots of death.

Brutus, encamped near Sardis in far-off Asia Minor, also needed money for war. He had sent to Cassius; but had been denied. Now, with his huge army stretched out across the fields like a monstrous harvest of steel, waving and glinting as far as the eye could see in the setting sun, he waited outside his tent for some explanation from his friend.

His old calmness had forsaken him. His heart, already heavy with bad news from home, had been stirred to anger by Cassius's doubtful behaviour, not only in denying him money, but because he had dared to plead for a man that he, Brutus, had punished for taking bribes. Even in war, their hands must be clean and their hearts unspotted.

"Most noble brother, you have done me wrong!" were Cassius's first words when they met, and spoken loud.

He had come with his officers, ahead of his marching legions, and now confronted Brutus. He, too, was an angry man; and, unlike his friend, made no effort to hide it. He had not liked the manner in which Brutus had reproached him for seeking to defend his guilty officer. He stood, breathing deeply, his brow dark and his fists clenched; and saw himself reflected, Medusa-like, in Brutus's too-bright breastplate: a frowning fellow in armour that was worn and soiled from hard fighting, very like the man himself.

Quietly, Brutus bade him come inside his tent. It was not wise for discord between generals to be in the public gaze. Accordingly, they dismissed their officers and, with an outward show of harmony, retired into Brutus's tent. But once the heavy, dim interior had enclosed them and shut them away from curious eyes, the division between them sprang wide apart.

The cause was money: money denied, and money got from bribery, which Brutus hated and despised. Private grief and the multiplying troubles of war had so stiffened his pride and encased him in the armour of his honour, that he could not forgive even the smallest falling away from honesty, least of all when he saw it in his friend.

"Let me tell you, Cassius," he said, as if to an underling, "you yourself are much condemned to have an itching palm . . ."

"I an itching palm!" cried Cassius, unable to believe that Brutus could address him so contemptuously.

"Remember March, the Ides of March remember. Did not great Julius bleed for justice' sake?" went on Brutus, as if careless of the deep hurt he had inflicted. "Shall we now contaminate our fingers with base bribes? . . . I had rather be a dog and bay the moon, than such a Roman."

"Brutus, bait not me," Cassius pleaded, striving with all his might to control his outraged heart. "You forget yourself. I am a soldier, I, older in practice, abler than yourself to make conditions!"

"Go on! You are not, Cassius."

"I am."

"I say you are not."

"Urge me no more!" warned Cassius, his hand going helplessly to his sword. "Have mind upon your health!"

"Away, slight man!" jeered Brutus; and, while Cassius spent himself in useless rage, he pricked and stabbed and hacked him with words as cold and sharp as steel, never giving him rest, ever accusing, ever condemning, until Cassius, staggering even as Caesar had staggered under the dagger-thrusts, could endure no more.

"Come, Antony, and young Octavius, come," he wept, sinking to his knees, "revenge yourselves alone on Cassius, for Cassius is aweary of the world . . ." He drew his dagger and offered it to Brutus. "Strike as thou didst at Caesar," he begged; "for I know, when thou didst hate him worst, thou lov'dst him better than ever thou lov'dst Cassius."

They stared at one another, these two friends who had come so far together since the Ides of March, and marvelled that it should have come to this: that one should now be begging his death of the other.

"Sheathe your dagger," muttered Brutus, suddenly ashamed; and, with an effort, thrust aside his private sorrow and confessed that he had been ill-tempered.

At once, Cassius, as quick to forgive as he was in everything, smiled. "Give me your hand!" he cried.

"And my heart too," answered Brutus gladly; and their hands were clasped once more in friendship. He called for his servant Lucius to bring a bowl of wine.

"I did not think you could have been so angry," murmured Cassius, as they waited.

"O Cassius," sighed Brutus, "I am sick of many griefs;" and then, unable any longer to hide the aching desolation in his heart, he told Cassius that Portia was dead.

Cassius drew in his breath sharply. "How 'scaped I killing when I crossed you so?" he whispered, in a rush of pity for his friend. "O insupportable and touching loss! Upon what sickness?"

No sickness but fear: fear for her husband, and fear of Antony and Octavius's growing strength. She had killed herself.

"Speak no more of her," pleaded Brutus, as Lucius came in with wine and with lighted tapers that changed the dark tent into a solemn golden cave.

The friends drank. There was a sound of voices outside. Lucius departed and a moment later, brought in two officers, Messala and Titinius. Brutus bade them be seated . . .

"Portia," sighed Cassius, his thoughts still with the lively lady whose dear love and sweet honesty had lightened Brutus's life, "art thou gone?"

"No more, I pray you!" whispered Brutus urgently; and, turning to the officers was, in a moment, his calm, unshaken self.

He had letters from Rome. Mark Antony and Octavius, with their armies, were marching towards Philippi. Messala nodded. He also had had letters confirming it. In addition, he had heard that a hundred senators had been put to death. Brutus had heard the same.

"Had you your letters from your wife, my lord?" asked Messala gently.

Brutus shook his head. Messala asked if his letters had contained any news of his wife? Again Brutus shook his head. Messala glanced quickly at Titinius, and in that glance it was plain that he knew of Portia's death and dreaded telling Brutus of it. Cassius scowled and turned away. His heart ached for his friend.

"Then like a Roman bear the truth I tell," said Messala steadily, "for certain she is dead . . ."

Brutus bowed his head. "Why, farewell, Portia," he murmured, and Messala and Titinius marvelled at his fortitude; but Cassius knew that such fortitude was paid for with a sea of inward tears.

"Well, to our work," said Brutus, abruptly dismissing all grief for the immediate necessity. "What do you think of marching to Philippi presently?"

Cassius was against it. It was wiser, he reasoned, for the enemy to come to them, and so waste himself with journeying. But Brutus knew better. The enemy was more likely to gain in strength from marching through a friendly countryside, whereas they themselves were already at the height of their power and could only decline.

"There is a tide in the affairs of men," he said, "which, taken at the flood, leads on to fortune; omitted, all the voyage of their life is bound in shallows and miseries." He paused; then went on: "We must take the current when it serves, or lose our ventures."

There was silence. Then one by one, his companions, their faces glowing in the tapers' yellow light, nodded. It was agreed. Tomorrow they were to set out for Philippi and the battle that would decide their fates. Quietly they took their leave.

Presently Brutus was alone. All but one of the tapers had been extinguished and the camp was quiet; but he could not sleep. He called for Lucius to play some music to him. The boy came, stumbling and clutching his lute, still half in his dreams.

"This is a sleepy tune," smiled Brutus as the music began. Then it ceased; the boy was fast asleep. Brutus gazed at him, enviously; but did not wake him. Gently he took the instrument from his hands and put it aside, lest it break in falling to the floor. He drew his seat close to the taper and tried to read; but the flame was sickly: it shook and trembled like a fevered spirit.

"How ill this taper burns!" he muttered, and laid his book aside.

61

The sleeping boy was smiling; he was in a happier time. Brutus sighed, and gazed into the crowding shadows that shifted, like uneasy thoughts, in the quiet tent. Smoke from the taper weaved up into the air, where it hovered curiously, as if it had met with an invisible obstruction. As he watched, it seemed to grow pale and form itself into the shape of a robe.

Drops of sweat gathered on Brutus's brow as, little by little, the robe became inhabited, and flowers of blood began to blossom amid the folds.

"Ha! Who comes here?" he whispered, as if to deny the fearful evidence of his senses.

"Thy evil spirit, Brutus," answered the apparition, fixing him with a pallid stare. It was Caesar, torn and bloody in his murder gown, even as Brutus had seen him when he'd stabbed him to death.

"Why com'st thou?"

"To tell thee thou shalt see me at Philippi."

"Well; then I shall see thee again?"

"Ay, at Philippi," came the solemn answer; and, with a gesture of farewell, the ghost of murdered Caesar faded and dissolved into the air.

The plains of Philippi swarmed with armed men, thick as bees.

"Mark Antony, shall we give sign of battle?" asked Octavius eagerly, his thin blood suddenly heated to a youthful rashness as a little group of horsemen, their breastplates glittering, came rapidly towards them, under the scarlet banner of war.

Antony, the seasoned soldier, smiled contemptuously, and shook his head.

"No, Caesar," he said, as Brutus and Cassius and their officers drew near, "the generals would have some words."

Presently they were face to face: the mighty enemies whose quarrel had divided the world. They stared at one another, silently noting the change that had been wrought by time and struggle; how much older and harsher they all looked, like men of rough-hewn stone! Their meeting was brief and bitter. Antony savagely denounced the murderers of Caesar, and they flung back his words with angry scorn.

"A peevish schoolboy," jeered Cassius, "join'd with a masker and a reveller!"

"Old Cassius still!" mocked Antony, yet with an unwilling affection for the man of passion who, in some ways, was more his fellow than was the bloodless youth by his side.

"Come, Antony," cried Octavius, wearied of insults and impatient for deeds, "away!" And so they parted, returning to their waiting legions, to make ready for the coming battle that for many would be their last.

"Messala," called Cassius, while Brutus was conferring apart with another of his officers.

Messala came to his side. Cassius smiled; but there was no pleasure in it. It was the saddened smile of a man suddenly tired of the fury of life. "This is my birthday," he confided; and, as Messala shook him by the hand, he charged him to bear witness that he had been compelled, against his better judgement, to risk all on the outcome of a single battle. He had strong forebodings of disaster.

"Believe not so," urged Messala; and Cassius, for a brief while, put on a cheerful face; but when he spoke with Brutus, it was of what should be done if the battle was lost, and how they should end their lives.

There was a grave solemnity between the friends as they spoke together. "This same day," said Brutus quietly, "must end that work the Ides of March begun, and whether we shall meet again I know not. Therefore our everlasting farewell take." He held out his hand, and Cassius took it firmly in his own. "For ever, and for ever, farewell, Cassius. If we do meet again, why, we shall smile; if not, why then this parting was well made."

"For ever, and for ever, farewell, Brutus," said Cassius, with a long and steady look. "If we do meet again, we'll smile indeed; if not, 'tis true this parting was well made."

Then they turned, and, with a last wave of the hand in a last farewell, rode away, each to his own command.

The bright morning grew still, as if, for a moment, all Nature was holding its breath. Then, with a sudden scream of trumpets and a roaring of drums, the legions began to move. As they did so, a vast cloud of dust rose up from the plain, and the earth shook under the tread of the opposing armies, like the mighty heart-beat of the world.

Now more clouds, tossed with pennants and pricked with sharp glints of steel, began to roll and billow down from the hills until, with a thunderous uproar, all met together like rushing waters, tumbling down, one upon another.

All day long the battle raged, with ever-changing fortunes, now inclining this way, now that, until the very sun was steeped in blood, and sank, dying, below the hills.

At last it was over, and a thankful darkness overspread the field, turning those who had died in triumph and those who had fallen in defeat, all alike into quiet black shapes. A single torch, like a flaring moth, wandered hither and thither, sometimes hovering to illumine upturned faces, like pale streaked flowers; then it moved on, with a little group of men wearily following after.

. . . the very sun was steeped in blood

"Come, poor remains of friends," sighed Brutus, "rest on this rock."

They halted, and, with heavy looks and aching hearts, sank down, some sitting with dazed head falling forward onto huddled knees, some leaning back against the rock and staring up at the cold stars. Brutus alone remained standing, sword in hand, as if to kill a ghost.

All was lost. Antony and Octavius had won the day. Cassius was dead. Rather than be taken by the enemy, he had killed himself with the very weapon that had stabbed Caesar.

"O Julius Caesar, thou art mighty yet," Brutus had wept when he'd looked down on the still face of his friend, whose eager fire was out, "thy spirit walks abroad and turns our swords in our own proper entrails."

Softly Brutus called to one of the pitiful few who seemed to cling about the rock like the sea-torn remnants of a wreck. The man came and Brutus whispered an urgent request. The man stared at him in dread. He shook his head and shrank away.

"What ill request did Brutus make of thee?" asked one of his companions.

"To kill him . . ."

Now Brutus summoned another, and made the same terrible request. But the man would not; and the third he asked, answered:

"That's not an office for a friend, my lord."

Suddenly there was heard a distant trumpet and a sound of shouting. Hastily, the friends arose . . . all save one who had been fast asleep: a fellow by the name of Strato, a thick-necked, sturdy fellow with an honest, albeit sleepy face.

Urgently, they begged Brutus to fly. He promised that he would; and, as his friends left him, he laid a hand on Strato's arm and asked him to stay behind. Strato, as slow to leave a friend in need as he was to save himself, stayed by Brutus's side.

"Thy life," said Brutus, to this last companion, "hath had some smatch of honour in it. Hold then my sword, and turn away thy face, while I do run upon it. Wilt thou, Strato?"

Strato, dull of wit but stout of heart, did not like the office; but he knew there was no other way. He was not a thinker, as Brutus was; but, like Brutus, he counted honour above mere life.

"Give me your hand first," he demanded; and, as Brutus clasped his hand, he took the sword and held it firmly. "Fare you well, my lord," he murmured, and turned away his face.

"Farewell, good Strato," whispered Brutus; and, with a last sad look about him, sighed: "Caesar, now be still. I killed not thee with half so good a will!"

Then, with one swift movement, he ran upon the sword; and, as the sharp steel entered him, his life rushed gladly out.

Gently, Strato withdrew the sword and laid it by his master's side. Then he arranged the body so that it should lie decently; and stood beside it to tell the world that Brutus had died as he had lived, with courage and with honour.

He was still there, the solitary sentinel, when the victors, their triumphant faces glowing in torchlight as they searched the battlefield for the chief of their enemies, at last came upon Brutus, dead.

"I held the sword," Strato told them proudly, "and he did run on it."

Mark Antony nodded. He understood such a death, even if he did not understand such a life.

"This was the noblest Roman of them all," he said, gazing down with respect upon the calm, proud face of his enemy, the man who had committed the worst of deeds for the best of reasons. "His life was gentle, and the elements so mixed in him, that Nature might stand up and say to all the world, 'This was a man!'"

Even as he said it, he glanced sideways at the cold, precise young man, who stood beside him; and slightly shook his head.

"According to his virtue let us use him," said Octavius, impatient to have done with wasteful generosity to the dead, "and let's away, to part the glories of this happy day."

Then together they left the field . . .

Antony and Cleopatra

Three men ruled the world: Octavius Caesar, Lepidus, and Mark Antony. Two were in Rome, where they belonged; the third, to his shame, was in Egypt, where he lay, gasping and wallowing like a huge fish in the luxurious net of the harlot Queen.

"Look, where they come!" In the gaudy hall of Cleopatra's palace in Alexandria, two Roman soldiers scowled angrily as Antony and Cleopatra appeared. It broke their hearts to see their master, the foremost soldier of the world, with the black-haired gipsy on his arm, and followed by all the squeaking eunuchs and tinsel girls of her court, waving their painted fans.

"If it be love indeed, tell me how much?" demanded Cleopatra, as if she was inquiring into some grave matter on which the fate of the world depended; and he, poor fool, answered with a wave of his lordly arm, "There's beggary in the love that can be reckoned!" and the gods alone knew how long they would have gone on with their bedroom chatter had not a servant come to tell them that ambassadors had arrived from Rome.

Antony brushed the news aside. What was Rome to him? But Cleopatra shook her head. "Nay, hear them," she urged; and with a mocking smile, suggested that they might be bringing word from Fulvia, his scolding wife, or even from young Caesar whose slightest command must be obeyed.

"Let Rome in Tiber melt, and the wide arch of the rang'd empire fall!" roared the old lion, stung by Cleopatra's taunts. "Here is my space!" and, to the applause of the idle court, clasped her in his arms and kissed her full upon the lips. "Come, my Queen!" he cried; and away went the shameless, laughing pair, in search of fresh distractions from the harsh, but necessary business of life.

Sadly, the watching Romans shook their heads . . .

There was a soothsayer in the palace, a magical old man who could tell fortunes. Eagerly, Charmian and Iras, the Queen's best-loved attendants, squabbled like a pair of sparrows over who should be first. Charmian won. "Good sir," she begged, holding out her palm like a child for sweets, "give me good fortune!"

The old man, seated on a cushion and wrapped in a blue robe embroidered with moons and stars, frowned as if his dignity had been offended. "I make not," said he, "but foresee."

"Pray then, forsee me one!" commanded Charmian, as imperiously as the Queen herself; and while the soothsayer bent his ancient head over her childish hand, she demanded, "Let me be married to three kings in a forenoon, and widow them all. Let me have a child at fifty—"

But the soothsayer shook his head. "You shall outlive the lady whom you serve," was all he would tell her; and he let go of her hand almost in haste.

Now it was Iras's turn. "Tell her but a worky-day fortune!" urged Charmian, not wanting to be out-fortuned by her friend. But Iras fared no better than she. "Your fortunes are alike," said the soothsayer quietly; and, though they plagued him with eager questions, he would say no more.

Antony was with the ambassadors. He had left Cleopatra's side abruptly. Angrily she'd guessed that a Roman thought had struck him. He was frowning heavily. The news from Rome was bad. Rebellion everywhere. Pompey, the ambitious son of Pompey the Great, had raised the flag of war; and Fulvia, Antony's meddlesome wife, had joined with factions against Caesar. The only crumb of comfort was that she had died . . .

He dismissed the ambassadors and began to pace to and fro. Everything demanded that he should return to Rome; everything except his heart. "I must from this enchanting Queen break off," he muttered. "Ten thousand harms my idleness doth hatch." He called for Enobarbus, his lieutenant and friend. Enobarbus was the only man to whom he could open his heart; he was a Roman, without a Roman thought in his head.

"What's your pleasure, sir?" inquired Enobarbus, appearing with his usual worldly smile.

"I must be gone."

Enobarbus's narrow, crinkled eyes grew round with surprise. "Why then we kill all our women!" he protested. "Cleopatra, catching but the least noise of this, dies instantly; I have seen her die twenty times upon far poorer moment."

This was no less than the truth. Her moods and passions were as wild and tempestuous as the sea itself. "Would I have never seen her!" sighed Antony.

"O, sir," said Enobarbus gravely, "you had then left unseen a wonderful piece of work."

Antony bowed his head. As always, Enobarbus spoke the truth. But nonetheless, he must return to Rome . . .

"Where is he?" Cleopatra was searching for her lover. "See where he is!" she commanded her minister, Alexas. "If you find him sad, say I am dancing; if in mirth, report that I am sudden sick: quick, and return!"

When Alexas had gone, Charmian reproached her royal mistress for being so contrary. Cleopatra stared at the girl in astonishment. "What should I do, I do not?"

"In each thing give him way, cross him in nothing," counselled the girl.

Cleopatra laughed. "Thou teachest like a fool: the way to lose him!"

"Tempt him not so too far," began Charmian; when Antony himself entered the apartment. Poor gentleman! he was smiling—

"I am sick and sullen!" cried the Queen instantly, and clung to Charmian for support. "Help me away!"

He had a letter in his hand. He came towards her. "My dearest Queen," he started to say; but she would not let him continue. Her quick eye had divined that he'd come to tell her that he was returning to Rome. "What, says the married woman you may go?" she demanded bitterly, and pointed to the letter. He pleaded to be heard. She shook her head. "Bid farewell and go; when you sued staying, then was the time for words; no going then; eternity was in our lips and eyes . . ."

At last she let him speak. He told her of the perilous state of the world that demanded his presence in Rome; and then, hoping to please her, he told her that Fulvia, his wife, was dead.

She stared at him. "Though age from folly could not give me freedom, it does from childishness. Can Fulvia die?"

Eagerly, he showed her the letter; but instead of the joy he'd hoped

for, she turned on him in a fury! She was outraged by his lack of grief! "Now I see, I see, in Fulvia's death, how mine received shall be!"

She'd gone too far! Charmian saw it. Antony was frowning. "You'll heat my blood: no more," he warned her. "I'll leave you, lady."

At once, Cleopatra's tempest subsided. She smiled sadly, and shook her head. "Courteous lord, one word: sir, you and I must part, but that's not it; sir, you and I have loved, but there's not it; that you know well. Something it is I would—" She paused and sighed: "O my oblivion is a very Antony, and I am all forgotten."

Antony's frowns fled, like snow before the melting sun; and Charmian marvelled to see how easily her royal mistress extended her sovereignty over the great Roman's heart.

There was anger in Rome, and fear. The Roman world was threatened. Every hour, it seemed, brought in news of fresh uprisings. Octavius Caesar strode furiously back and forth across his wide marble floor, on which was depicted, like a private garden, the world. At one moment, his thin foot was upon Sicily, then Athens, then Lydia, while his billowing gown swept the seas between. Puffing and panting in his wake, and childishly trying not to tread on the lines, sweated fat old Lepidus, the third and feeblest of the three world rulers. "'Tis pity of him," he urged, striving to find excuses for the absent Antony.

Octavius glanced at his partner with contempt. "Let his shames quickly drive him to Rome," he said, his foot poised above Egypt. Then he brought it down, grinding it heavily, as if to crush something unclean . . .

Cleopatra yawned. "Give me to drink mandragora," she commanded.

"Why, madam?" asked Charmian.

"That I might sleep out this great gap of time my Antony is away." She sighed and smiled. "Did I, Charmian, ever love Caesar so?" she wondered, dreamily remembering the mighty Julius Caesar, who had been her lover, long ago.

"O! that brave Caesar!" sighed Charmian.

"Say the brave Antony!"

"The valiant Caesar!"

71

"By Isis," cried Cleopatra, raising a clenched fist, "I will give thee bloody teeth!"

"By your most gracious pardon," pleaded Charmian, skipping back, "I sing but after you."

"My salad days," said Cleopatra, with a careless wave of her hand, "when I was green in judgement." She called for ink and paper. Her Antony must have another letter. Every day since he had gone, her messengers had sped after him, swift as Cupid's arrows.

Antony was in Rome. He had brought Enobarbus with him. They were in the house of Lepidus, who had provided a great feast to celebrate the meeting of Antony and Caesar, in the firm belief that nothing is so conducive to good fellowship as good food and wine. But he was wrong. No sooner had the two men met than they were at each other's throats. It was the worldly Enobarbus alone who helped himself to Lepidus's feast, looking up from time to time with dry amusement as angry words, sharp as Lepidus's fruit-knives, flew across the table.

"It cannot be we shall remain in friendship," said Octavius at length, "our conditions so differing in their acts. If I knew what hoop would hold us—"

"Give me leave, Caesar," suddenly interposed Agrippa, one of Caesar's men. Everyone looked at him, inquiringly. Agrippa reached out and took hold of a peach. Carefully he studied it. Caesar had a sister, the fair and lovely Octavia, he observed thoughtfully; and now that Mark Antony was a widower—

"If Cleopatra heard you—" warned Octavius, mockingly; but Antony shook his head. "I am not married, Caesar," he said quietly. "Let me hear Agrippa further speak."

Agrippa continued. If words could not heal the division between Caesar and Antony, let it then be healed by the ties of blood. Let Antony marry Octavia!

Enobarbus watched his master. Antony's face was grave and thoughtful. He was no longer the careless lover, but the shrewd politician. His Roman head had conquered his Egyptian heart. He looked at Caesar. Caesar nodded. Antony rose to his feet, and held out his hand. At once, Caesar responded. "A sister I bequeath you," he loudly proclaimed, "whom no brother did ever love so dearly!"

"Happily, amen!" cried Lepidus, as Caesar and Mark Antony clasped each other firmly by the hand. Then the new-made brothers, together with their host, went off to seek out the fair Octavia, and tell her of her good fortune.

Three remained behind: Enobarbus, Agrippa, and Maecenas, another of Caesar's men. Eagerly, the Roman pair plied their visitor with questions about Egypt, its fabled feasts, and its fabled queen. What was Cleopatra really like? Had she been, as men reported, so wonderful a sight when first she'd met Mark Antony on the River Cydnus?

Enobarbus smiled. "I will tell you," he said softly. "The barge she sat in, like a burnished throne, burned on the water; the poop was beaten gold, purple the sails . . ." and as he conjured up the marvellous scene, his two listeners drew close, as Rome dissolved and Cleopatra filled the air. "For her own person," sighed Enobarbus, "it beggared all description."

"Royal wench!" breathed Agrippa.

"Now Antony must leave her utterly," murmured Maecenas.

Enobarbus shook his head. "Never; he will not: age cannot wither her, nor custom stale her infinite variety; other women cloy the appetites they feed, but she makes hungry where most she satisfies . . ."

The three men were silent. Then Maecenas said quietly, "If beauty, wisdom, modesty can settle the heart of Antony, Octavia is a blessed lottery to him," and all agreed.

In Caesar's house, where the world lay stretched across the marble floor, 'the blessed lottery', pale as milk, walked between her mighty brother and her mighty husband-to-be. Antony, bestriding the East, solemnly promised Octavia that he would be true to his marriage vows, and wished her goodnight.

"Goodnight, sir," said she, curtseying low; and Caesar led her away.

Antony stared after the gentle lady. She was the price he'd paid for an empire. Suddenly he became aware he was not alone. An old man in a blue robe was watching him. It was the soothsayer. Antony had brought him to Rome as a rare wonder of the East. "Now, sirrah," asked Antony, tracing the snaky Nile with his foot, "do you wish yourself in Egypt?"

"Would I had never come from thence," answered the old man, "nor you thither."

Antony shrugged his shoulders. On an impulse, he held out his palm. "Say to me, whose fortune shall rise higher, Caesar's or mine?"

Obediently the soothsayer studied the palm that held a third of the world in its grasp. He looked up. "Caesar's," he said. "Stay not by his side."

Antony frowned. "Speak no more of this," he said. The old man nodded, and withdrew. The soothsayer had spoken the truth, and Antony knew it. Though he was ten times Caesar's superior in soldiership, Caesar would always win. He had the luck. And no man could prevail against luck. He stared after the departed Octavia. He sighed heavily. "Though I make this marriage for my peace," he whispered, "i' the East my pleasure lies."

But Antony's peace proved worse than war, and the news of it made Egypt tremble. In terror, her court looked on as Cleopatra stormed and raged and screamed horrible revenges on the luckless messenger who'd uttered the words, "He's married to Octavia!" She beat him with her tight fists, she seized him by the hair, she dragged him up and down the room, scattering cushions and courtiers alike, she snatched up a dagger—and the man fled for his life!

She stood swaying, as if she would fall. She stared at the dagger she still held in her hand. She shook her head and laid it aside. She picked up a golden mirror and gazed into it. Little by little, her spirits began to rise. Her weapon was not a dagger, but the strange magic of her person. "Go to the fellow, good Alexas," she commanded her minister; "bid him report the feature of Octavia, her years, her inclination, let him not leave out the colour of her hair; bring me word quickly!"

While Cleopatra, in her fashion, was preparing for war, Antony, Caesar and Lepidus were celebrating a peace. They had concluded a treaty with Pompey and his ally, Menas the pirate, and were aboard his galley in the harbour at Misenum, roaring and singing and drinking each other's healths. Swinging lanterns made a tipsy day of night, and

clustering faces, like a windfall of red-cheeked apples, rolled and tumbled about the deck. But one of them was green. "I am not so well as I should be," moaned Lepidus, clasping Antony fondly about the neck; "but I'll ne'er out!" and he held out his cup to be filled as if, by drinking yet another health, he could restore his own.

A single figure stood apart: Menas, the pirate. He leaned against the side of the vessel and watched the great ones of the world, all drunk; and in their midst, his captain, Pompey, pitifully trying to be the man his father had been. Quietly, he approached him. "Pompey," he murmured, "a word." But Pompey waved him aside, and filled up Lepidus's cup.

Lepidus had grown studious. "What manner o' thing is your crocodile?" he inquired, suddenly displaying an interest in the natural world, of which he was part commander.

Carefully, Antony explained. "It is shaped, sir, like itself, and it is as broad as it hath breadth; it is just so high as it is, and it moves with its own organs . . ."

"What colour is it of?" pursued Lepidus, intelligently.

"Of its own colour too," Antony informed him.

Lepidus nodded wisely. "'Tis a strange serpent," he said; and Antony agreed. "'Tis so, and the tears of it are wet." This extra weight of knowledge proved too much for Lepidus. He slid gently from his place and vanished below the table.

While efforts were being made to restore Lepidus to the world, Menas again approached his captain. "Rise from thy stool!" he muttered; and Pompey, with a frown, followed his ally to the side of the vessel. He looked inquiringly at him. Menas put his face close. "Wilt thou be lord of all the world?" Pompey stared. "How should that be?" Menas pointed to the ship's cable, then to the three rulers of the world. Cut the cable, then cut the throats of Antony, Caesar and Lepidus.

Pompey caught his breath. A tempting prospect. But he shook his head. "Ah! this thou should'st have done, and not spoken on't," he murmured regretfully. "In me, 'tis villainy; in thee't had been good service . . . desist and drink," he advised, and returned to the feast.

Menas stared after his captain with contempt. He no longer had the stomach to follow a man who lacked the courage to be a villain himself, but who would have been ready enough to profit by another's crime. Grimly he watched Pompey the Fool, son of Pompey the Great, being danced off his feet by Antony and Caesar, while Lepidus, a heap of snoring flesh, was carried away.

Next day, Pompey, full of false success, sailed away, and Antony, Caesar and Lepidus returned to Rome, like three thieves, to share out the spoils. Their business concluded, Antony and his new wife prepared to depart for Athens. "You take from me a great part of myself," Caesar warned Antony, much moved by his sister's tears. "Use me well in't."

Stoutly, Antony protested his good faith, and, in parting, embraced Caesar as a brother. "Adieu; be happy!" Caesar wished him; and Lepidus, still green from Pompey's feast, called down blessings upon the departing pair. Then ceremonial Roman trumpets sounded and Caesar, giving up his sister, raised his arm in Roman salute. Antony returned it, and, ever the gallant gentleman, comforted Octavia with gentle smiles and a courteous arm.

"Is she as tall as me?" Cleopatra, like a shrewd general seeking to know the enemy's strength, closely questioned the cowering messenger about Octavia's charms.

"She is not, madam," came the satisfactory reply.

"Is she shrill-tongued, or low?"

"She is low-voiced."

"That's not so good. He cannot like her long."

"Like her?" cried Charmian loyally. "O Isis! 'tis impossible!"

"I think so, Charmian," agreed the Queen: "dull of tongue and dwarfish. What majesty is in her gait?"

"She creeps," answered the messenger.

"The fellow has good judgement," said Cleopatra, and Charmian agreed. "Guess at her years, I prithee?"

"Madam, she was a widow—" began the messenger cautiously; and when the Queen showed pleasure at the news, he went on, "I do think she's thirty."

An unlucky number. He should have doubled it. The Queen was biting her lip with vexation. He dreaded another tempest. Desperately he sought to undo the harm that 'thirty' had done; and it was only by representing Octavia as being so deficient in womanly grace and beauty as to be an object of pity, that he was able to restore himself to the Queen's favour.

"A proper man," pronounced Charmian when the messenger had gone. Cleopatra nodded. Such a woman as Octavia could never hold her Antony.

In Athens, Octavia trembled, not for herself, but for the world. The division between her brother and her husband, that her marriage should have healed, had gaped open like a wound. She begged Antony's leave to travel to Rome as a supplicant for peace.

"As you requested, yourself shall go between us," said Antony, his fists clenched and his brow thunderous; "the meantime, lady, I'll raise the preparation of a war!"

He was enraged. While he'd been safely in Athens, Caesar had swept all opposition aside. Pompey had been murdered; Lepidus was in prison, awaiting death; and Antony himself had been publicly derided and spoken of with contempt.

"Provide your going," he said, subduing his anger and speaking kindly to his wife; "chose your own company, and command what cost your heart has mind to."

She thanked him; but though she had an empire for her purse, she was no Cleopatra: she travelled simply, and at small expense.

"You are come a market-maid to Rome!" cried Caesar, his dignity offended when his sister presented herself before him, humbly attended and stained and weary from her many days of travel. "The wife of Antony should have an army for an usher!"

Gently she protested that both the time and manner of her coming had been of her own choosing. It was to halt the headlong rush to war that she had begged her husband's leave to come—

"Which soon he granted," said Caesar grimly, "being an obstruct 'tween his lust and him!"

"Do not say so, my lord!" cried Octavia, quick to defend her husband's honour. But Caesar knew better. "I have eyes upon him, and his affairs come to me on the wind. Where is he now?"

"My lord, in Athens."

Caesar shook his head. "No, my most wronged sister; Cleopatra hath nodded him to her. He hath given up his empire to a whore!" She did not answer. "You are abused beyond the mark of thought," went on Caesar, and told her that, no sooner had she left Athens, than Antony had rushed to Egypt, and into the arms of its lustful Queen. There, in Alexandria, in the public market-place, the adulterous pair, seated on golden thrones, had summoned all the kings of the East to join with them in war against Rome.

Octavia bowed her head to hide her tears. Her love, for she did indeed love Antony, had failed. The war that she so dreaded had begun; and it would not end until either her husband or her brother lay dead, together with the many thousands who would fall in their cause.

The world was prepared for war. High up, on the promontory of Actium, the kings of the East had assembled their armies in a shining host; and far below, the sea was dancing with galleys of war. Cleopatra, glittering with excitement, gazed down proudly on her ships; but Enobarbus, who stood by her side, frowned and shook his head. Though she was attired in warlike fashion, with golden breastplate and helmet with gorgeous plumes, she was more like the goddess of love than the goddess of war. Plainly he told her that her presence was ill-timed and would distract Antony from the stern business of battle.

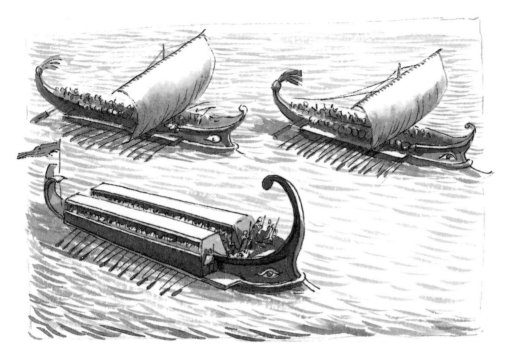

"'Tis said in Rome—"

"Sink Rome, and their tongues rot that speak against us!" she cried angrily. "I will not stay behind!"

Enobarbus shrugged his shoulders. "Nay, I have done," he said. "Here comes the emperor."

Antony, with Canidius, his chief commander, approached. Antony was wearing his old armour, and the shrewd eye of Enobarbus observed that the straps were strained: Antony had put on flesh.

The news was not good. Caesar's advance had been far swifter than had been expected. Already he had crossed the Ionian Sea and captured a town to the north. "You have heard on't, sweet?" Antony asked, turning to Cleopatra. "Celerity," said she sharply, feeling Enobarbus's critical eye upon her, "is never more admired than by the negligent."

"A good rebuke," admitted Antony. "Canidius, we will fight with him by sea."

"By sea! What else?" cried Cleopatra, in high delight. "I have sixty sails, Caesar none better!" But Enobarbus thought otherwise. Antony's ships were poorly manned; he should fight by land. And Canidius agreed.

79

"O noble emperor! do not fight by sea, trust not to rotten planks. Let the Egyptians and the Phoenicians go a-ducking; we have used to conquer standing on the earth, and fighting foot to foot!"

It was a common soldier who'd spoken up, a fellow whose scarred limbs bore witness to many a battle he'd fought for Antony in the past. But Antony, laying a kindly hand on the fellow's shoulder, shook his head. He would fight by sea. He went down to the ships with Cleopatra by his side.

Enobarbus, no lover of sailing, remained on the promontory, and gazed down on the tiny vessels far below. Suddenly, he saw that they were thrown into a commotion. They began to bustle among the busy waves like a flock of warring gulls. The cause of the commotion was approaching from round the headland to the north. It was Caesar's fleet! It was approaching at immense speed! Ten thousand oars were driving his galleys across the water, like a host of venomous insects, churning up a chain of silver drops with their rapid insect legs.

In moments, it seemed, the smaller, swifter Roman vessels were darting among the white and golden ships of Egypt. Glints and flashes pricked the air like furious stitchwork, as arrows flew from decks and rigging, piercing necks and eyes and hearts and faintly screaming lungs. For a while, the advantage lay neither way; if anything, it was with the larger, more heavily armed Egyptians.

Then came an action that even the worldly Enobarbus could not bear to watch. Old Scarus, a general of Antony's, an honest soldier brought up in the countryside and steadfast as an oak, wept openly. "Gods and goddesses!" he cried. "We have kissed away kingdoms and provinces!" The accursed Egyptian whore had fled from the battle, taking her sixty sails with her! "I' the midst of the fight," groaned Scarus, "the breeze upon her, like a cow in June, hoists sails and flies!" And Antony had followed after. "I never saw an action of such shame!"

The day was lost. Antony had thrown away the world for his Egyptian dish. His ships, suddenly leaderless, took fright and scattered. Some escaped; but many, pursued by the swift Roman galleys, were hit by balls of blazing pitch and burned on the water till, like a crowd of setting suns, they sank, hissing, into the sea.

★

. . . they sank, hissing, into the sea

There was a heavy quiet in the palace at Alexandria, and a slow shuffling along the passages as the fearful Cleopatra was led unwillingly to face the giant whose ruin she had brought about.

Antony was not alone. Some soldiers were seated about him, a forlorn encampment amid the idle cushions on the floor. They rose, wearily, as the Queen approached; but Antony did not move. "Go to him, madam, speak to him!" urged Iras, supporting her trembling mistress by the arm; and Antony's servant, Eros, knelt beside his master and begged, "Most noble sir, arise; the Queen approaches . . ."

Antony shook his head. "O whither hast thou led me, Egypt!" he sighed.

"O my lord, my lord!" cried Cleopatra, as she was gently pushed forward by Charmian. "Forgive my fearful sails: I little thought you would have followed."

"Egypt, thou knewst too well my heart was to thy rudder tied by the strings, and thou should'st tow me after—"

"O! my pardon!"

"Now must I to the young man send humble treaties," said Antony bitterly, "dodge and palter in shifts of lowness—"

"Pardon, pardon!"

She knelt beside him. Her marvellous eyes were filled with tears. Helplessly, Antony stretched out his hand and touched her cheek. "Fall not a tear, I say, one of them rates all that is won and lost. Give me a kiss . . ."

Antony sent an envoy to Caesar, who was encamped outside Alexandria, with proposals for peace. They were as humble as was the envoy himself. Antony had sent his children's schoolmaster.

Coldly, Caesar listened as the schoolmaster recited the message he had learned by heart. For himself, Antony requested only that he should be allowed to live, a private man, in Athens; and for Cleopatra, that she should be permitted to keep the crown of Egypt for herself and for her heirs.

Caesar smiled. He had somewhat different terms in mind. Antony's request was refused utterly; nor would anything be granted to Cleopatra unless she drove "her all-disgraced friend," as he described the fallen Antony, from Egypt, or had him killed. He had nothing more to say.

When the schoolmaster had departed, Caesar turned to his officers. Now was the time to strike at Antony where he was most vulnerable. He beckoned to Thidias, a smooth young man with a ready tongue. He bade him go to Cleopatra and try to win her away from her lover. He was to offer anything that he judged would tempt her to abandon Antony. It should not prove difficult . . .

Enobarbus, who, together with Scarus and his legions, had followed Antony from Actium to Alexandria, stayed on in the palace, as if to warm himself at the dying fire of his master's greatness. The schoolmaster had returned with Caesar's harsh terms, and Antony, in a raging fit of self-pity, had shouted to the Queen, "To the boy Caesar send this grizzled head, and he will fill thy wishes to the brim with principalities!" And when his mad offer was greeted with the amazement it deserved, he'd rushed off to write a letter, challenging Caesar to single combat!

Briefly Enobarbus wondered who was the greater fool: himself or Antony? "Yet he that can endure to follow with allegiance a fallen lord," he murmured, "earns a place i' the story."

There was a messenger from Caesar. Enobarbus knew him, and did not like him. He was Thidias, a young man on whom the gods had spread charm like oil. He was a young man well-calculated to win the hearts of ladies with his silver smiles and golden promises. He begged leave to speak with the Queen in private. She declined; she was among friends. But one friend was missing, thought Enobarbus, and went in search of Antony.

When he returned, accompanied by his master, the handsome Thidias was kneeling and gallantly kissing the extended hand of the Queen. Enobarbus smiled inwardly. The moment could scarcely have been better chosen.

"Favours? By Jove that thunders!" roared Antony. "What art thou, fellow?"

"You will be whipped," murmured Enobarbus, with pleasurable anticipation. Haughtily, Thidias proclaimed himself Caesar's envoy.

He might have saved his breath. "Take hence this Jack and whip him!"
Antony commanded; and, as the protesting Thidias was dragged away,
Enobarbus reflected, "'Tis better playing with a lion's whelp than with
an old one dying."

Then Antony turned his fury on Cleopatra, the universal whore,
who had so readily let the hand she'd given to Antony be soiled by
another's kisses. "You were half blasted ere I knew you!" he shouted,
and flung in her face the salty catalogue of her past lusts, breaking off
only when Thidias was brought back, supported between guards. "Is
he whipped?"

"Soundly, my lord."

"Get thee back to Caesar, tell him thy entertainment," Antony commanded the moaning Thidias. "Hence with thy stripes; begone!"

"Have you done yet?" quietly asked the Queen, when the messenger
had been helped away. Antony began to accuse her again. She shook
her head. "Not know me yet?" she asked, with a sad smile.

Antony faltered. "Cold-hearted toward me?"

"Ah! dear, if I be so, from my cold heart let heaven engender hail
and poison it in the source; dissolve my life!"

In an instant, all her past misdeeds were forgiven and forgotten. Antony was smiling eagerly. Suddenly he was full of plans for the battle to come. He still had troops, he still had ships—

"That's my brave lord!"

"When mine hours were nice and lucky, men did ransom lives of me for jests; but now I'll set my teeth and send to darkness all that stop me!" cried Antony defiantly. "Come, let's have one other gaudy night!"

"It is my birthday," said she, laughing as Antony embraced her. "I had thought to have held it poor; but since my lord is Antony again, I will be Cleopatra!"

"Come on, my Queen; there's sap in't yet!" promised Antony; and together they left the room.

Sadly Enobarbus watched them go. He shivered. "I will seek some way to leave him," he whispered. The dying fire was out.

Antony's challenge to single combat had been laughed at. "Let the old ruffian know," Caesar had said, "I have many other ways to die!" It was plain that Antony's end was near. Already his soldiers were deserting him. They were coming over to Caesar in sufficient numbers for them to be set upon their old master like dogs, and bring him down. "Poor Antony!" murmured Caesar, and sighed.

But Antony, though poor in luck, was still rich in love; and the glimmering palace heaved and murmured in the heavy, perfumed air of Antony and Cleopatra's gaudy night.

Outside, in the dark, soldiers were talking quietly together. They spoke of rumours, of strange sights seen in the streets, and of the chances of victory in the coming battle. "Tomorrow is the day," murmured one, testing the edge of his sword against his thumb; when suddenly another held up his hand. "Peace! What noise?"

They fell silent. There was a sound of strange music. It was very soft, and seemed to be moving from place to place. It was a lively, dancing music, of pipes and cymbals, that somehow seemed to make the heart long to follow. The soldiers stared at one another. "What should this mean?"

Even as the words were spoken, the music died away, as if invisible dancers were departing, leaving a cold and sullen world behind.

"'Tis the god Hercules, whom Antony loved, now leaves him."

The soldiers nodded. "'Tis strange."

The morning was bright, and the lovers full of laughter and hope.

"Nay, I'll help too!" cried Cleopatra, as Antony's servant, Eros, began attiring his master in armour. "What's this for?" she demanded, seizing up an article of steel with a spider's nightmare of straps. "Ah! let be, let be!" protested Antony as she set about buckling onto his arm what was meant for his leg. "Sooth, la! Thus it must be!" she exclaimed, discovering her error and setting it to rights. "Is not this buckled well?"

"Rarely, rarely!" said he; and so it continued until, at last, between the efforts of Eros and the busy Queen, he was ready for battle. "O love!" he declared, standing before her with the sunshine flashing on his breast-plate. "That thou could'st see my wars today!" He took her in his arms. "Fare thee well, dame, whate'er becomes of me, this is a soldier's kiss."

The busy camp looked up from its stern preparations to smile a greeting as the well-loved figure of Mark Antony walked among his soldiers, exchanging old memories, and giving fresh hope.

"The gods make this a happy day to Antony!" He halted. He recognized the soldier who'd addressed him. It was the same man who begged him, before the battle of Actium, not to trust to rotten planks. Antony smiled ruefully, and confessed he wished he'd taken that good advice.

"Hadst thou done so," went on the man, not to be stopped from speaking his mind, "the kings that have revolted, and the soldier that has this morning left thee, would have still followed at thy heels."

"Who's gone this morning?"

"One ever near thee. Call for Enobarbus, he shall not hear thee."

Antony bowed his head. "Sir," said Eros softly, "his chests and treasure he has not with him."

Curiously the soldier watched his general, and waited for the outburst of bitterness and anger that must surely come. Antony looked up. There was neither anger nor bitterness in his face; only a great sorrow. "Go, Eros," he said quietly, "send his treasure after. Write to him—I will subscribe—gentle adieus and greetings: say that I wish he never find more cause to change a master." He paused, and sighed deeply, "O! my fortunes have corrupted honest men!"

Enobarbus was in Caesar's camp. He hovered on the outskirts of a throng of officers about Caesar; but no man spared him so much as a glance. He listened as Caesar gave orders that Antony was to be taken alive, so that he might be led in chains through the streets of Rome. Then he heard Caesar order that those who had deserted from Antony should be sent into battle first. A shrewd move. Nothing would dismay Antony more than to be met by the swords of yesterday's friends.

Caesar was a clever young man, no doubt about it. He was cleverer by far than the careless, ageing Antony. Very soon now, he would be the sole ruler of the world. Any sensible man would choose to follow him; yet, when Caesar and his officers moved away, Enobarbus did not follow. "I have done ill," he whispered miserably. "I have done ill . . ."

"Enobarbus!" A soldier had approached him. The man looked at him coldly and said, "Antony hath after thee sent all thy treasure, with his bounty overplus."

"I give it you," said Enobarbus, and smiled, as if he'd expected no less. The soldier frowned. "Mock not, Enobarbus. I tell you true. Your emperor continues still a Jove."

When the soldier had gone, Enobarbus considered his good fortune, and wept. Antony's generosity had broken his heart. "O Antony!" he cried out, "thou mine of bounty! I fight against thee? No: I will go seek some ditch wherein to die . . ."

Against all expectation, the old ruffian was victorious! The fury of his assault, and his superior skill in generalship, had scattered Caesar's troops and sent them flying from the field of battle. "O thou day o' the world!" he cried, holding out his arms to Cleopatra as she came running to meet him on his triumphant return.

"Lord of lords!" she wept joyously. "O infinite virtue, com'st thou smiling from the world's great snare uncaught?"

"Mine nightingale, we have beat them to their beds! What, girl," he laughed, "though grey do something mingle with our younger brown, yet ha' we a brain that nourishes our nerves, and can get goal for goal of youth!"

The years seemed to fall away from Antony like a discarded garment. He called for fierce music and feasting to celebrate the victory achieved, and the greater one to come.

That night, there was dancing in the streets of Alexandria; but in Caesar's camp, there was a heavy quiet. A man lay dying. Two soldiers, near at hand, heard him whispering and sighing strangely. "O Antony, nobler than my revolt is infamous, forgive me . . . but let the world rank me . . . a master-leaver and a fugitive. O Antony! O Antony . . ." Then no more.

Cautiously the soldiers approached. "He sleeps," said one. "Awake, sir, awake!" said the other. "Hear you, sir?" But Enobarbus was dead.

The soldiers looked up. Already grey was beginning to mingle in the blackness of the sky. There was a mutter of thunder in the air. Drums were beginning to beat to rouse the sleeping army to the second day of battle.

Antony was filled with excitement. The war had moved from land to sea, and he'd sent his best troops to man Cleopatra's galleys. Now, on a hilltop outside Alexandria, he and Scarus impatiently awaited the outcome of the battle. "Yet they are not joined," muttered Antony, for the long stillness was unsettling him. "Where yond pine does stand, I shall discover all!" and away he galloped, leaving Scarus alone.

Scarus frowned. He was deeply troubled. He'd heard that swallows had built their nests in Cleopatra's sails. It was an unlucky sign; and Antony's moods were as changeable as the sky: one moment bright with hope, the next, clouded over with uncertainty and doubt.

He was returning, and an iron fist clutched at Scarus's heart! There was ruin in his master's face!

"All is lost!" howled Antony, mad with rage. "This foul Egyptian hath betrayed me!"

His fleet had surrendered to Caesar! Cleopatra's galleys had yielded themselves up as if by design! "Triple-turned whore, 'tis thou hast sold me to this novice, and my heart makes only wars on thee! Bid them all fly," he shouted to Scarus; "for when I am revenged upon my charm, I have done all!" For a moment, Scarus hesitated; then, with a soldier's farewell, he galloped away.

Antony was alone. He looked up at the sky. "O sun, thy uprise shall I see no more, fortune and Antony part here, even here do we shake hands. Betrayed I am."

Slowly he rode back to Alexandria. He came to the palace and heavily dismounted from his horse. "Eros, Eros!" he called; but instead of his servant, it was the whore herself who appeared. He cursed her violently, and she, shrinking back, all false innocence and wide-eyed, wondered, "Why is my lord enraged against his love?"

"Vanish!" he screamed at her, "or I shall give thee thy deserving!"

He drew his sword, and Cleopatra fled in terror!

"The witch shall die!" she heard Antony shouting as she rushed for safety to her apartment. "Help me, my women!" she begged, with fearful backward looks, as if the maddened Antony was at her heels.

"To the monument," instantly advised Charmian. "There lock yourself and send him word you are dead."

"To the monument!" Cleopatra eagerly agreed; and bade her servant Mardian tell Antony that she had killed herself. "Say that the last I spoke was 'Antony', and word it, prithee, piteously!" Then, hearing the noise of approaching footsteps, she and her frightened girls rushed away.

Antony entered with Eros by his side. His sword was still in his hand, but his rage had flickered out. He looked round the empty room. He caught sight of Cleopatra's golden mirror. He picked it up and stared into it, as if puzzled by what he saw. "Eros," he murmured, "thou yet behold'st me?"

"Ay, noble lord."

"Sometime we see a cloud that's dragonish, a vapour sometime, like a bear or lion, a towered citadel, a pendant rock . . ."

"Ay, my lord."

"That which is now a horse, even with a thought the rack dislimns, and makes it indistinct, as water is in water."

"It does, my lord."

Antony sighed. "Now thy captain is even such a body: here I am Antony; yet cannot hold this visible shape . . ." He shook his head and laid the mirror aside. "I made these wars for Egypt; and the Queen, whose heart I thought I had, for she had mine—she, Eros, has packed cards with Caesar, and false-played my glory—"

He paused. Mardian, Cleopatra's fleshy servant, had appeared in the doorway. At once, Antony's face grew dark with anger. "O! thy vile lady, she has robbed me of my sword!"

"No, Antony," bleated the wretched eunuch, "my mistress loved thee—"

"She has betrayed me and shall die the death!"

"Death of one person can be paid but once," cried Mardian anxiously, "and that she has discharged. What thou wouldst do is done unto thy hand. The last she spake was 'Antony! most noble Antony!' She rendered life, thy name so buried in her.''

Eros watched his master with a breaking heart; but Antony received the news of Cleopatra's death with Roman calm. He turned to Eros and held out his sword, as if it was suddenly too heavy for him. "Unarm, Eros, the long day's task is done, and we must sleep."

He dismissed Mardian and, when Eros had helped him take off his armour, he bade his servant leave him for awhile. Obediently, Eros withdrew.

Antony gazed round the room. Its emptiness seemed to have stretched till it encompassed all the world. "I will o'er take thee, Cleopatra," he whispered, "and weep for my pardon. So it must be, for now all length is torture; since the torch is out, lie down and stray no farther." His gaze fell upon his sword. "I come, my Queen! Stay for me! Where souls do couch on flowers, we'll hand in hand, and with our sprightly port, make the ghosts gaze!" He called for Eros. He was eager to make an end.

Eros came. "What would my lord?"

"Since Cleopatra died," said Antony quietly, "I have lived in such dishonour that the gods detest my baseness. Thou hast sworn, Eros," Antony reminded him, "that, on my command, thou then would'st kill me. Do't, the time has come."

"The gods withhold me!" cried Eros, filled with pity and dread; but Antony would not release him from his oath.

"Come then, draw that thy gentle sword . . ."

"Turn from me then—" begged Eros.

Antony turned away his head.

"My dear master, my captain, my emperor: let me say before I strike this bloody stroke, farewell."

"'Tis said, man, and farewell."

"Shall I strike now?"

"Now, Eros."

"Why, there, then: thus I do escape the sorrow of Antony's death."

Antony heard him fall. Rather than kill his beloved master, Eros had killed himself.

"Thrice-nobler than myself," cried Antony, ashamed, "thou teachest

me, O valiant Eros, what I should, and thou could'st not. But I will be a bridegroom in my death, and run into't as to a lover's bed." He took up his sword, and, making a hoop of his body, like a runner about to begin a race, thrust until he felt the blade pierce his entrails, and he fell, bleeding to the ground.

But he had not been so skilful as Eros. His sword, like all his glorious fortunes, had failed him in the end. "O despatch me!" he cried out piteously and when guards came running, he begged them to put him out of his misery and pain. But there was no man who would kill Antony. Frightened by the hugeness of the calamity, they melted away. All save one, who saw some profit to be had. He crept forward and, avoiding Antony's dying gaze, drew the sword out of the wound. He heard someone coming. Hastily he hid the sword under his cloak.

"Where's Antony?" It was Diomedes, a servant of Cleopatra. The sword-thief pointed and, as Diomedes rushed to Antony's side, he vanished away.

"Most absolute lord," cried Diomedes, kneeling beside the dying man in terror, "my mistress Cleopatra sent me to thee!"

"When did she send thee?"

"Now, my lord."

"Where is she?"

"Locked in her monument," said the servant miserably, and told how Cleopatra, fearing Antony's anger, had sent word that she'd killed herself; and then, fearing even more the consequences of her lie, had sent to tell him the truth.

"Too late, good Diomed," sighed Antony. He was beyond caring about truth or lies. Nothing mattered to him but Cleopatra. He asked for the guards to be called back, and when they came, he begged to be carried to the Queen. "'Tis the last service that I shall command you."

They bore him gently to the tall black house of the monument, that Cleopatra had built to be her own tomb. They laid him down beneath the high balcony, from which the white faces of the Queen and her women looked down.

"Is he dead?" cried Cleopatra.

"His death's upon him," answered Diomedes, "but not dead."

Cleopatra's eyes grew huge with despair. "O sun, burn the great sphere thou mov'st in, darkling stand the varying shore o' the world! O Antony, Antony, Antony!"

Diomed raised his hand for quiet. Antony was speaking, and his voice came faintly up: "I am dying, Egypt, dying; only I here importune death awhile, until of many thousand kisses, the poor last I lay upon thy lips."

But even for that last kiss, Cleopatra would not leave the monument; she was frightened that she would be captured by Caesar. Instead, she rushed to drag out ropes, and fling them down, pleading, "Help me, my women—we must draw thee up: assist, good friends!"

"O quick, or I am gone!" urged Antony as, little by little, the Queen and her women hoisted him aloft in a net of ropes, like royal fishermaids with a marvellous catch.

"Welcome, welcome!" wept Cleopatra, as at last Antony rested in her arms, and she greeted him with a thousand frantic kisses.

"Let me speak a little—"

"No, let me speak—"

"One word, sweet Queen—" There were important matters to confide, before it was too late. With all his remaining strength, he begged her to seek her honour and safety of Caesar. Violently, she shook her head. He warned her to trust none about Caesar but his officer,

Proculeius. She would not listen. He sighed. His life was almost gone. With his last breath, he asked her to remember him as he once had been, "the greatest prince o' the world." Then he died.

Cleopatra stared in terrible disbelief. "Woo't die? Hast thou no care of me? Shall I abide in this dull world, which in thy absence is no better than a sty?" Then those below heard a cry of such wild and world-destroying misery, that they trembled and knelt. "O! withered is the garland of the war, the soldier's pole is fall'n! Young boys and girls are level now with men; the odds is gone, and there is nothing left remarkable beneath the visiting moon!"

"Lady . . . Madam!" cried her women, for the Queen had fallen, as if dead. They rubbed her cold hands, they smoothed away her tangled hair from her eyes . . .

At last she stirred. She looked suddenly weary and forlorn, as if all her great storms and tempests had blown themselves out. "No more but e'en a woman," she sighed, "and commanded by such poor passion as the maid that milks . . ." She touched the dead Antony's lips. "Ah women, women! Look, our lamp is spent, it's out. We'll bury him: and then what's brave, what's noble, let's do it after the high Roman fashion, and make death proud to take us. Come, away, this case of that huge spirit now is cold."

The war was over. Caesar, swelling with triumph, dispatched Dolabella, his chief officer, to demand Antony's surrender without delay. But no sooner had Dolabella left on his errand, than a man forced his way through the crowd and knelt before Caesar. He held out a sword and cried out:

"Antony is dead! This is his sword; I robbed his wound of it!"

There was silence. Eagerly the man looked up, for the joyful smile, the heartfelt thanks. But Caesar's face was marble as he stared at the blood on the blade. Already it was speckled with flies, buzzing with wonderment at so rich a feast. At length, Caesar spoke: "The breaking of so great a thing should make a greater crack. The round world should have shook lions into civil streets, and citizens to their dens. The death of Antony is not a single doom; in the name lay a moiety of the world."

"He is dead, Caesar—"

Caesar turned away. He had paid his tribute to his great rival, and it had come from his heart. Now other matters occupied him. Cleopatra was still living. She must not be allowed to follow her lover. She must live to walk in chains behind Caesar's chariot through the streets of Rome. Without the Queen of Egypt, his triumph would be a hollow affair. He sent Proculeius to reassure the Queen that he meant her well. Then, fearing that Proculeius might become another Antony in Cleopatra's cunning hands, he sent Gallus, an eager young officer, to safeguard his intent.

The sword-thief stood by, forgotten. The size of the news had swallowed up the bringer of it.

Cleopatra was resolved to die. Securely locked in her monument, she tried to comfort her fearful women. "It is great to do that thing that ends all other deeds; which shackles accidents and bolts up change, which sleeps, and never palates more the dung, the beggar's nurse and Caesar's—"

There came a knocking on the outer door. Cleopatra started in alarm. A voice called out: "Caesar sends greetings to the Queen of Egypt!"

"What's thy name?"

"My name is Proculeius."

Cleopatra frowned. She went to the door and stared through the iron lattice at the tall Roman who waited outside. "Antony did tell me of you," she said doubtfully, "bade me trust you, but I do not greatly care to be deceived . . ."

"Be of good cheer, y'are fallen into a princely hand," Proculeius assured her, "fear nothing."

"Pray you, tell him I am his fortune's vassal."

"This I'll report, dear lady. Have comfort—" But even as he spoke, the inner doors burst open and, in a moment, the monument was full of Caesar's soldiers with Gallus at their head!

"You see how easily she may be surprised!" laughed that sharp young officer. While Proculeius had parleyed, he and his men had mounted on ladders to the high balcony, and slipped inside. He unbolted the door and let Proculeius in.

Cleopatra, mad with fear and fury, snatched up a dagger to stab herself. "Hold, worthy lady, hold!" cried Proculeius, preventing her. "Do not yourself such wrong, who are in this relieved, but not betrayed."

"What, of death too, that rids our dogs of languish?" she screamed.

"Cleopatra—"

"Where art thou, death? Come hither, come! Come, come, and take a Queen worth many babes and beggars!"

She rushed from soldier to staring soldier, offering her breast to their swords. "O temperance, lady!" begged Proculeius; but nothing would calm her, and she wept and raged until, at last, Dolabella came to set him free from the frantic, captured Queen. "Be gentle to her," he urged his successor; and, taking young Gallus and his men with him, thankfully left her in the firm hands of Caesar's most trusted officer.

Dolabella bowed courteously. He had come to prepare the way for his master. "Most noble empress, you have heard of me?"

"I cannot tell."

Dolabella was surprised. He was a person of some importance. "Assuredly you know me."

Cleopatra shrugged her shoulders. "No matter, sir, what I have heard or known." She paused, and then said strangely, "You laugh when boys and women tell their dreams; is't not your trick?"

"I understand not, madam." He was puzzled by this sudden change in the Queen. Her fury was gone, and she was smiling.

"I dreamt there was an Emperor Antony," she sighed. "O, such another sleep that I might see but such another man!"

"If it might please ye—"

"His face was as the heavens," she went on, her eyes shining brightly, as she remembered a man whose being was so vast that it encompassed all the world. "In his livery walked crowns and crownets, realms and islands were as plates dropped from his pocket—"

"Most sovereign creature! . . . Cleopatra! . . ." pleaded Dolabella, trying to bring her back to the world as it really was.

"Think you there was, or might be, such a man as this I dreamt of?" she asked him. He shook his head. "Gentle madam, no."

"You lie up to the hearing of the gods! But if there be, or ever were, one such, it's past the size of dreaming!"

Dolabella bowed his head. "Hear me, good madam: your loss is, as yourself, great," he began; then, hearing sounds of the approach of Caesar, quickly warned her that, whatever his master might promise, he meant to lead her in chains through the streets of Rome. He had come to reassure her, to lie to her, but his heart had overruled his head.

With a clash of steel and a tramp of iron feet, Caesar and his officers entered the room. The stern young ruler of the world stared about him. He saw three women. "Which is the Queen of Egypt?" he demanded.

"It is the emperor, madam," murmured Dolabella to one, and she knelt. Caesar smiled. "Arise, you shall not kneel. I pray you, rise, rise,

"*. . . rise, rise, Egypt.*"

Egypt." She looked up at him. He was surprised. She was not young, nor was she more beautiful than many another woman. It was hard to believe that she had conquered so great a man as Antony. She stood up. She was taller than he'd supposed, and bore herself like a queen. Magnanimously he promised her gentle and honourable treatment. She smiled, faintly, and gave him a scroll on which was a full account of all her treasure.

"'Tis exactly valued," she told him, "no petty things omitted," and summoned her treasurer to confirm her word. "Speak the truth!" she commanded the fat fellow who came before her. "What have I kept back?"

Alas! he told her. "Enough to purchase what you have made known," he muttered, dividing his piteous looks between Caesar and his furious mistress.

"O slave, of no more trust than love that's hired!" cried Cleopatra, and would have scratched her treasurer's eyes out had he not retreated in haste. "O Caesar, what a wounding shame is this!" she wept, and protested that all she'd kept back were some trifling articles to present to Octavia and to Caesar's wife.

Caesar laughed, and told her he was no merchant; she might keep all her treasure for herself. At once, she knelt in gratitude: "My master and my lord!"

"Not so," said Caesar, amused that Cleopatra should attempt to practise her famous deceitfulness on him. He was no Antony, to be taken in by a woman's tears and lies. He took his leave of her, well-satisfied that a woman who had tried to cheat him out of money was not the woman to cheat him out of his triumph, and take her own life.

"He words me, girls, he words me, that I should not be noble to myself," said Cleopatra contemptuously, when Caesar and his iron tribe had gone. "But hark thee, Charmian—"

"Finish, good lady; the bright day is done, and we are for the dark," said Iras sadly, as her mistress whispered in Charmian's ear.

"It is provided. Go put it to the haste," commanded Cleopatra, and despatched Charmian on her secret errand.

"Madam!" Dolabella had returned. His look was anxious. Little time remained. Caesar was preparing to depart, and Cleopatra was to be sent to Rome before him. "Make you best use of this," he urged her. "Adieu, good Queen." Then he hastened away.

Charmian returned. She nodded, and Cleopatra smiled. "Show me, my women, like a queen; go fetch my best attires," she bade Iras. "I am again for Cydnus, to meet Mark Antony! When thou hast done this chare, I'll give thee leave to play till doomsday."

There was a commotion outside the door. A guard entered. "Here is a rural fellow that will not be denied your highness' presence," he informed the Queen. "He brings you figs."

"Let him come in."

The guard went away. Cleopatra and Charmian looked at one another. "He brings me liberty," murmured the Queen.

The guard returned with a grinning, shuffling countryman. He was carrying a basket. "Avoid, and leave him," ordered the Queen; and the guard returned to his post.

Cleopatra beckoned, and the fellow approached. She pointed to the basket. "Hast thou the pretty worm of Nilus there, that kills and pains not?"

His grin grew broader. "Truly I have him, but I would not be the party that should desire you to touch him, for his biting is immortal; those that do die of it do seldom or never recover."

"Remember'st thou any that have died on't?"

"Very many, men and women too. I heard of one of them no longer than yesterday, a very honest woman, how she died of the biting of it, what pain she felt. Truly, she makes a very good report o' the worm," he confided; and Charmian shook her head in wonderment as the great Queen and the simple countryman talked easily together of life and death.

"Get thee hence, farewell," said Cleopatra.

"I wish you all joy of the worm," said the countryman, setting down the basket but showing no sign of departing. It was not every day he talked with a queen; it was something to remember and tell to his grandchildren. "Look you," said he, "the worm is not to be trusted. Give it nothing, I pray you, for it is not worth the feeding."

"Will it eat me?"

The fellow tapped the side of his nose knowingly. "You must not think I am so simple but I know the devil himself will not eat a woman; I know that a woman is a dish for the gods . . ."

"Well, get thee gone, farewell."

"I wish you joy o' the worm," he mumbled, and unwillingly shuffled away.

Iras returned, richly laden. Cleopatra held out her arms: "Give me my robe, put on my crown, I have immortal longings in me," she cried joyfully, as her women began to attire her. "Methinks I hear Antony call; I see him rouse himself to praise my noble act. Husband, I come! Now to that name, my courage prove my title! I am fire and air: my other elements I give to baser life. So, have you done?"

They stood back and gazed proudly at their splendid queen. "Farewell, kind Charmian, Iras, long farewell." Tenderly she embraced and kissed them.

"Have I the aspic in my lips?" Iras had fallen. She lay at her mistress's feet. Cleopatra gazed down at the dead girl in wonderment. "If thou and nature can so gently part, the stroke of death is as a lover's pinch, which hurts, and is desired. Dost thou lie still? If thus thou vanishest, thou tell'st the world it is not worth leave-taking." She frowned. "This proves me base. If she first meet the curled Antony, he'll make demand of her, and spend that kiss which is my heaven to have."

Impatiently she opened the countryman's basket. She thrust her hand inside and drew out the little writhing serpent that was to set her free. "Come, thou mortal wretch, with thy sharp teeth this knot intrinsicate of life at once untie: poor venomous fool, be angry, and despatch!"

She put the serpent to her breast. She cried out, softly; and Charmian saw her brows contract, as if in sudden pain. The girl caught her breath.

"O eastern star!"

Cleopatra shook her head, and put her finger to her lips. "Peace, peace, dost thou not see my baby at my breast that sucks the nurse asleep?"

"O, break! O, break!"

"As sweet as balm, as soft as air, as gentle—O Antony! What, should I stay—" Then silence.

"In this vile world?" whispered Charmian. Weeping, she closed Cleopatra's gazing eyes. "Now boast thee, death, in thy possession, lies a lass unparalleled. Your crown's awry, I'll mend it, and then play . . ."

As she began her last task, she heard footsteps approach. Quickly she snatched the coiled serpent from Cleopatra's breast and thrust it against her own.

A soldier entered. "Where's the Queen?"

"Speak softly," Charmian warned him, "wake her not."

"Caesar hath sent—"

"Too slow a messenger!"

The soldier stared at the throne. "What work is here, Charmian? Is this well done?"

"It is well done, and fitting for a princess descended of so many royal kings. Ah, soldier!" she sighed triumphantly, and fell dead.

The Romans entered the chamber, where the silent Queen and her quiet women awaited them. "That you did fear, is done," murmured Dolabella; then he saw the anger on Caesar's face change to admiration. He spoke quietly: "Bravest at the last, she levelled at our purposes, and being royal took her own way. She looks like sleep, as she would catch another Antony in her strong toil of grace." His tribute paid, Caesar and his officers left the chamber. But Dolabella lingered. His heart ached for the glorious brightness of a world that was no more.

Measure for Measure

It happened one day in long-ago Vienna, when the city was ruled over by a Duke. There was disturbing news. The council had been summoned and the councillors, perched on their high seats, like dusty old crows, flapped their black gowns in distress. Their Duke was leaving the city. None knew why, or for how long. But this was not to be wondered at: their Duke had always been a mysterious gentleman, whose comings and goings were as sudden as a duke in a dream.

He stood before them in his long furred travelling coat and deep velvet cap that overshadowed his face. In his absence, he announced, all power to govern the city was to be vested in the hands of Lord Angelo. "What think you of it?" he asked, turning to Lord Escalus, the oldest and wisest of his councillors.

With a loud cracking of stiff joints, the old gentleman rose to his feet. "If any in Vienna be of worth to undergo such ample grace and honour," he replied, "it is Lord Angelo."

There was a general nodding of heads and fluttering of pale, assenting hands. The Duke could not have made a better choice. Lord Angelo, though young, was famous for his strict virtue and upright way of life. Accordingly, he was summoned and, as he entered the chamber, all eyes turned upon him admiringly.

Tall, lean, and firm of step, he approached the Duke. "I come to know your pleasure," he said with quiet dignity; and, with bowed head, awaited the Duke's command.

For a few moments, the Duke observed the young man from under the shadow of his cap; then, seemingly satisfied by what he saw, he pronounced his decision. "Mortality and mercy in Vienna live in thy tongue and heart."

The young man flushed with pleasure and pride. Modestly he protested that he was not yet ready for so great an honour—

"No more evasion!" commanded the Duke; and, bidding a brief farewell to the council, departed from the chamber. Soon after, he vanished from the city as mysteriously as if he had been taken up to heaven in a fiery chariot. But he had left his city in good hands . . .

Vienna had become a sinful city, noisy with love's laughter, and the groans of love's diseases. It was a city ripe for a man like Lord Angelo to pluck out its rotten fruit. So he rolled up his sleeves and set to work . . .

"But shall all our houses of resort in the suburbs," wailed Mistress Overdone, the owner of a famous bawdy-house, "be pulled down?"

"To the ground, mistress," confirmed Pompey, her strong-smelling assistant.

Tears dribbled down the lady's seasoned cheeks. "What shall become of me?" she wept; but before Pompey could tell her, another victim of the Duke's strict deputy appeared in the street.

It was a young man by the name of Claudio. Grey as death itself, he was being escorted to prison by grim officers of the law. Mistress Overdone and Pompey were about to lose their livelihoods; he was about to lose his life.

Lord Angelo had condemned him to death. His crime was unlawful love; and the evidence was plain for all to see. Behind him walked his companion in sin: a young unmarried woman by the name of Julietta. She was almost fainting under the double burden of public shame and Claudio's swelling child within.

"Why, how now, Claudio!" called out Lucio, an elegant young propper-up of door-posts and a cheerful ruiner of young women. "Whence comes this restraint? What's thy offence? Is't murder?"

Claudio shook his head, and gazed mournfully back at the wretched Julietta. Lord Angelo had invoked the old neglected law that punished unmarried love with death.

Lucio listened with sympathy and concern. "Send after the Duke," he advised, "and appeal to him."

"I have done so, but he's not to be found," said Claudio; and then, most piteously, begged a favour. He had a sister, by name of Isabella, who was about to become a nun. "Acquaint her with the danger of my state," he pleaded; "implore her, in my voice, that she make friends to the strict deputy. I have great hope in that; she hath prosperous art when she will play with reason and discourse, and well she can persuade."

"I pray she may!" said Lucio with all his heart. "I'll to her!" he called out as his friend was led away. Claudio waved, and his eyes shone with hope.

The monastery bell was ringing. Wearily Friar Peter rose from his supper and, taking a lantern, went to answer the summons. Outside the gate, a heavily muffled figure awaited him. He raised his lantern. Sharp eyes glittered warily; then, seeing there was none else by, the stranger revealed himself. The friar took a pace back. His visitor was the Duke!

Hastily, the friar opened the gate and the Duke, raising a finger to his lips, slipped inside like a thief. Discreetly the friar lowered his lantern and glanced beyond the Duke for some female companion of the night.

The Duke, catching the look and guessing its meaning, frowned angrily. "No," he muttered. "Holy father, throw away that thought, believe not that the dribbling dart of love can pierce a complete bosom." The purpose of his visit was quite different.

For too many years he had been a duke of books and libraries, quite removed from the world. But now he had awoken to the corruption into which his city had fallen. His decrees were mocked, his laws neglected. "Liberty plucks Justice by the nose," he said bitterly, "the baby beats the nurse, and quite athwart goes all decorum!" It was for this reason that he had set up the strict Lord Angelo in his place, to bring the law back into respect.

Mildly, the friar suggested that this was something the Duke might have done for himself; but the Duke shook his head. If he were to become suddenly severe after so many years of neglect, it would seem like mad tyranny, and he would lose the love of his people. It was wiser for another to do it . . .

The friar shrugged his shoulders, but kept his opinion to himself, and listened as the Duke revealed his plan. Far from abandoning his city, he intended to return in disguise, and secretly observe the actions of his deputy. "Lord Angelo is precise," he murmured thoughtfully, "stands at a guard with envy, scarce confesses that his blood flows, or that his appetite is more to bread than stone. Hence shall we see, if power change purpose, what our seemers be."

He begged Friar Peter to furnish him with the hooded gown of a holy order and to instruct him how a priest should conduct himself.

Even as the Duke was at the gate of one religious house, Lucio was at the gate of another: the Convent of St Clare. Somewhere within its stern grey walls was Claudio's last hope: his sister Isabella. Lucio peered through the close ironwork and dimly observed two nuns walking together across a quiet green.

"Hail virgin!" he called. The nuns halted. Briefly they conferred; then one came towards him, shadowy and demure. "Bring me to the sight of Isabella."

"I am that Isabella," the nun replied.

Lucio stared. He had expected something drab and shrivelled, like fruit withered on the bough; but the nun was young and beautiful, and the severity of her black set her off like a pearl in velvet, a pearl of great price.

The loose and amorous chatter that was Lucio's stock-in-trade with young women quite forsook him; he could scarcely bring himself to name Claudio's crime.

"Someone with child by him?" she whispered, when she understood. "My cousin Juliet?"

Lucio nodded.

"O, let him marry her!"

Sadly Lucio shook his head. He explained the Duke's absence and his strict deputy who had condemned Claudio to death. "All hope is gone," he concluded, "unless you have the grace by your fair prayer to soften Angelo. Assay the power you have."

"My power?" sighed Isabella. "Alas, I doubt."

"Our doubts are traitors," urged Lucio, "and make us lose the good we oft might win, by fearing to attempt. Go to Lord Angelo . . ."

Isabella bowed her head. "I'll see what I can do."

"But speedily!"

"I will about it straight," she promised. "Commend me to my brother; soon at night I'll send him certain word of my success!"

Lord Angelo, proud and eager in his fine robes and heavy gold chain of office, strode into the hall of Justice with his fellow judge, old Lord Escalus, hobbling to keep up with him. Escalus had been pleading for the life of Claudio, even suggesting that Angelo himself might once have been tempted even as Claudio had been tempted—

"''Tis one thing to be tempted, Escalus," said Angelo, "another thing to fall. Sir, he must die." He summoned the provost of the prison and ordered execution to be carried out on Claudio by nine o'clock tomorrow morning.

"Well, heaven forgive him, and forgive us all," murmured the old gentleman, under his breath, as they mounted the steps to the high seat of Justice, "some rise by sin, and some by virtue fall . . ."

Sternly Lord Angelo looked down on the shuffling crowd of hollow-eyed sinners who thronged the court, some seeking justice, most seeking to escape it. He settled back in his seat and, fingering his chain, prepared to weigh the evidence brought before him, find out the truth and pronounce on life or death.

Unluckily, it was not so easy. The very first cause concerned an action brought by one Elbow, a half-witted constable, against Pompey, a brothel-keeper, for something or other that had been done, or not done, to Elbow's wife. With mounting impatience, Angelo listened as the wretched Elbow stuttered and stammered and wandered from the point, dragging in—God knew how!—two stewed prunes, a threepenny dish that wasn't china, and somebody's father who had died at Hallowmas. At length, he could endure it no longer. Angrily, he rose to his feet. "This will last out a night in Russia when nights are longest there! I'll take my leave," he said to Escalus, "and leave you to the hearing of the cause, hoping you'll find good cause to whip them all!"

Clutching his robe about him, like a man crossing a filthy street, he swept from the hall and retired to his apartment. To his surprise, the provost of the prison was awaiting him. "Now what's the matter, provost?" he demanded irritably.

The provost looked uncomfortable. "Is it your will that Claudio shall die tomorrow?"

"Did I not tell thee yea?" said Angelo. "Why dost thou ask again?"

"Lest I might be too rash," said the provost: "I have seen, when after execution, judgement hath repented o'er his doom."

"Do your office, or give up your place," came the stern reply.

The provost bowed his head. He was about to withdraw, when a servant entered. There was a young woman desiring to see Lord

Angelo. It was the condemned man's sister who had come from her convent to plead for her brother's life.

Angelo shrugged his shoulders. "Well, let her be admitted," he said; and bade the provost stay awhile.

The door opened and Isabella entered. She was accompanied by Lucio. For a moment, she remained in the doorway, timid and demure. Lucio gave her a little push. Shrewdly he observed that both the stern deputy and the provost seemed taken aback by Isabella's beauty. Plainly her looks would get her further than her words . . .

"Y'are welcome," said Angelo, courteously; "what's your will?"

"I am a woeful suitor to your honour," answered Isabella, "please but your honour hear me."

"Well, what's your suit?"

Her suit was her brother's life. Gently she pleaded for him, and Lucio listened in despair. Her words were so soft and feeble that they would not have stirred a feather, let alone the stony-hearted deputy. Angelo shook his head. The law must take its course—

"O just but severe law: I had a brother then," whispered Isabella, bowing her head in submission. "Heaven keep your honour."

She began to withdraw. "Give't not o'er so! You are too cold," whispered Lucio, losing all patience with this girl who seemed to value her own modesty above her brother's life. "If you should need a pin, you could not with more tame a tongue desire it!"

Her pale cheeks flushed; the reproach had struck home. She turned again to Angelo. "Must he needs die?" she asked, and this time her voice was firmer.

"Maiden, no remedy."

"Yes: I do think that you might pardon him—"

"I will not do't."

"But can you if you would?"

"Look what I will not, that I cannot do."

"But might you do't—?"

"He's sentenced, 'tis too late."

"Too late?" she cried, and fiercely denounced the deputy for his unyielding coldness and lack of mercy. Lucio listened, lost in admiration for her spirit, and, for the first time, understood why her brother had hoped for so much from her powers.

"Pray you be gone," muttered Angelo when she paused for breath; but she swept him aside. "How would you be," she demanded, "if He, which is the top of judgement, should but judge you as you are? O think on that—"

"Be you content, fair maid, it is the law, not I, condemn your brother. Be satisfied. Your brother dies tomorrow. Be content."

But Isabella was far from content. "O, it is excellent to have a giant's strength, but it is tyrannous to use it like a giant!"

"That's well said!" whispered Lucio, delightedly. Now the demure young girl had become a passionate woman.

"Man, proud man, dressed in a little brief authority," she cried, pointing an accusing finger at the deputy in his fine robes and gold chain, "most ignorant of what he's most assured, like an angry ape plays such fantastic tricks before high heaven as makes the angels weep!" Then, in softer tones she urged: "Go to your bosom, knock there, and ask your heart what it doth know that's like my brother's fault. If it confess a natural guiltiness, such as is his—"

Lord Angelo had risen to his feet. Lucio could see that he was deeply agitated. His fists were tightly clenched, and he almost pleaded, "Fare you well." He turned to go—

"Gentle my lord!" Isabella had fallen to her knees. "Turn back!"

Helplessly he turned. "I will bethink me. Come again tomorrow."

"At what hour tomorrow shall I attend your lordship?"

"At any time 'fore noon."

"Save your honour!" breathed Isabella thankfully; and Lucio drew her away. She had done enough. The icy Angelo had begun to melt; but whether it was the warmth of her words or the heat of her passion that had turned him to water was hard to say . . .

When the young woman had gone, the provost looked inquiringly at Lord Angelo. But the deputy was lost in thought. Silently, the provost withdrew. From what he had heard, it was plain that the execution was to be delayed . . .

"What's this? What's this? Is this her fault, or mine?" Angelo, alone in his bedchamber, paced to and fro. He was bewildered and frightened

by what had happened to him. It was as if he had taken a poison that now raged in his blood, turning his grey thoughts red. He desired Isabella passionately, and she inhabited every dark corner of his mind. Night, when it came, brought him no peace, only hot dark fancies that tormented him further . . .

At last, it was morning. He rose and dressed himself with fanatical care. Then he went to his apartment.

"One Isabel, a sister, desires access to you."

His heart leaped violently as a servant brought him the news. She entered.

"How now, fair maid?"

"I come to know your pleasure," she murmured, with an anxious smile.

His pleasure? "That you might know it would much better please me than to demand what 'tis!" breathed Angelo, desire almost suffocating him; but aloud he said: "Your brother cannot live," and watched her eyes fill with tears.

"Even so. Heaven keep your honour." She bowed her head and began to withdraw.

"Yet he may live a while," said Angelo quickly, "—and it may be as long as you or I—yet he must die."

She paused, frowning. "Which had you rather," asked Angelo softly: "that the most just law now took your brother's life, or to redeem him, give up your body to such sweet uncleanness as she that he hath stained?"

"I had rather give up my body than my soul!" answered Isabella instantly. "Better it were a brother died at once, than that a sister, by redeeming him, should die for ever!"

"Were you not then as cruel as the sentence you have slandered so?" accused Angelo. Isabella bit her lip; and Angelo, seizing his advantage, hastened to entrap her, skilfully proving that sin was virtue if its purpose was mercy, the very mercy she herself had pleaded for.

"I have no tongue but one," she protested, confused by the skilful deputy's arguments. "Gentle my lord, let me entreat you speak the former language."

She had not understood him! With a quick motion, he took her hand in his, and, fixing his hot gaze upon her, muttered, "Plainly conceive, I love you!"

Amazed, Isabella stared at him. A flush of shame and anger spread across her cheeks. At last she understood the monstrous bargain! To save her brother's life, she was to give herself to Angelo's vile lust!

She snatched back her hand and, raising it, pointed a fierce accusing finger.

"I will proclaim thee, Angelo, look for't," she cried. "Sign me a present pardon for my brother, or with an outstretched throat I'll tell the world aloud what man thou art!"

"Who will believe thee, Isabel?" challenged Angelo, inflamed still further by Isabella's fury. "Fit thy consent to my sharp appetite. Redeem thy brother by yielding up thy body to my will!" and he threatened that if she still denied him, her brother's death would be most horribly prolonged by torture. "Answer me tomorrow," he bade her, and abruptly left the room.

Isabella sank to her knees in despair. "To whom should I complain?" she wept. "Who would believe me?"

The Duke in darkness. The good Friar Peter had provided well. Profoundly hidden in the deep-hooded gown of a ghostly father, the Duke walked the dark streets of his city to learn how his people were faring under the rule of the strict deputy.

Presently he came to the prison, a huge gloomy place of neither night nor day, where Time slept in a never-ending nightmare; a place of locks and bolts and weeping stones, of weary curses, shouts and tears, and drunken snores. Here he learned of Claudio and his crime . . .

"A young man more fit to do another such offence," sighed the kindly provost, "than die for this."

"When must he die?"

"As I do think, tomorrow . . ."

The Duke nodded; then, drawing back from the prying light of the provost's lantern, asked if he might be taken to Claudio, to confess him and prepare his soul for heaven. Willingly, the provost consented; and conducted his holy visitor along the echoing passages and down the stony steps to Claudio's cell.

The prisoner, hearing footsteps approach, started up from his bed of straw. Isabella had succeeded! His pardon had come! But then, seeing the provost's grave looks, and the hooded figure by his side, he returned to his bed of despair.

"So then you hope of pardon from Lord Angelo?" the Duke asked gently.

"The miserable have no other medicine, but only hope," came the forlorn reply.

"Be absolute for death: either death or life shall thereby be the sweeter," counselled the Duke, drawing close to the bars; and, faithfully playing his part as holy comforter, he drew upon all his library wisdom to prepare the young man for the dread solemnity of death. "Reason thus with life," he bade him: "if I do lose thee I do lose a thing that none but fools would keep . . . The best of rest is sleep, and that thou oft provok'st, yet grossly fear'st thy death, which is no more . . ."

The youth half-smiled and nodded, and by the time the Duke had finished, all his fears were laid to rest. Warmly, he clasped the holy father's hands through the bars and thanked him for the comfort he had brought. Now he was ready to die.

"I'll visit you again," promised the Duke, well-pleased to have per-formed his office with such success. He was about to leave, when a woman's voice called out. It was Isabella, come to visit her brother. Quickly the Duke whispered to the provost: "Bring me to hear them speak where I may be concealed."

There was a cell opposite whose tenant had recently died. Here the provost concealed the friar, and, having conducted the young woman to her brother, joined him in the dark.

"Now, sister, what's the comfort?" asked the young man eagerly, after embracing her, as best he could, through the bars. Sadly, she shook her head . . .

The Duke leaned forward. Though, as he had assured Friar Peter, his bosom was not to be pierced by the dribbling dart of love, he, like all who saw her, was struck by Isabella's beauty . . .

"Is there no remedy?" asked Claudio, and managed a pitiful smile.

Isabella hesitated. She turned away. Plainly she was in great distress. "Yes, brother, you may live," she confessed most miserably; and revealed the price that was to be paid to Lord Angelo to save his life. "If I would yield to him my virginity thou might'st be freed!"

"O heavens, it cannot be!" cried Claudio in outrage and in horror.

"Yes, he would give't thee. This night's the time that I should do what I abhor to name, or else thou diest tomorrow."

"Thou shalt not do't!" declared the young man valiantly, and to Isabella's vast relief.

"O, were it but my life," she sighed, tenderly stroking his pale moist brow, "I'd throw it down for your deliverance as frankly as a pin!"

"Thanks, dear Isabel," said he, striving to sound grateful; then, a demon of hope rising within him, he murmured, "Sure it is no sin, or of the deadly seven it is the least . . . ?"

She drew back. She stared at him. "What says my brother?"

"Death is a fearful thing."

"And shamed life a hateful!"

"Ay, but to die and go we know not where, to lie in cold obstruction and to rot!" cried Claudio. With the faint prospect of clinging onto life, however dishonourably, all the friar's philosophy was blown to

. . . embracing her, as best he could

the winds. In frantic desperation, Claudio poured out his naked human terror of dying. "Sweet sister, let me live!" he begged; and falling to his knees, clutched her holy gown. "What sin you do to save a brother's life, nature dispenses with the deed so far that it becomes a virtue!"

The very argument of Angelo! With a cry of loathing she snatched her gown from her brother's grasp and turned on him like a blazing Fury! "O dishonest wretch! Wilt thou be made a man out of my vice? Take my defiance, die, perish! I'll pray a thousand prayers for thy death, no word to save thee!"

"Nay hear me, Isabel!"

"Thy sin's not accidental, but a trade! 'Tis best that thou diest quickly!"

"O hear me, Isabella!"

But she had gone, leaving her brother sunk in misery and remorse.

The watchers came out of their concealment. The Duke was filled with anger at Angelo's monstrous betrayal of trust. Leaving the provost to comfort the prisoner, he hastened after Isabella. "Vouchsafe a word, young sister," he called to the hurrying, black-robed figure ahead, "but one word!"

She turned; and seeing that it was a holy father who had addressed her, she paused. "What is your will?" she asked, as the hooded friar approached.

He beckoned her aside. "I have no superfluous leisure," she protested. She longed to return to the holy quiet of the convent, and shut herself away for ever from the hateful dangers of the world.

"The assault that Angelo hath made to you, fortune hath conveyed to my understanding," confided the friar. At once, Isabella felt a great relief that her terrible situation was known. She listened eagerly, and with mounting excitement, as the holy father unfolded a strange and wonderful plan that would bring the corrupt deputy to justice.

There was a young woman, by name of Mariana, he told her, who lived in a moated grange not far from the city. Once, she was to have been married to Angelo, but unluckily her dowry was lost at sea, so Angelo had turned his back upon her—

"Can this be so? Did Angelo so leave her?"

"Left her in her tears," said the holy father; and went on to tell how the lady, still loving the cold Angelo, was sighing away her life in self-imposed seclusion. It was her love, made frantic by Angelo's denial, that was now to resolve everything.

"Go you to Angelo," the friar instructed Isabella, "agree with his demands, only refer yourself to this advantage: first, that your stay with him may not be long; that the place may have all shadow and silence in it . . ." Then he revealed that it would not be Isabella, but Mariana, silent and cloaked in darkness, who would go to Angelo's bed! "And here, by this," concluded the friar, "is your brother saved, your honour untainted, the poor Mariana advantaged and the corrupt deputy scaled! What think you of it?"

Isabella's eyes shone with wonderment and gratitude. The mysterious friar who had appeared to her out of the darkness of the prison, seemed like the intervention of a kindly Providence. With all her heart, she thanked him; and hastened away to Angelo, to do the friar's bidding.

For some moments, the Duke gazed after her, his admiration divided between her passionate purity, and the grace and lightness of her step. Then he, too, departed, to seek out Mariana in her moated grange, and prepare her for the part she was to play.

The deepest time of the night, moonless, starless . . . Within its encircling wall of brick, crouched Angelo's garden-house, black, silent, waiting . . . A faint noise broke the heavy quiet: a key turning in a lock. A door opened in the wall. A vague shape slipped within, drifted uncertainly to and fro, as if driven by conflicting winds, then approached the blackness ahead. With a quick sigh, it was swallowed up. There was no outcry. Silence and contentment. Angelo had been deceived.

In the prison, preparations were afoot for the execution of Claudio. The block was ready, the axe was sharpened, and the provost, seated at his table with the lantern light streaming over him, awaited the striking of the terrible hour with a heavy heart.

A shadow fell across the papers before him. He looked up. The ghostly father had returned. "Have you no countermand for Claudio yet," he inquired, "but he must die tomorrow?"

"None, sir, none," sighed the provost. "It is a bitter deputy."

"As near the dawning, provost, as it is, you shall hear more ere morning," promised the Duke, confident of the success of his plan.

Scarcely had he spoken than a messenger arrived. He came with a letter from Lord Angelo. Eagerly the Duke waited while the provost, having dismissed the messenger, read the letter. "Now, sir, what news?" he asked impatiently.

The provost stared at him; then he read from the letter. "Whatsoever you may hear to the contrary, let Claudio be executed by four of the clock, and in the afternoon, Barnardine. For my better satisfaction, let me have Claudio's head sent me by five . . ."

Sharply the Duke drew in his breath. This he had not counted upon, that Angelo's villainy could be so complete!

"What say you to this, sir?" muttered the provost, blinking unhappily at the flame within his lantern that, with the approach of its death in the coming dawn, had begun to burn as pale as the poor prisoner in his cell.

"What is that Barnardine who is to be executed in th'afternoon?" asked the Duke thoughtfully. "Hath he borne himself penitently in prison?"

The provost shook his head. Barnardine had been a prisoner for nine long cursing drunken years . . . "A man," he said, as if to remind the friar of his wise words to Claudio, "that apprehends death no more dreadfully but as a drunken sleep."

"He wants advice," said the Duke abruptly; and then confided his plan. Barnardine was to be executed directly and his head sent to Angelo in place of Claudio's—

"Angelo hath seen them both," objected the provost, "and will discover the favour."

"O, death's a great disguiser," the Duke assured him; but the provost remained unconvinced; so the Duke set his mind at rest. He explained he was carrying letters telling of the Duke's immediate return. In proof of this, he showed a letter in the Duke's own hand, and sealed with the Duke's own seal.

The provost examined the seal and writing, and nodded. "Call your executioner, and off with Barnardine's head!" commanded the Duke briskly; and then, recollecting that he was a holy father in the business of divine forgiveness, added that he would prepare Barnardine to meet with God.

Barnardine, summoned to his instant death, came forth from his cell, cursing and clanking his chains. More beast than man, with matted beard and half his bed of filthy straw still clinging to his ragged garments, he swore at the executioner for waking him. Then he saw the hooded friar approaching, like the grim figure of Death itself. He rubbed his sleep-encrusted eyes, hiccuped and spat.

"I am come to advise you, comfort you, and pray with you," said the holy one, nimbly avoiding the sudden shower.

"Friar, not I," grunted the drink-sodden wretch, swaying on his feet and putting out a dazed hand for support from an imaginary wall. "I have been drinking hard all night, and I will have more time to prepare me. I will not consent to die this day, that's certain."

"O, sir, you must!" insisted the Duke.

"I swear I will not die today for any man's persuasion."

"But hear you—"

"Not a word," said Barnardine, with a look of sovereign contempt. "If you have anything to say to me, come to my ward, for thence will not I today." With that, he turned on his heel and trudged, clanking, back to the comforts of his cell.

"Unfit to live or die!" cried the Duke, enraged by the brutish unwillingness of Barnardine to oblige him by dying. "After him, fellows!" he commanded the executioner and his assistant. "Bring him to the block!"

He stood, breathing deeply, when the provost appeared and gently inquired, "Now, sir, how do you find the prisoner?"

"A creature unprepared, unmeet for death," confessed the Duke, already repenting of his unpriestly anger, "and to transport him, in the mind he is, were damnable."

The provost smiled; and then revealed that Providence had come to the aid of the friar's plot, and had supplied another death. That very morning, one Ragozine, a notorious pirate, had died of a strange fever. "A man of Claudio's years, his beard and head just off his colour . . ."

"O, 'tis an accident that heaven provides!" cried the Duke, overjoyed by this stroke of good fortune. "Quick, dispatch, and send the head to Angelo!"

The juggling with heads done with, away went the provost, thankfully, to cut off the dead man's, leaving the Duke alone to plot, plan and contrive the public downfall of Angelo—

"Peace, hoa, be here!" A woman's voice broke in upon his thoughts. It was Isabella. "Hath yet the deputy sent my brother's pardon?" she asked.

The Duke turned away. "He hath released him, Isabel, from the world," he told her quietly: "his head is off, and sent to Angelo."

He heard her cry out in disbelief, and then give way to wretchedness and despair. "O, I will to him and pluck out his eyes!" she wept, frantic for revenge. "Most damned Angelo!"

The Duke shook his head. "You shall not be admitted to his sight," he said; and comforted her as much as he dared by promising that the Duke was coming home directly, and that justice would be done. "Nay, dry your eyes," he begged her; and, putting his arm about her trembling shoulders, softly instructed her in what she was to do . . . Still weeping for her murdered brother, she nodded; but before she could escape from the hated prison, another visitor appeared.

It was Lucio. His face was long, his step was solemn: he had been told of Claudio's death. "O pretty Isabella," he cried, hastening forward to comfort her, "I am pale at mine heart to see thine eyes so red: thou must be patient. By my troth, Isabel, I loved thy brother," he called out as she departed; then confided to the friar, "If the old fantastical Duke of dark corners had been at home, he had lived."

"Sir," said the Duke indignantly, "the Duke is marvellous little beholding to your reports."

"Friar, thou knowest not the Duke so well as I do," said Lucio, his natural high spirits overcoming his grief. "Ere he would have hanged a man for the getting a hundred bastards, he would have paid for the nursing a thousand. He had some feeling of the sport, he knew the service—"

"You do him wrong, surely!" said the Duke, his anger increasing.

"Sir, I know him and I love him. I was once before him for getting a wench with child," boasted Lucio happily; and went on to relate how he had perjured himself to escape being married to "the rotten medlar".

Vainly the Duke tried to rid himself of the impudent young man, but Lucio, who delighted in polishing his wit by blackening names, like shoes, continued to slander the Duke, and would not be shaken off. "Nay, friar," he said as they left the prison, "I am a kind of burr, I shall stick."

They walked together to the lane's end, where they parted, Lucio with a careless smile, the Duke with a grim one.

Letters had been received informing the council of Vienna that the Duke was returning. They were commanded to meet him at the city gates and there deliver up the authority that they had held in his absence. Nor was this all. Lord Angelo, looking up from the paper before him, frowned. "And why," he asked old Lord Escalus, "should we proclaim it in an hour before his entering, that if any crave redress of injustice, they should exhibit their petitions in the street?" Uneasily, he shook his head; but nonetheless bade old Escalus carry out the Duke's command.

Once alone, Angelo sank back in his chair. He clasped his burning head in his icy hands. He had satisfied his lust, but far from being content, he was filled with horror and remorse. At four o'clock that morning, his order had been carried out. Claudio had been executed and his head had been brought to him, wrapped in a bloody cloth. He had waved it away, not daring to look the murdered man in the face.

Yet the execution had been necessary. If Claudio had been allowed to live, he would have demanded revenge for his dishonoured sister. "Would yet he had lived!" whispered Angelo hopelessly. "Alack, when once our grace we have forgot, nothing goes right: we would, and we would not."

In a single night, he had fallen from the highest virtue into the blackest pit of sin.

The morning sun stared down upon the city of Vienna as if in bright astonishment to find it still standing after so long a night. Foremost among the great crowd that had assembled at the city gates, stood the two judges, Lord Angelo and Lord Escalus, with a light breeze ruffling their hair.

Suddenly, trumpets announced the coming of the Duke. At once, there was a murmuring and a stirring and a jostling as the crowd pressed forward for a better view. Then, with a thunder of hoofs, the Duke's golden coach appeared, like a fiery chariot come down from heaven in a cloud of dust.

The coach halted, the door opened, and the tall, dignified figure of the Duke, in his long furred travelling coat and deep velvet hat, stepped out into the sun. The people cheered, and the two judges moved forward to greet their royal master.

The sun was warm and Angelo was smiling; but it was with a tremendous effort. Indeed, everything seemed an effort to him, even breathing. Only yesterday, when he'd walked, the old gentleman at his side had had to hobble to keep up with him; now he could scarcely keep pace with Escalus: his feet were like lead.

The Duke was gracious. He held out his hands in greeting to his judges, and thanked them warmly for having upheld his laws in his absence; and when Angelo offered up his chain of office, the Duke waved it aside, and invited his judges to walk with him on either side as he entered through the gates.

They had not gone above a dozen paces, when there was a disturbance in the crowd. The Duke halted, gazed curiously in the direction of the disturbance. Angelo longed to hurry him on; but he was powerless and could only stand in inward terror as two figures stumbled out of the crowd and into the Duke's path. One was old Friar Peter; the other was Isabella! What he had dreaded had come to pass.

"Justice, O royal Duke!" she cried, kneeling before him. "Justice, justice, justice!"

Angelo swayed and would surely have fallen, had not the Duke taken him by the arm and urged him forward. "Here is Lord Angelo shall give you justice," he said.

She stared at him, her eyes blazing with hatred. Then she turned to the Duke. "O worthy Duke," she said, "you bid me seek redemption of the devil!"

Angelo tried to brush her aside—to silence her—to prepare the Duke—"My lord," he said rapidly, "her wits I fear me are not firm; she hath been a suitor to me for her brother, cut off by course of justice . . . She will speak most bitterly and strange."

"Most strange, but yet most truly will I speak!" She had risen to her feet. She was pointing at Angelo. "That Angelo's forsworn, is it not strange? That Angelo's a murderer, is't not strange? That Angelo is an adulterous thief, an hypocrite, a virgin-violater, is it not strange, and strange?"

Then out it came! In a terrible voice, she shouted his foul and hateful crime to all the world!

There was silence. She had finished. She was breathing deeply. He could hear her. The Duke was watching him. Old Escalus was frowning. He felt bitterly cold, as if he had been stripped naked—

"By heaven, fond wretch, thou know'st not what thou speak'st!"

It was the Duke! He had not believed her! He was angry! Angelo's eyes began to fill with tears of huge relief. His reputation had saved him, even against the word of a holy sister! 'Who would believe thee, Isabel?' he had told her; and it was true!

"To prison with her!" commanded the Duke, outraged that his deputy should have been so vilely slandered. An officer came forward to arrest her. She bowed her head. "Who knew of your intent and coming hither?" the Duke asked her. She looked up and answered that it had been a certain friar by the name of Lodowick.

"Blessed be your royal Grace!" Old Friar Peter had come forward. He had something to say. Angelo looked at him uneasily. But all was well. Friar Peter had come forward in support of him.

"I have heard your royal ear abused," he said. "First hath this woman most wrongfully accused your substitute, who is as free from touch or soil with her as she from one ungot."

"We did believe no less," said the Duke; and Isabella was led away, all her fire and fury spent. Angelo stared after her. 'Who would believe thee, Isabel!' he shouted triumphantly, inside his head.

"Know you that Friar Lodowick that she speaks of?" the Duke was asking Friar Peter.

"I know him for a man divine and holy," answered the friar, and explained that Friar Lodowick was confined to his bed with a strange fever, and so was unable to be present.

The Duke smiled at Angelo, and Angelo smiled at the Duke. They were both familiar with those strange fevers that so conveniently laid a man low.

But now there was something more. Friar Peter was saying that he had come on behalf of this mysterious Lodowick, who knew the falseness of Isabella's claim. He knew that she had never submitted her body to Angelo's lust, and there was a witness whose testimony would prove it!

"Good friar, let's hear it," said the Duke. He turned to Angelo. "Come, cousin Angelo," he said most affably, "in this I'll be impartial: be you judge of your own cause."

Angelo was bewildered. A witness? He did not know what to make of it. Friar Peter was beckoning. The crowd stirred, made way—

"Is this the witness, friar?" asked the Duke.

A woman had stepped forward. She was heavily veiled, and all in black. She stood quite still in the bright sunshine, her shadow stretching towards Angelo, like a spilled finger of ink. He looked at her searchingly, but could make out nothing. His bewilderment increased; at the same time, he could not suppress a gnawing fear, as if he had a secret enemy who was moving round him, stealthily, in the shadows . . .

"Let her show her face," ordered the Duke.

"Pardon, my lord," she answered, in a low voice, "I will not show my face until my husband bid me."

"What, are you married?"

"No, my lord."

She answered in riddles. She was neither married, maid, nor widow; yet she claimed, "I have known my husband, yet my husband knows not that he ever knew me."

"This is no witness for Lord Angelo," said the Duke impatiently.

"Now I come to't, my lord," she said. "She that accuses him of fornication in self-same manner doth accuse my husband, and charges him, my lord, with such a time when I'll depose I had him in mine arms with all th'effect of love!"

Her husband? She was mad! What she said was impossible! "Let's see thy face!" muttered Angelo.

"My husband bids me," she said quietly, "now I will unmask."

She threw back her veil. Angelo was amazed. The lovely face that was revealed was not unknown to him. He felt a pang of guilt. It was the lady Mariana who, long ago, he had loved, and even promised marriage to—

"This is that face, thou cruel Angelo," she sighed, "which once thou swor'st was worth the looking on . . ." She paused, and then, holding out her arms in a gesture of helpless love, she said, "This is the body that took away the match from Isabel and did supply thee at thy garden-house, in her imagined person."

Fiercely Angelo denied it. He swore to the Duke that he had never spoken with, seen nor heard from the woman for five years . . . "Upon my faith and honour!"

"Noble prince!" cried Mariana, kneeling before the Duke, "but Tuesday night last gone, in's garden-house, he knew me as a wife!"

There was a plot against him! He was sure of it. The feeling of a secret enemy lurking in darkness grew stronger, an enemy who, for some mysterious reason, had conspired with the two women to bring him down. But the plot had failed!

"Think'st thou thy oaths," said the Duke sternly to the kneeling Mariana, "were testimonies against his worth and credit?"

Once more his reputation had saved him! But who was his enemy?

"There is another friar that set them on," said the Duke; and at once Angelo knew. It was the shadowy, elusive Friar Lodowick! "Let him be sent for."

At once the provost was ordered to fetch the friar from his all-too-convenient sick-bed. No sooner had he gone, than the Duke addressed Angelo: "Do with your injuries as seems you best; I for a while will leave you."

With that, he turned and strode abruptly back to his coach. He'd spoken in a loud, clear voice; and it was plain to Angelo that he'd wanted all the world to hear that his faith was unshaken and his trust was firm enough to leave everything in his deputy's hands. Angelo rejoiced—

"But stir not you till you have well determined upon these slanderers," commanded the Duke; and, with a swirl of his long furred coat, vanished inside the coach with the suddenness of a conjuror. Then the coach drove rapidly away.

Old Escalus had been busy. He'd been asking if anyone knew of this Friar Lodowick. Lucio knew him, and knew him well. "'Tis a meddling friar," he was saying contemptuously, "a very scurvy fellow . . . honest in nothing but in his clothes, and one that hath spoke most villainous speeches of the Duke."

Angelo nodded. So this was his mysterious enemy: a wretched plotting friar who bore a grudge . . .

"Come on, mistress, here's a gentlewoman denies all that you have said."

Old Escalus was still interfering. He'd called back Isabella and confronted her with Mariana. She did not answer; instead, both women were staring at Angelo, and one of them seemed to be smiling. He could not understand it—

"My lord, here comes the rascal I spoke of," said Lucio suddenly, "here with the provost."

At last, Friar Lodowick! Tall and profoundly hooded, he walked beside the provost, still fastening the cord of his gown as if he had indeed been snatched untimely from his bed.

"Come, sir, did you set these women on to slander Lord Angelo?" demanded Escalus as the friar stood before him. "They have confessed you did."

"'Tis false," answered the friar, in gruff, contemptuous tones. "Where is the Duke? 'Tis he should hear me speak."

"The Duke's in us; and we will hear you speak," said Escalus.

"Is the Duke gone? Then is your cause gone too: the Duke's unjust—"

"Why, thou unreverend and unhallowed friar!" cried Escalus angrily.

"Is't not enough thou hast suborned these women to accuse this worthy man, but in foul mouth, to glance from him to th'Duke himself, to tax him with injustice? Take him hence," he commanded the provost; "to th'rack with him! What? Unjust?"

"Be not so hot!" The friar held up a warning hand, and with such authority that the provost, who had moved to seize him, fell back. He was no subject of the Duke, he said, but an onlooker in Vienna, where he had seen "corruption boil and bubble till it o'errun the stew!"

"Slander to th'state!" shouted Escalus, outraged. "Away with him to prison!"

Again, the provost put out a timid, uncertain hand. "Stay, sir, stay a while!" commanded the strange friar; and the provost obeyed.

"What, resists he?" cried Angelo, fearing that his enemy would escape. "Help him, Lucio!"

Eagerly, Lucio came forward. At one stroke he might ruin the friar, whom he disliked, and ingratiate himself with the Duke's deputy. "Come, sir, come, sir, come, sir!" he cried, struggling with the holy fellow. "Foh, sir! Why, you bald-pated, lying rascal, you must be hooded, must you? Show your knave's visage, with a pox to you! Show your sheep-biting face, and be hanged an hour! Will't not off?" and with a violent effort, he dragged off the friar's hood.

There was silence. The Duke stood revealed.

"Thou art the first knave that e'er mad'st a duke," he said to Lucio; and then, "Sneak not away, sir," as that gentleman showed every sign of modestly seeking to escape the honour that had so horribly befallen him. Lucio halted, a frozen man.

The Duke turned to Angelo, who stood like a man already dead. The Duke knew all. The darkest corners of his soul were pitilessly exposed. He could utter no more than, "Death is all the grace I beg."

The Duke made no answer. Instead, he summoned Mariana. "Say, wast thou e'er contracted to this woman?" he asked.

"I was, my lord," whispered Angelo, not daring to look at the woman by his side, for fear of meeting with her scorn and loathing.

"Go, take her hence and marry her instantly!" commanded the Duke; and, to his wonderment, the ruined Angelo felt Mariana take his hand gently in her own.

"Come hither, Isabel," said the Duke, offering his hand with a warm and tender smile. She came, and humbly knelt before him. "Your friar is now your prince," he said, gallantly raising her up: "not changing heart with habit, I am still attorneyed to your service."

Then, in sorrowful tones, he spoke of the death of her brother, which he had been unable to prevent.

He turned sternly to Angelo the murderer, and pronounced: "An Angelo for Claudio, death for death; haste still pays haste, and leisure answers leisure; like doth quit like, and measure still for measure. We do condemn thee to the very block where Claudio stooped to death—"

"O, my most gracious lord, I hope you will not mock me with a husband?" cried Mariana in terror.

"It is your husband mocked you with a husband," answered the Duke. "For his possessions, although by confiscation they are ours, we do instate and widow you with all, to buy you a better husband."

"O my dear lord, I crave no other, nor no better man!"

But the Duke was not to be moved: justice must be done. A death for a death: Angelo must die.

In desperation, Mariana turned to Isabella to help her save her Angelo—

"Against all sense you do importune her!" cried the Duke, amazed.

"Should she kneel down in mercy of this fact, her brother's ghost his paved bed would break and take her hence in horror!"

But Mariana was past all reason in her terror for Angelo's life. "Isabel!" she pleaded, clutching Isabella's gown, "Sweet Isabel, do yet but kneel by me, hold up your hands, say nothing; I'll speak all! They say best men are moulded out of faults, and, for the most, become much more the better for being a little bad: so may my husband! Oh Isabel! Will you not lend a knee?"

"He dies for Claudio's death," said the Duke.

Isabella looked down, and saw the wild, despairing love in Mariana's eyes. She remembered how her brother had once clutched her gown and begged for a mercy she had refused. Must she refuse again? She knelt before the Duke. "Most bounteous sir," she pleaded, "look, if it please you, on this man condemned as if my brother lived. I partly think a due sincerity governed his deeds till he did look on me. Since it is so, let him not die . . ."

The Duke shook his head. He turned to the provost and demanded to know why Claudio had been beheaded at so unusual an hour?

"It was commanded so," said the provost, and then confessed that there was another prisoner who was to have been executed, but him he had spared. His name was Barnardine—

"I would thou hadst done so by Claudio," said the Duke. "Go fetch him hither. Let me look upon him."

Lord Escalus approached the wretched Angelo. Sadly, he shook his head. "I am sorry one so learned and so wise as you, Lord Angelo," he murmured, "should slip so grossly . . ."

"I am sorry that such sorrow I procure," said Angelo, for the old gentleman's distress moved him deeply. "I crave death more willingly than mercy. 'Tis my deserving, and I do entreat it."

He felt Mariana's hand tighten upon his in sudden fear; and his eyes filled with tears as he thought of what he had lost . . .

The provost had returned, and with him was Barnardine and another prisoner, whose head was muffled, as if for execution. The Duke looked at Barnardine. By light of day, he appeared even fouler than in the dark of the prison. His eyes were horribly screwed up against the painful sun, and every curse and sinful thought seemed to have left its blotchy mark upon his villainous face.

"Sirrah," said the Duke sternly, "thou art said to have a stubborn soul that apprehends no further than this world, and squar'st thy life accordingly. Thou'rt condemned—" He paused and smiled. He could not find it in his heart to condemn the squinting, still-drunken Barnardine, who, even in the darkness of his cell, clung to life so sturdily: "but, for those earthly faults, I quit them all, and pray thee take this mercy to provide for better times to come. Friar, advise him—"

Whether or not Barnardine understood that he had been pardoned, was hard to say. He hiccuped, spat, and suffered himself to be led away. The Duke looked curiously at the muffled prisoner who remained.

"This is another prisoner that I saved," said the provost, "who should have died when Claudio lost his head, as like almost to Claudio as himself." He took off the muffling. Isabella cried out. It was Claudio who stood before her!

Brother and sister gazed at one another. They had parted in bitterness; but since then they had endured much. Now there was nothing

. . . and with him was Barnardine

but joy and forgiveness in their eyes.

"If he be like your brother," said the Duke softly to Isabella, "for his sake is he pardoned, and for your lovely sake give me your hand, and say you will be mine, he is my brother too."

She made no answer; and the Duke, dreading that she would choose the cool cloister instead of the warmth of his heart, turned away. He spoke to Angelo: "Well, Angelo, your evil quits you quite."

Angelo nodded. He, too, was unable to speak. Claudio was alive! He, Angelo, had murdered in thought alone. It was as if all his evil had been a wicked dream. He had been given a second chance.

"Look that you love your wife," commanded the Duke; and it was a command that Angelo gladly obeyed.

Amid all the rejoicing, there was one who, thankfully, believed he had been overlooked. With infinite caution, he began to tiptoe away—

"You, sirrah!" Lucio halted. The Duke gazed at him sternly. "You, sirrah, that knew me for a fool, a coward, one all of luxury: wherein have I so deserved of you that you extol me thus?"

"'Faith, my lord," said Lucio uncomfortably, "I spoke it but according to the trick: if you will hang me for it, you may—but I had rather it would please you I might be whipped."

"Whipped first, sir, and hanged after," said the Duke. "Proclaim it, provost, round about the city, if any woman wronged by this lewd fellow, as I have heard him swear himself there's one whom he begot with child, let her appear, and he shall marry her!"

"I beseech your highness, do not marry me to a whore. Your highness said, even now, I made you a duke: good my lord, do not recompense me in making me a cuckold!"

"Slandering a prince deserves it," said the Duke. Then he turned to those who were happy. "She, Claudio, that you have wronged, look you restore. Joy to you, Mariana! Love her, Angelo!"

Now, at last, he dared to look to Isabella for her answer; and most wonderfully she had given it. It was the last unveiling. She had thrown back her hood and unbound her hair. It fell about her shoulders in a storm of gold.

Isabella, like the Duke, had made the long and arduous journey from justice to mercy, to forgiveness, and thence to love. She had chosen the warmth of his heart.

As You Like It

It began upon a winter's morning in an orchard in France. A cold sun was slanting down between the naked trees, and a cold wind was making them shiver and shake their skinny fists at an unnatural Nature that had stripped them of their clothing when most they had need of it. At the same time a poorly dressed young man was pacing back and forth, and likewise shaking his fists at an unnatural nature. Against all the obligations of blood, his eldest brother had cheated him out of his rights and left him to stink in the mire like a beast of the field!

"His horses are bred better!" he cried out bitterly. "I will no longer endure it!"

A withered old tree—or so, at first glance, it seemed—creaked into motion and laid a comforting branch upon the young man's sleeve. It was an aged servant by the name of Adam, who, by his bent back and his pecked and wrinkled cheeks, might have been that very Adam who had been booted out of Eden. Sadly, he shook his frosty head. The lad was right, and it was a bad business. If ever a lad had just cause for complaint, it was Orlando, the youngest son of good Sir Rowland de Boys. Even before the old gentleman had been cold in his grave, Oliver, the eldest son and the new master, had shoved Orlando from his rightful place at table, and lorded it over the estate alone. Truly, the world had fallen away from the goodly place it once had been . . .

Suddenly, a shadow fell across the path. "Yonder comes my master, your brother!" warned the old man as Oliver, swaggering in furs and velvet, appeared among the trees. As quickly as he could, the old servant took himself off and watched, from a little distance, the meeting of the brothers: the one, a rich and costly gentleman, the other, a rough-hewn peasant in coarse woollen, with anger in his eyes like a half-smothered fire in straw, threatening a sudden blaze. Nor was it long in coming! Angry words passed between them, then Oliver shouted: "What, boy!" and raised his hand to strike his brother!

"Sweet masters, be patient!" cried out Adam, rushing forward to prevent murder being done, for Orlando had seized his brother's wrist, twisted his arm behind his back, and secured him with an elbow around his throat! And all in an instant! Already Oliver's face was purple with choking, as he kicked and struggled like a dog in a sack. "For your father's remembrance, be at accord!" pleaded Adam; but Orlando would not let his brother go until he had squeezed a promise out of him that his inheritance would be paid.

"And what wilt thou do? Beg, when that is spent?" muttered Oliver savagely, rubbing his bruised throat and his bruised arm. "Leave me!" His eye fell upon the old servant. "Get you with him, you old dog!"

"Is 'old dog' my reward?" protested Adam indignantly. "Most true, I have lost my teeth in your service. God be with my old master! He would not have spoke such a word!" Then, seeing Orlando's fists clench in anger at such treatment of a faithful servant, and fearing more violence, he tugged him away.

There was someone waiting to speak with Sir Oliver de Boys. A strange visitor indeed. A mountainous fellow, who might have broken the back of a bear with his powerful arms, or killed a lion with one blow of his huge fist. He was Monsieur Charles, the Duke's wrestler, and the strongest man in France. Despite his great strength, the wrestler was a humble fellow and easily tongue-tied in the presence of a gentleman of rank.

"Good Monsieur Charles," said Oliver pleasantly, and meaning to put the fellow at his ease, "what's the new news at the new court?"

"There's no news at the court, sir, but the old news," answered the wrestler; and then, gaining courage, went on to tell that the new Duke was still the new Duke, and his elder brother, whom he had over-thrown, had fled for safety into the Forest of Arden, "and a many merry men with him," he related with growing eloquence; "and there they live like the old Robin Hood of England. They say many young gentlemen flock to him every day, and fleet the time carelessly as they did in the golden world." He paused, and a small sigh crept out of him, like a mouse coming forth from a mountain . . .

"You wrestle tomorrow before the new Duke?" inquired Oliver, impatient to bring the fellow out of the golden world and to the purpose of his visit, which, he supposed, must be to do with his trade. He was not mistaken. At once, a deeply serious look came over Monsieur Charles's large countenance, and Oliver, his heart beating rapidly, listened in silence as the wrestler unburdened his troubled spirit. He had heard that, among the foolhardy youth who had put themselves forward to challenge him, there was none other than his lordship's own younger brother, Orlando! It was for this reason that he had come. Earnestly, he begged his lordship to persuade his brother against so foolish a course. He, Charles, had no wish to break the young gentleman's limbs.

"I had as lief," murmured Oliver, "thou didst break his neck as his finger!" And, as Monsieur Charles looked amazed at so unbrotherly a wish, he went on to represent Orlando as so black and treacherous a villain, that it would be a good deed to rid the world of him!

Monsieur Charles sighed with relief. "I'll give him his payment," he promised; and, as the huge fellow departed, well-pleased to be doing his lordship a service, Oliver smiled with satisfaction. He hated his brother with all his heart; and for no stronger reason than that Orlando had always been loved better than himself. But it was reason enough . . .

The new court, like a woman in a new gown, was proud, but inclined to be uneasy, as if wondering if all was secure behind. This shadow of unease had even darkened the ordinarily high spirits of the two young women who walked together in the great hall of the new Duke's palace. They were Princesses, both. One was Celia, daughter of Frederick, the new Duke; the other was Rosalind, daughter of his brother, the overthrown Duke in the forest. Although Duke Frederick had protested that he loved Rosalind as tenderly as he loved his own daughter, it was impossible for Rosalind to forget her dearly loved father, living like an outlaw in Arden.

"I pray thee, Rosalind," pleaded Celia, for the hundredth time, "be merry!" But neither she nor Touchstone, the court jester—a fellow who, in his own opinion, could have squeezed laughter out of a lemon—could persuade her into more than the mouse of a smile, and a promise that she would try to do better.

"Here comes Monsieur Le Beau!" said Celia; and Rosalind's smile did indeed grow a little as that willowy gentleman of the court wafted towards them, like a flower in velvet boots.

"Fair Princess," he cried, addressing Celia with a twinkle of yellow stockings and a sweep of his feathered hat, "you have lost much good sport!"

"Sport?" inquired Celia, upon which the courtier eagerly informed the ladies that Monsieur Charles, the Duke's wrestler, had already broken the ribs of three young men who had been rash enough to answer his challenge. And the ladies had missed it!

"It is the first time," marvelled Touchstone, "that ever I heard breaking of ribs was sport for ladies!" But Monsieur Le Beau, ignoring the jester, assured the Princesses that they had not missed all. The best was yet to come. Another young man had come forward—

Even as he spoke, there was a murmuring commotion and the Duke and his court flowed into the great hall like a perfumed silken tide. Among them towered the huge figure of Monsieur Charles and, beside him, like a frail sapling next to a mighty oak, walked the new challenger, a humbly dressed youth whose proud looks and straight limbs made the heart ache for the ruin that was to become of them. It was Orlando.

Celia heard a sigh, a sigh that was deep enough to drown a world in. She turned. Her cousin was gazing, with enormous eyes, at the doomed young man; and her face was pale as death. "Alas," she whispered, "he is too young!"

Nor was Rosalind the only one to be affected. Duke Frederick himself had sought to persuade the young man from his foolhardy course; but to no avail. "Speak to him, ladies," he urged his daughter and his niece; "see if you can move him."

So Orlando was brought before the two Princesses who, one after another, begged him to abandon the unequal contest.

"Do, young sir!" pleaded Rosalind, and with a passion that seemed, to Celia, to have been stirred by something stronger than a mere wish to please the Duke. But the young man was resolved. He declared it did not matter to him whether he lived or died . . . although his eyes, as he gazed at Rosalind, seemed, to the curious Celia, to tell a very different tale. "The little strength that I have, I would it were with you!" breathed Rosalind, as the young man bowed to the two princesses and departed to do battle with the cruel giant.

Rosalind could not bear to watch. She covered her face with her hands. But, at the same time, could not bear *not* to watch, and her eyes kept sparkling through a lattice-work of fingers. "You shall try but one fall," she heard the Duke command; and she glimpsed the wide seated circle of the eager court.

"But come your ways!" the young man shouted defiantly; and the contest began!

She shut her eyes. She could hear grunts and gasps and cries, and the scrape and thump of staggering feet . . . She opened her eyes . . . caught a sudden sight of the giant's face, swollen with fierce triumph . . . then the young man, his poor head in a halter of mighty arms. The Duke was leaning forward, his fists were tightly clenched. A lady of the court had fainted clean away; a gentleman was sprinkling her with water, and a lady by her side was frantically tugging to free her gown. There was a loud cry! Then came a great shout. The Duke was on his feet, amazed—

Fearfully, Rosalind took her hands away from her face. She stared. "O excellent young man!" she cried out. Most marvellously, he was standing upright and unharmed! Beside him, like a fallen mountain, lay Monsieur Charles. The contest was ended. The youth had over-thrown the giant!

Everyone was on their feet and applauding, and, while half a dozen servants carried the groaning Charles away, the Duke himself, all smiles, was shaking the young man by the hand and asking his name. "Orlando, my liege," he answered proudly; "the youngest son of Sir Rowland de Boys."

At once, the Duke let go of his hand. Sir Rowland de Boys had been the good friend of the Duke in the forest; therefore his son was the new Duke's enemy. In an instant, smiles were changed to frowns, and joy to darkness and anger. "I would thou hadst told me of another father," he said abruptly, and departed from the hall, with the suddenly alarmed court hastening after.

Orlando and the two Princesses were alone in the great hall, with some awkward yards of silence between them.

"Let us go thank him," said Celia, feeling that, if she did not speak, her cousin and the young man would remain motionless, like two posts in a field, for ever and a day. Gently but firmly she urged Rosalind forward.

"Gentleman," murmured Rosalind, "wear this for me." And, impulsively taking a gold chain from her neck, offered it to Orlando. He stared at it. Impatiently, Rosalind put it over his head; and then, overcome with confusion at her own boldness, she turned to Celia. "Shall we go, coz?"

"Ay. Fare you well, fair gentleman," said Celia with a smile, and took her cousin by the arm.

They were half-way to vanishing from the hall before Orlando recovered the power of speech.

"Can I not say, I thank you?" he whispered, marvelling at the suddenness of the affliction that had struck him dumb.

"He calls us back!" cried Rosalind, catching the whisper and dragging Celia nearly off her feet in her haste to return. "Did you call, sir?" she asked eagerly; but Orlando was speechless again. "Sir, you have wrestled well, and overthrown more than your enemies," she went on, with such warmth in her voice and honesty in her eyes that a stone would have been moved to speak. But not Orlando.

"Will you go, coz?" murmured Celia, seeing it was a hopeless case. Reluctantly, Rosalind agreed, and with a sad shake of her head, accompanied her cousin out of the hall. Helplessly, the young man gazed after her.

"O poor Orlando," he sighed, "thou art overthrown!" The God of Love had shot him, not with a single arrow, but with his whole quiverful!

But the God of Hate was also aiming his arrows at Orlando. He felt a touch upon his shoulder. Startled, he turned. Monsieur Le Beau, on his velvet feet, had tiptoed up beside him. "Good sir," muttered the courtier, with anxious looks behind, "I do in friendship counsel you to leave this place!" Orlando frowned in puzzlement, and the courtier went on to confide that the Duke, who trusted no one, had suddenly taken it into his head that the youngest son of Sir Rowland de Boys was a threat to him. "Sir, fare you well," he urged; and, as he spoke, the mask of smiles that he, like everyone else in the new Duke's court habitually wore, slipped to reveal an honest man with an honest care for the young man's safety. "Hereafter, in a better world than this," he murmured softly, "I shall desire more love and knowledge of you."

Orlando thanked him warmly; and, cursing the cruelty of fortune that had offered him love with one hand only to snatch it back with the other, he hastened away. Sadly, Monsieur Le Beau watched him go; then, adjusting his courtier's mask of smiles, he trotted off to wait upon his master.

The Duke was in a fever of enemies. He saw them all around him. Every smile hid a frown; every word of love hid a thought of hate. No one was beyond suspicion; and least of all Rosalind, the daughter of the brother he had wronged, and whose presence in the court he had only tolerated on account of the love his own daughter had for her. But that was all over—"Mistress!" he shouted, bursting into the apartment where his daughter and the hated one were laughing together. "Get you from our court!"

"Me, uncle?" cried Rosalind, amazed.

"You!" answered the Duke in a mounting rage; and he swore that if she should be found within twenty miles of the court, she would die for it! Celia, outraged by her father's cruel injustice, declared that she would go wherever her cousin went.

"You are a fool!" said the Duke contemptuously; and, with his palely smiling courtiers, swept out of the room.

The cousins stared at one another in fear and stark amazement. "Whither shall we go?" whispered Rosalind at length.

"To seek my uncle in the Forest of Arden," decided Celia, without hesitation.

The forest! At once, the image of a dark and dreadful place of savage beasts and lurking robbers presented itself to the cousins' imagination. Surely it was no place for a pair of tender Princesses! "I'll put myself in poor and mean attire," proposed Celia. "The like do you."

"Were it not better," suggested Rosalind, "because I am more than common tall, that I do suit me all points like a man?" So it was agreed: Rosalind, in man's attire, would be known as Ganymede, and Celia, dressed like a shepherdess, would be his sister, Aliena. Then Rosalind had another thought. Should they not take Touchstone, the court jester, with them for company?

Celia nodded. "He'll go along o'er the wide world with me," she promised; and straightway the cousins set about making ready for their flight.

While the two Princesses, in secret haste, were stuffing their purses with gold and their satchels with clothing, and Touchstone, gnawing his fingernails, was waiting below their window to steady the ladder for their night-time descent, Orlando, that other victim of the Duke's frantic suspicions, returned to his lodging.

As he approached, all was dark. A shadow stirred. "Who's there?"

It was old Adam, his face as white as his hair. "O unhappy youth, come not within these doors!" he cried out, barring Orlando's path. In a shaking voice, he warned the young man that his brother Oliver, enraged by his success, meant to burn down his lodging that very night, with the sleeping Orlando inside it! "This house is but a butchery," he whispered. "Do not enter it!"

Orlando, his life now threatened in his own home, asked bitterly what was to become of him: must he get his living by robbing on the highway, or by begging in the town? The old servant shook his head. He had five hundred crowns, he said, that he had saved up during his long years of service; and now at last he had found a better use for his little fortune than ever he could have supposed. He offered it to Orlando and asked no more in return than that the young man should take him as his servant. "Though I look old, yet I am strong and lusty," he protested, as Orlando looked sadly at his white hair and frail limbs. "Let me go with you; I'll do the service of a younger man . . ."

"O good old man!" cried Orlando, his eyes filling up with tears. "Thou art not for the fashion of these times, where none will sweat but for promotion . . ." Adam bowed his head. "But come thy ways," said Orlando with a smile, "we'll go along together!" and with lifting hearts and sturdy pace, they set off side by side into the night.

The palace was in an uproar! The Princesses had gone, and the jester with them! Their beds had been unslept in, and none knew when or where they had fled. All that could be found out was from a gentle-woman who had overheard the Princesses warmly praising the youth who had overthrown the wrestler. Find that youth, was her shrewd advice, and you will find the others.

"Fetch that gallant hither!" commanded the Duke. "If he be absent, bring his brother!" and, as frightened courtiers hastened to obey, the search went on, high and low, for the runaways.

The day was ending, and in the forest the gathering gloom turned every tree into a lurking robber, and every bush into a bear. "O Jupiter, how merry are my spirits!" cried Rosalind, for all the world as if she meant it; but her companions were not of her mind.

"I care not for my spirits, if my legs were not weary," groaned Touchstone, his melancholy countenance drooping onto the bright patchwork of his jester's coat; and Celia, a Princess of burrs and scratches, limping far behind, wailed:

"I pray you, bear with me: I can go no further."

"Well, this is the Forest of Arden!" said Rosalind, determined to be cheerful; for now she was in man's attire, with her golden hair crammed up inside her feathered cap, she was resolved, against all private inclin-ation, to be a prop and a comfort to her frailer friends.

"Ay, now am I in Arden," moaned Touchstone, sitting down on a

tree-stump and nursing his blistered feet, "the more fool I; when I was at home I was in a better place—"

There came a sound of footfalls and a murmur of voices! The three travellers looked to one another in alarm; and then, forgetful of their aching limbs, skipped, brisk as lambs, into the concealment of the trees.

No sooner had they vanished from the clearing, than two inhabitants of the forest appeared. They proved to be nothing more alarming than a pair of shepherds: one sturdy and grey-haired; the other, young and tender, and full of sighs. They were talking of love, and the elder was gently advising his young companion against being too slavish in his courtship of his beloved. But his words went unheeded. "O Corin," cried the afflicted one, clapping a hand to his pale brow, "that thou knew'st how I do love her!"

"I partly guess," smiled Corin, "for I have loved ere now." But the youth would not have it. He could not believe that any man had loved as he loved, and not bear the scars for all to see.

"Thou hast not loved!" he cried indignantly; and, clutching his hair as if to pull it out by the roots, rushed off into the forest, calling: "O Phebe, Phebe, Phebe!" to the unfeeling bushes and trees.

Rosalind, in concealment, felt an ache in her heart. The shepherd's passion for his Phebe reminded her sharply of her own for Orlando; and such was the power of visible love, that even the ever-mocking Touchstone was driven to recollect a time when he, too, had been laid low by the same madness. "We that are true lovers," he sighed, "run into strange capers."

Celia alone felt differently. True, she felt pangs; but they were in her stomach, not in her heart. "I pray you," she begged, "one of you question yond man, if he for gold will give us any food: I faint almost to death."

"Holla, you clown!" called out Touchstone, with a courtier's contempt for simple countrymen who were little better than the beasts they tended.

"Who calls?" asked Corin; and he stared in wonderment as the trees disgorged themselves of strange fruit indeed: a haughty jester, a lady dressed as a shepherdess who, he would have taken his oath, had never tended sheep save with a knife and spoon, as mutton, and a swaggering young huntsman with villainous sword and fearsome spear, whose complexion was as soft as a flower.

"Good even to you, friend," said the huntsman, with a mildness that belied his fierce ironmongery; and he went on to beg, for his fainting sister's sake, food and shelter for which he was willing to pay. Sadly, Corin shook his head. He was not his own master, but served a man who cared nothing for hospitality, and wanted only to sell his cottage, pasture and flock, and have done with them.

On hearing this, the young huntsman glanced at his sister; and she, poor famished soul, eagerly nodded her head. Without more ado, the huntsman offered to buy the property and pay Corin his wages for tending the sheep. "Assuredly the thing is to be sold," said Corin, well-pleased at the prospect of so pleasant and monied a young master; and they all went off together, new landlords of a piece of Arden.

But in another part of the forest, two travellers were not so fortunate. They had journeyed far, and one, the elder, was almost at his end. "Dear master, I can go no further," gasped old Adam, his piled-up years at last overcoming his willing spirit. "O I die for food. Here lie

I down," he sighed, sinking to the ground, "and measure out my grave. Farewell, kind master."

"Why, how now, Adam?" cried Orlando, rushing back to help the old man, "no greater heart in thee?" Desperately he chafed the old man's freezing hands and smoothed his brow. He gathered moss and leaves to make a pillow for his head, and laid his coat over the old man to keep him warm. "Live a little; comfort a little!" he pleaded; and hoping that the habit of long service would make the old servant obey, he sternly bade him keep death away while he, Orlando, went in search of food. "Thou shalt not die for lack of a dinner," he promised, and, drawing his sword, set off into the forest. "Cheerly, good Adam!" he called back encouragingly, but could not subdue the dread in his heart that when he returned, old Adam would no longer be alive.

As he crept among the darkening trees, he paused from time to time to listen for a rustling, or the crackling of a twig, that would betray some wild creature that would serve them for food. But the forest was as quiet as a grave. Then, suddenly, he heard, very faintly, a strange sound. He strained his ears. It was a voice, singing! With beating heart, he hastened towards it . . .

> "Under the greenwood tree
> Who loves to lie with me . . ."

It was a young man's voice, full of easy confidence, and seemed to be moving from place to place. Eagerly Orlando followed it, sometimes mistaking the echo for the substance, but ever drawing nearer . . .

"Come hither, come hither, come hither," tempted the wandering voice,

> "Here shall he see
> No enemy
> But winter and rough weather
> Come hither, come hither . . ."

Stumbling over roots, scratched and torn by spiteful branches, Orlando pursued the song. Suddenly, it ceased. Lanterns were gleaming among the trees, and there was a murmur of voices. Orlando stopped, amazed.

143

In a golden clearing, like a little summer's day, a company of outlaws were gathered together; and in their midst were spread enough good things to eat to save a dozen dying men! With a wildly desperate cry, Orlando rushed into the clearing, fiercely brandishing his sword. "Forbear, and eat no more!"

The outlaws turned in astonishment. "Why, I have eat none yet,"

protested one, a long-faced melancholy fellow, pointing to his empty plate. Then another, who, from the respect accorded him, seemed to be the leader of the band, reproached Orlando for his show of needless force. "What would you have?" he asked courteously.

"I almost die for food," answered Orlando; to which the other replied: "Sit down and feed, and welcome to our table."

Strange forest! where fury was answered by gentleness, and outlaws spoke with the tongues of kindness! Ashamed, Orlando laid his sword aside. "There is an old poor man," he told them, "who after me hath many a weary step limped in pure love. Till he be first sufficed I will not touch a bit."

"Go find him out," said the leader kindly, "and we will nothing waste till you return."

"I thank ye!" cried Orlando, weeping with gratitude, and hastened back to his old servant, praying with all his heart that he would not be too late.

"Thou seest we are not all alone unhappy," observed the Duke when the wild young man had gone; for this leader of the outlaw band was indeed the banished Duke, and the outlaws gathered round him were the young men who had flocked to join him and live the greenwood life. "This wide and universal theatre," continued the philosophical Duke, "presents more woeful pageants than the scene wherein we play in."

"All the world's a stage," instantly observed the melancholy one, whose name was Jacques, "and all the men and women merely players. They have their exits and their entrances, and one man in his time plays many parts, his acts being seven ages." He paused and, picking up his empty plate, polished it on his sleeve till it shone like a mirror, and studied his reflection. Then, suiting his expression to his words, he expounded the seven ages of man, from, "the infant, mewling and puking in the nurse's arms" and continuing on his relentless journey to the grave, concluding with, "second childishness and mere oblivion, sans teeth, sans eyes, sans taste, sans everything."

But no sooner had his bleak and dreadful vision of man's old age been presented, than, in an instant it was overthrown! Orlando returned, bearing old Adam on his back. The good old man had obeyed his young master, and remained alive! Here was the visible evidence of age not useless, but wonderfully enriched by courage, loyalty and love! "Welcome!" cried the Duke, mightily glad to see it. "Set down your venerable burden and let him feed!"

At once, willing hands assisted the old man to a place at the feast, and helped him to food; and, while his guests were satisfying their hunger, the Duke called for music, and the singer who had been heard in the forest, obliged the company with another song.

> "Blow, blow, thou winter wind,
> Thou art not so unkind
> As man's ingratitude,"

he sang, while the courtiers in the forest sighed and nodded: it was a truth they had learned only too well.

> "Then heigh-ho! the holly!
> This life is most jolly!"

and all were agreed.

Even as Orlando found gentleness in the savage forest, so his brother Oliver found savagery in the gentle court. The maddened Duke Frederick, still seeking his daughter, had learned that Orlando had also fled. "Find out thy brother!" he shouted at the fearful Oliver. "Bring him dead or living within this twelvemonth!" and, with bloodshot eye and direst threats, despatched him to obey or lose all that he possessed. So Oliver, like many another bewildered by sudden adversity, turned his desperate steps towards the Forest of Arden . . .

A strange malady had begun to afflict the trees of the forest. It first appeared as Touchstone and the good countryman Corin were walking together, near to the cottage that Celia and Rosalind had newly bought. "Here comes young Master Ganymede," said Corin, interrupting the jester's unending flow of wit as Rosalind, still in her man's attire, came winding slowly among the trees. She was deep in the study of a paper, and, unaware of her audience, was reading aloud:

"From the East to western Ind,
No jewel is like Rosalind . . ."

"This is the very false gallop of verses!" cried Touchstone, unable
to endure such poor stuff. "Why do you infect yourself with them?"

"Peace, you dull fool!" cried Rosalind, blushing to have been overheard reciting her own praises. "I found them on a tree."

"Truly, the tree yields bad fruit!" said the jester, to which Rosalind
returned as good as she got, and the battle of wits would have continued
had not another deep reader appeared among the trees. It was Celia,
likewise with her nose in a paper that declared still more wonders of
Rosalind.

"O most gentle Jupiter!" protested Rosalind (when it was plain there
was no more to come), "what tedious homily of love . . ."

Startled, Celia turned, to discover an audience crowding at her heels.
She was no better pleased than Rosalind at being overheard reciting,
not her own praises, but another's. Sharply, she dismissed the jester
and the countryman. Then she turned to Rosalind and held out the
paper. "Didst thou hear these verses?" Humbly Rosalind confessed she
had, but hastened to add that she did not think highly of them. Celia
gazed at her cousin thoughtfully; and asked if she had not wondered
how it had come about that half the trees in the forest had been stricken
by the same poetic malady? Again, Rosalind confessed it, and held out
her own paper in evidence. Celia ignored it, and inquired if Rosalind
knew who had hung up her name so far and wide?

"Is it a man?" ventured Rosalind, striving to keep a mounting excitement out of her voice.

Celia nodded. "And a chain," she said, striving to keep a bubbling
up of laughter out of hers, "that you once wore, about his neck. Change
you colour?"

A needless question. At once Rosalind began to plague Celia for
more particulars, which Celia laughingly withheld, like sweets from a
child, until, having been pursued round trees and bushes by her wildly
importuning cousin, she gave up and confessed that the poet had been
none other than the young man who had wrestled so well: Orlando!
But far from contenting her, the news drove Rosalind at first into a
frantic dismay that Orlando should see her in man's attire and not at

147

her best, and then into another tempest of questioning that was only stopped when Celia cried: "Soft! comes he not here?"

Rosalind's eyes grew huge. "'Tis he!" she whispered, and jerked Celia into concealment as her beloved approached.

He was not alone. He was walking with a long-faced melancholy fellow, a wretch who was daring to complain that Orlando's love-songs were spoiling the trees. But Orlando defended his verses with spirit. "Rosalind is your love's name?" the wretch inquired; and, on receiving confirmation, most impertinently declared, "I do not like her name!"

To which Orlando justly replied, "There was no thought of pleasing you when she was christened!" The fellow sniffed and asked, "What stature is she of?"

"Just as high as my heart!" came back the answer, which, in Rosalind's opinion, could not have been bettered by any man. At length, they parted with expressions of mutual disdain, and Orlando was left alone.

"I will speak to him like a saucy lackey!" determined Rosalind; and, before Celia could stop her, she had strutted out with a swagger and a manly frown. Uneasily, Celia followed. She could not believe the young man would fail to recognize his Rosalind, no matter what she wore. But love proved blind, not only to the loved one's faults, but to her virtues as well! True, once or twice he looked curiously at 'Master Ganymede', as if a recollection was stirring; but it was plain he never saw, in the impudently posturing youth before him, the gently bred Princess of the court.

"I pray you, what is't o'clock?" she began; and thereafter Celia was lost in wonderment as she found herself audience to the strangest courtship in the world! Lacking the assistance of a gorgeous gown, rich golden hair and speaking eyes, Rosalind had only her wit with which to dazzle her lover, to entangle and bewitch him with a thousand whirling words. "Love is merely a madness," she was saying, having at last, like a skilful shepherd, guided her unruly flock of words to that very subject; "yet I profess curing it by counsel."

"I would not be cured, youth," sighed Orlando; upon which, Rosalind, concealing her joy, insisted that her remedy at least be tried. Then, sailing so near to the wind of discovery that Celia held her breath, she proposed that Orlando call her Rosalind and come to court her every day, when she would be so wild, so fantastical, so changeable and contrary in her moods, that the very name of Rosalind would become a torment rather than a delight. "And this way I will take it upon me," she promised, "to wash your liver as clean as a sound sheep's heart that there shall not be one spot of love in't!" Orlando smiled at the youth's confidence, but assured him that the remedy would have no success. But Rosalind insisted, and Orlando, with a laugh, gave in. "With all my heart, good youth!"

"Nay," cried Rosalind, raising her hand in stern rebuke, "you must call me Rosalind!" and, extending a brotherly arm to Celia, stalked away before solemnity was blown to the winds.

Love lay upon the forest like a blight. The very trees, as if they had sucked in sugar from the verses that had been hung upon them, seemed to twine together in gnarly embraces; and Jacques, who had just parted from one love-sick fool, now found himself witness to a pair of them, like cock and hen, crowing in a glade. One was a fool by nature, the other, a fool by profession.

Touchstone, wearied of country life, and finding nothing to aim his wit at, save a few sagely nodding bushes and a philosophical sheep or two, had decided to take unto himself a wife. It seemed to be in the fashion, and he was nothing if not fashionable. He had chosen, for this high office, one Audrey, a country wench, thick of speech and stinking like a goat. The union suited him very well. As male and female, they agreed as readily as the beasts of the field; and as courtier and foul slut, they were worlds apart. In this manner, he found satisfaction both as a man and as a gentleman: for Audrey never understood a word he said and, accordingly, held him in high respect. But yet there were moments when he could not help having his doubts . . .

"Truly," he sighed, gazing at Audrey, whose mouth stood open, like a kitchen door, blasting forth stale cabbage and onions, "I would the gods had made thee poetical."

"I do not know what 'poetical' is," pleaded Audrey, humbled by the wondrous mystery of language. "Is it honest in deed and word? Is it a true thing?"

"No, truly, for the truest poetry is the most feigning," returned Touchstone; then, perceiving that his pearls had been cast away, sadly shook his head. "But be it as it may be," he sighed, having weighed Audrey against a lonely life, which was something against nothing, "I will marry thee." And Audrey laughed and clapped her hands. "Well, the gods give us joy!" she cried.

Orlando had not come. The morning sun, bursting through the forest in misty beams and sudden glares, made a thousand flickering phantoms of him; but none proved real, and Rosalind, disgracing her man's attire, wept. Celia, who knew nothing of the pangs of true love, tried to comfort her cousin by abusing Orlando for lack of constancy—

"Nay, certainly, there is no truth in him," she declared.

"Not true in love?" wailed Rosalind.

"Yes, when he is in," said Celia; "but I think he is not in."

"But you heard him swear downright he was!"

"'Was' is not 'is'," pointed out Celia, and would have said a great deal more, had not their shepherd, old Corin, interrupted the argument.

He came in haste, his weathered face all aglow. With twinkling merriment, he told his mistress and his master of an entertainment nearby in the forest that was well worth their attendance. The young shepherd, who, as they remembered, was so in love that he was almost dying of it, was even now pleading his cause before his Phebe! "Go hence a little," he urged, "and I shall conduct you . . ."

"O! come," cried Rosalind eagerly: "the sight of lovers feedeth those in love!" and the cousins followed after the beckoning old countryman.

The lovers were in a clearing, like a tragical picture framed in tangled hawthorn and sharp briar. The young shepherd, whose name was Silvius, was on his knees before his Phebe, who sat on a tree-stump, a rustic queen upon a rustic throne. "Sweet Phebe, do not scorn me!" he pleaded; while she, proud impossible she, her black eyes sparking like coals in a grate, dealt him blow after blow of sovereign disdain.

At length, Rosalind could endure her unkindness and arrogance no longer. "Who might be your mother," she cried, striding into the clearing and confronting the lofty shepherdess, "that you insult, exult, and all at once, over the wretched?"

The wretched fell over backwards, and the rustic queen gaped in amazement at the sudden youth whose eyes out-flashed her own. Quite dazzled, she sat in silence as he indignantly rebuked her for her pride. Nor was Silvius spared. "You foolish shepherd," the youth declared, more in pity than in anger, "wherefore do you follow her, like foggy South puffing with wind and rain? You are a thousand times a properer man than she a woman; 'tis such fools as you that make the world full of ill-favoured children; 'tis not her glass, but you that flatters her!" Then he turned again on Phebe, and, pointing an accusing finger, cried: "But, mistress, know yourself. Down on your knees, and thank heaven, fasting, for a good man's love; for I must tell you friendly in your ear—" He beckoned, and she most willingly left her throne and inclined her head to the youth's red lips as he softly advised, "Sell when you can; you are not for all markets. Cry the man mercy; love him; take his offer!" Then, with a last injunction of Silvius to take his Phebe to himself, the youth and his two companions departed from the glade.

Long after the youth had gone, Phebe sat gazing after him. No youth had ever spoken to her so sternly before; and she was full of bewilderment and sighs. She looked at Silvius, who loved her dearly, and she sighed again. Then she thought of the youth, and her sighs came fast as a blacksmith's bellows. "I'll write to him a very taunting letter," she said thoughtfully, "and thou shalt bear it; wilt thou, Silvius?" she asked, with such a smile at her lover that he, feeling he had been paid in better than gold, could deny her nothing. "I will be bitter with him," she said; and Silvius believed her!

Marching through the forest, with a festive sprig of holly in his cap and whistling an air that was all the fashion with the banished Duke and his companions, Orlando came at last to where the youth and his sister dwelt. "Good day and happiness, dear Rosalind," he announced to his pretended love, with a flourish of his cap and a gallant bow; only to be greeted by a frown, severely folded arms and a tapping of the foot. He was late. "My fair Rosalind," he protested, in answer to her reproaches, "I come within an hour of my promise!"

"Break an hour's promise in love!" cried she; and he, contrite as a crocodile, hung his head and pleaded, "Pardon me, dear Rosalind!" She thought about it; and pardoned him. She was no more able to keep sullen than a child could keep still in church. "Come, woo me, woo me," she commanded, with a royal clap of her hands; "for now I am in a holiday humour, and like enough to consent!" and so once again Celia found herself witness to this strangest of strange courtships in which pretended love hid honest love, and false words were true.

"Am not I your Rosalind?" demanded Rosalind; and Orlando, with a wishful smile, answered, "I take some joy to say you are." Then Rosalind, true to her promise of being contrary, said she would not have him; and he, true to his lover's part, swore it would kill him. But this was too much for Rosalind's good sense. "Men have died from time to time," she said, "and worms have eaten them; but not for love."

He frowned. "I would not have my right Rosalind of this mind," he said, and instantly she changed about. She would indeed have him . . . "And twenty such," she added for good measure.

"What sayest thou?" he cried, outraged. She gazed at him with wide, innocent eyes. "Are you not good?" she asked. He said he hoped he was. "Why then," she declared triumphantly, "can one desire too much

of a good thing?" She laughed and turned to Celia. "Come sister, you shall be the priest and marry us!"

Celia stared. Truly, this strange courtship had passed beyond all bounds! "I cannot say the words," she muttered uneasily.

"You must begin," instructed Rosalind, "'Will you Orlando—'" Celia sighed and, shrugging her shoulders, married off the false, yet true, couple who stood hand in hand before her, feeling all the while that a high solemnity was being mocked.

"Now tell me," demanded Rosalind of Orlando after the ceremony was concluded, "how long you would have her after you have possessed her?"

"For ever, and a day," he answered very properly; but she shook her head.

"Say 'a day', without the 'ever'," she advised. "No, no, Orlando; men are April when they woo, December when they wed. Maids are May when they are maids, but the sky changes when they are wives." But Orlando would not believe his Rosalind would ever change, and he put a stop to all arguments that proved the contrary, by remembering that he was to wait upon the Duke at dinner. "For these two hours, Rosalind, I will leave thee."

"Alas! dear love," she cried, clutching him fiercely by the sleeve, "I cannot lack thee two hours!" But there was no help for it; so, after threatening him with her direst displeasure if he should be so much as a minute late in returning, she let him go.

Celia was bursting with indignation over her cousin's outrageous display of female perversity. "You have simply misused our sex in your love-prate!" she cried. "We must have your doublet and hose plucked over your head, and show the world what the bird hath done to her own nest!"

But Rosalind did not care. "O coz, coz, coz," she laughed, flinging out her arms and dancing on the green, "my pretty little coz, that thou didst know how many fathom deep I am in love!" Then, remembering that two long hours must pass, she said, "I'll go find a shadow and sigh till he come."

"And I'll sleep," said Celia, who was not in love.

The two hours came and went, but brought no Orlando. Instead, they wafted another lover through the forest: the breathless Silvius doing his Phebe's bidding. He had brought her letter and faithfully delivered it into Master Ganymede's hand, with humble apologies for the bitter and taunting words that Phebe said she had written. Impatiently, and with many an anxious glance for the coming of Orlando, Rosalind read the letter. Her brow grew dark with anger, and Silvius trembled that his Phebe should have written so cruelly. Rosalind looked up. "Will you hear the letter?" she asked.

"So please you," answered Silvius; so she read it to him. As he listened, his eyes grew big with tears. Phebe had deceived him! The words she had written were bitter, but only to him. The letter he had carried was full of a wild and tender passion; but not for him. She had fallen in love with Ganymede!

"Alas, poor shepherd!" sighed Celia; but Rosalind felt no pity for the foolish youth who was weeping for so worthless a creature as Phebe. "Well, go your way to her, for I see love hath made thee a tame snake!" she cried, angry that love, which should have ennobled, had reduced this lover to so crawling a condition. "Say this to her: if she love me, I charge her to love thee. If she will not, I will never have her—" She stopped. She had glimpsed a familiar figure approaching through the trees. Hastily she dismissed Silvius, and made herself ready for—

But once again, it was not Orlando . . . yet there had been something about the stranger that had, for a moment, deceived her. He was handsome enough (but no Orlando!) and his manner was gentle . . . though inclined to be awkward, like a new garment, not yet worn in. He was looking for a cottage near a clump of olive trees, where a brother and sister dwelt together. As he spoke, he looked curiously at Rosalind and Celia, and wondered if they could be the pair who owned the cottage? "It is no boast, being asked, to say we are," answered Celia; and a sudden summer of roses bloomed in her cheeks as she met the stranger's inquiring gaze.

Nor was the stranger unaffected. He seemed, for a moment, to forget the purpose of his errand. He faltered, looked confused . . . then, recovering himself, began, "Orlando doth commend him to you both—" and at once Rosalind understood why he had reminded her of her love! He had come from Orlando, and therefore bore his imprint! "And to the youth he calls his Rosalind," the stranger continued, "he sends this bloody napkin." He held out a handkerchief, streaked with red.

Rosalind stared at it. "What must we understand by this?" she whispered, suddenly pale. The stranger sighed; then, seating himself cross-legged on the turf, with his audience, like eager children, kneeling before him, he told a story so strange, so wild and wonderful, that the cousins scarcely dared to breathe . . .

It began with Orlando on his way to keep his promise to his imagined Rosalind. As he walked through the forest, full of dreams, he came upon a ragged man, asleep under an ancient tree. About the sleeper's neck, like a lady's bright scarf, was coiled a deadly serpent, which, on hearing Orlando's approach, glided harmlessly away. But a more terrible danger was near at hand. Under a bush crouched a hungry lioness, waiting to leap upon the sleeper with savage teeth and claws! Orlando drew close; then stopped in amazement. He recognized the man! It was his brother, his elder brother Oliver!

"O! I have heard him speak of that same brother," breathed Celia,

155

staring at the stranger as if wondering how he could know so much without having been present himself; "and he did render him the most unnatural that lived amongst men!"

"But to Orlando," cried Rosalind, impatient of brothers and all else, save Orlando. "Did he leave him there—?"

The stranger shook his head. Though sorely tempted to leave his brother to the lioness, and so be revenged for all the ill-usage he had suffered, he could not do so. As the lioness roared and sprang, Orlando, without a thought for his own danger, met her in mid-career! They wrestled, and in a moment he had overthrown the savage beast as readily as he had once overthrown the mighty Charles! Here the stranger paused; and then said quietly, "In which hurtling from miserable slumber I awaked!" He himself had been that sleeping man; he was Oliver, Orlando's wicked brother!

The cousins stared at him: Rosalind with anger, but Celia more with sorrow that so fair a young man should turn out to be so black a villain. But no longer! With earnest looks he told them of his most wonderful conversion: of how, having been despatched by the tyrant Duke to bring back Orlando, he had wandered in the forest, becoming more and more wretched until the moment he had awakened from sleep to see Orlando endangering his own life to save his brother's. At once, all envy and malice had vanished from his heart, and now there was only love and forgiveness between himself and Orlando . . .

Celia listened with shining eyes; but Rosalind was still troubled. She had not forgotten the strange token that Orlando had sent. "But, for the bloody napkin?" she asked; and Oliver resumed his story. Orlando had taken him to the banished Duke, where he had been received with great kindness and given fresh clothing; but as Orlando himself was changing his torn attire, he suddenly fainted! The lioness had ripped open his arm, and he had lost much blood. But he quickly recovered and begged Oliver to seek out the brother and sister in the forest to explain to them the reason for his failure to keep his promise. "And," concluded Oliver with a smile, "to give this napkin, dy'd in his blood, unto the shepherd youth that he in sport doth call his Rosalind." He rose, and courteously presented Orlando's crimson gift.

"Why, how now, Ganymede! Sweet Ganymede!" cried out Celia in a fright; for Rosalind, seeing Orlando's blood, had fainted clean away!

"Many will swoon when they do look on blood," said Oliver; but Celia, vigorously chafing her cousin's cold hands, shook her head. "There is more in it," she muttered. "Cousin! Ganymede!"

Rosalind opened her eyes. "I would I were at home," she murmured; and suffered herself to be helped to her feet. Then, fearful that her sudden weakness had betrayed her sex, she assured Oliver that her fainting had been pretence, that she had not fainted at all, that she had never felt better . . . and that he was to be sure to tell his brother how skilfully she had pretended. She looked to see how well her assurances had been received, and could not help noting some resemblances to Orlando in his elder brother's features: but they were prentice-work compared with what Nature had accomplished when she'd tried again! Celia, on the other hand, as she and Oliver assisted Rosalind back to their cottage, could not help wondering, as she kept glancing at the young man, if Nature, like a lucky player, had not done her best at the first throw! "Good sir," she murmured, as he showed signs of departing, "go with us . . ."

"We shall find a time, Audrey," sighed Touchstone, as the sun went down among the trees, and marriage, like Monday after Sunday, threatened ahead. "Patience, gentle Audrey," he urged as, gazing at his

chosen bride ambling foolishly among her goats, he wondered yet again about the wisdom of his choice. But even as he puzzled over it, and would have given much to find some means of delay, there was another in the forest ready to give up all to hasten it!

"My father's house and all the revenue that was old Sir Rowland's will I estate upon you!" cried Oliver distractedly, as he dragged Orlando back to the cottage where Ganymede and his sister Aliena dwelt. He had fallen in love with Aliena, and she with him! It had happened in an instant, in the merest twinkling of eyes; and now, all he desired was to marry Aliena, poor as she was, and live and die by her side, a humble shepherd in the forest.

Orlando marvelled at the swiftness of it all, although why he, who had been struck dumb with love for Rosalind with a suddenness that made his brother's courtship seem almost tedious, should be surprised was a mystery. Nonetheless, he would not stand in their way, and promised to bring the banished Duke and all his followers to celebrate their forest wedding on the morrow. "Go you and prepare Aliena," he advised; "for look you, here comes my Rosalind."

Warmly, Oliver clasped his brother by the uninjured hand; then, greeting the approaching Ganymede as "fair sister", he laughed and hastened to Aliena's cottage.

"O! my dear Orlando," cried Rosalind, regarding his bandages with concern, "how it grieves me to see thee wear thy heart in a scarf!"

"It is my arm!" he protested. She expressed surprise, then inquired if, by any chance, his brother had told him how well she had pretended to faint on seeing his blood?

"Ay," nodded Orlando, "and greater wonders than that," he said, with a smiling look towards the departed Oliver. She took his meaning, and at once confirmed that Aliena's passion was fully the equal of his brother's.

"They are in the very wrath of love," she declared, "they will together: clubs cannot part them!"

"They shall be married tomorrow," Orlando promised; then he sighed, "But O! how bitter a thing it is to look into happiness through another man's eyes!"

"Why then, tomorrow," asked Rosalind softly, "I cannot serve your turn for Rosalind?"

"I can no longer live by thinking," said he.

"I will weary you then no longer with idle talking," said she, much moved by the honesty of Orlando's love and the deepness of his distress. The time was near for truth. Her own heart could scarcely hold out against it. But it must be revealed with proper solemnity and mystery . . . "Believe then, if you please, I can do strange things," she told her lover gravely. "I have, since I was three year old, conversed with a magician . . ." He smiled; but she reproved him with a frown, and continued: "If you do love Rosalind so near the heart as your gesture cries it out, when your brother marries Aliena, shall you marry her."

Orlando stared. "Speakest thou in sober meanings?" he demanded.

"By my life, I do," returned she. "If you will be married tomorrow, you shall; and to Rosalind, if you will . . ."

He would have pressed further, but there were others in the forest who had come to seek out Ganymede. Phebe, the vain and foolish shepherdess, her black eyes screwed up in anger, like rivets in a plank, and with her poor love following after, had come to reproach that youth for reading aloud her very private letter. "You have done me much ungentleness," she complained.

"I care not if I have!" answered Rosalind, wearied by such persistence in folly. "You are there followed by a faithful shepherd; look upon him, love him. He worships you!"

But Phebe shook her silly head. "Tell this youth," she bade the doting Silvius, "what 'tis to love!"

"It is to be all made of sighs and tears," responded Silvius hopelessly; "and so am I for Phebe."

"And I for Ganymede," echoed Phebe, with a yearning look.

"And I for Rosalind," sighed Orlando, adding his link to the chain.

Then all turned to Ganymede, who smiled, and ended the chain most mysteriously with, "And I for no woman!"

Then mystery upon mystery! The strange youth raised a hand and solemnly commanded, "Tomorrow meet me all together;" then spoke to each in turn: first, to Phebe, "I will marry you, if ever I marry woman, and I'll be married tomorrow." Then to Orlando: "I will satisfy you, if ever I satisfied man, and you shall be married tomorrow." And last, to Silvius: "I will content you, if what pleases you contents you, and you shall be married tomorrow!" Then, making a magical sign in the air, doubtless learned from the magician, the youth vanished among the trees, leaving the three lovers to stare and wonder, to hope and doubt if these marvels could ever be brought to pass.

Two little pages from the banished Duke's court, all in green like leaves of holly, with faces bright as berries, came marching through the dawning forest, singing as they went:

> "It was a lover and his lass,
> With a hey, and a ho, and a hey nonino,
> That o'er the green corn-field did pass,
> In spring time, the only pretty ring time,
> When birds do sing, hey ding a ding, ding,
> Sweet lovers love the spring."

As they marched along, keeping time in song and step, all the birds of the forest obliged with a shrill and chattering chorus, from hawthorn, oak and holly . . .

"Dost thou then believe, Orlando," asked the Duke, as he and his followers, with Oliver and his Aliena among them, crowded into the misty chapel of sunshine that was the place appointed for the lovers' meeting, "that the boy can do all this that he hath promised?"

"I sometimes do believe," said Orlando, and then with a sigh, "and sometimes do not." And the little pages went on singing:

> "These pretty country folks would lie,
> In spring time, the only pretty ring time . . ."

until suddenly they fell silent as, like a bright phantom passing through the golden pillars of the sun, Ganymede appeared, leading Silvius and Phebe by the hand. Gravely the youth surveyed the assembled congregation, and then addressed the Duke: "If I bring in your Rosalind, you will bestow her on Orlando here?"

"That would I," returned the Duke gladly, "had I kingdoms to give

. . . marching through the dawning forest

with her!" Ganymede nodded, and turned to Orlando: "And you say you will have her when I bring her?"

"That would I," promised Orlando, "were I of all kingdoms king!" Now was the turn of Phebe. "You say you'll marry me if I be willing?"

"That will I," cried Phebe, all aglow with hope; but Ganymede raised a warning finger. "But if you do refuse to marry me, you'll give yourself to this most faithful shepherd?" Phebe thought; she frowned, she sighed; she looked at Silvius and she smiled. "So is the bargain," she said. Then Ganymede, reminding each and all of their solemn promises, beckoned to Aliena; and, hand in hand, the mysterious brother and sister departed into the forest.

"I do remember in this shepherd boy," frowned the Duke, "some lively touches of my daughter's favour." Orlando agreed. He too had fancied he'd seen something of Rosalind in Ganymede, and had wondered if he could have been Rosalind's brother. "But my good lord, this boy is forest-born," he began to assure the Duke, when Jacques, his melancholy face crumpling into smiles, announced, "Here comes a pair of very strange beasts, which in all tongues are called fools!"

Sniffing out weddings, like dogs to a dinner, Touchstone and Audrey emerged from among the trees; he, crowned with a chaplet of ivy leaves, and she in her best attire, with her shining happy face poking out from ruff and bonnet, like a festive mutton chop.

"Salutation and greeting to you all!" cried Touchstone grandly, perceiving that he had fallen among courtiers and gentlemen; then, feeling that his choice required some explanation, presented her to the Duke: "A poor virgin, sir, an ill-favoured thing, sir, but mine own: a poor humour of mine, sir, to take that that no man else will." He gave Audrey a shove to indicate that she, in acknowledgement of the tribute paid her, should curtsey gracefully; so down she went, as if to milk her goats. "Bear your body more seeming, Audrey," urged her lord as he engaged in a battle of courtly wits with Jacques; but she could only gape in wonderment as his words, of which she understood not one, flew as fast as fat from a pan. And he, seeing her looks, was well content with his choice: admiration was much to be preferred to equality.

Suddenly, there was a noise in the forest, a strange noise that stilled the birds and hushed the waiting throng. It was a slow, mysterious music, accompanied by solemn drumbeats, like the beating of the forest's heart. A soft breeze began to blow and the air was filled with the scents of spring. The music grew louder and the trees trembled; then the sunbeams seemed to part like golden curtains, making way for a tall, smiling youth in marvellous yellow robes, and bearing a torch. It was Hymen himself, the God of Marriage, who had come to bless the day. Gently, he led by the hand two shining Princesses to complete the fourfold forest wedding, and so bring the promised marvels about!

Amazed and joyful, the Duke recognized in the two Princesses, his daughter and his niece: Oliver, his poor shepherdess Aliena in the Princess Celia, and Orlando, his true love in the one-time Ganymede. "If there be truth in sight," he breathed, "you are my Rosalind!"

"If sight and shape be true," sighed Phebe, no less amazed, but not so joyful to see her Ganymede lost for ever in the fair Rosalind, "why then, my love adieu!" She sighed again, and, turning to the ever-loving Silvius as the better bargain and most true, promised, "I will not eat my word, now thou art mine," and Silvius nearly died of joy!

Then Rosalind united all the lovers' hands, and they knelt for the god to bless their marriages, while the little pages sang:

> "High wedlock then be honoured.
> Honour, high honour and renown,
> To Hymen, god of every town!"

All promises had been kept; but the forest was not yet done with its wonders. The last was still to come. Even as the god departed, and a multitude of joyful explanations broke out, there came a gentleman, flushed with haste and stuffed with news from Duke Frederick's court. That wicked man had taken it into his mad head to set out with a mighty force to seize his brother and put him to death! But no sooner had he come within the charmed circle of the forest than he, like Oliver, had been changed and converted . . . not by means of serpent and lioness, but by an old religious man. So powerful had been the words of this venerable person, that the storms that had raged within the unhappy Duke were calmed. He had dismissed his forces, relinquished his crown to his wronged brother, and desired no more than a life of contemplation in the Forest of Arden!

So now all wrongs were righted, and banishment was at an end. The restored Duke turned to his faithful followers and promised: "Every of this happy number that have endured shrewd days and nights with us, shall share the good of our returned fortune!"

At this, there was loud rejoicing, and many a cap was flung into the air. Although in their forest days the courtiers had learned to find, as the wise Duke had once told them, "tongues in trees, books in the running brooks, sermons in stones and good in everything," there was no doubt that soft beds were to be preferred to hard turf, and a sound roof to a leaking sky. The melancholy Jacques alone was of another mind. He, in his time, had seen everything under the tired old sun;

and looked only for something new. He chose to remain in the forest, and seek out the company of the changed Duke Frederick: there being more to amuse him in a bad man made good, than in a good man made merely better.

"Stay, Jacques, stay," begged the Duke; but he would not. With a smile and a bow he departed, leaving dancing and merriment behind; and the two little pages singing their hearts out:

> "And therefore take the present time,
> With a hey, and a ho, and a hey nonino;
> For love is crowned with the prime
> In spring time, the only pretty ring time,
> When birds do sing, hey ding a ding, ding,
> Sweet lovers love the spring."

Cymbeline

Long ago, when Rome still ruled the world, there was a king of Britain whose name was Cymbeline. He was a man consumed with anger. Misfortune had struck him again and again with the mindless venom of a post striking a blind man. His two sons had been stolen away in infancy by a man he'd wronged, never to be seen again. Then his Queen had died in childbirth, leaving him with a daughter as his only heir.

He'd taken another wife, a clever, handsome, widowed lady who'd brought him a full-grown son of her own: Prince Cloten was his name; and it was the King's fondest hope that Imogen, his daughter, should marry this prince. But Imogen, scorning her father's wishes, had married young Posthumus, who, though a thousand times the better man, was not the prince's equal in birth.

The King flew into a violent rage. He banished Posthumus, shut up his daughter, and set the Queen, dragon-like, to guard her close; and so matters stood, upon a certain morning in the springtime of the year, as the brocaded Queen, her fair prisoner, and the banished Posthumus, walked together in the high-walled palace garden, between the flowers and green.

Imogen and Posthumus had eyes only for each other; while the Queen, a diligent pupil of Cornelius, the royal physician, fixed her gaze upon the earth, as if she would unravel the sleepy mysteries of the clustering herbs. She heaved a sigh over the plight of the unlucky lovers, and shook her head. "No," she murmured, casting a glance towards a tuft of hemlock that grew beside the wall, "be assured you shall not find me, daughter, after the slander of most stepmothers, evil-eyed unto you." Earnestly she advised Posthumus, for his own safety, to leave the country without delay; and promised that in his absence, she would do all within her power to soften the King's heart.

She begged them to be brief in their farewells, and, with a gentle smile, left them to make their adieus in private. "I'll fetch a turn about the garden," she said, and rustled away.

Posthumus gazed after the honey-sweet lady, much moved by her compassion; but Imogen was not deceived. She knew that beneath the Queen's flowery smiles there lurked a serpent, thick with poison, and that the Queen hated her and desired only her death. But she was prepared to endure her stepmother's enmity and her father's anger so long as she had the love of her husband, and the hope of seeing him again.

"Look here, love," said she, taking a ring from her finger, "this diamond was my mother's. Take it, heart, but keep it till you woo another wife, when Imogen is dead."

"How, how? another?" cried he, and swore by all he held holy that he would die before he took another wife. "For my sake wear this," he begged her, and gave her a golden bracelet: "it is a manacle of love, I'll place it upon this fairest prisoner!"

Tenderly they exchanged their love-tokens; but before they could embrace, there came a violent interruption! The King appeared, in a sudden blaze of fury.

"Thou basest thing!" he shouted, confronting the wretch who had dared to marry his daughter. "Away! Thou'rt poison to my blood!" Hastily, Posthumus departed, and the King turned bitterly upon the weeping Imogen. "O disloyal thing, that should'st repair my youth, thou heap'st a year's age on me!"

The lords who attended the King looked on with mingled feelings. Those who had daughters, felt for the father; the others trembled for the Princess. But Imogen, far from shrinking before the King's anger, seemed to draw strength from it. She answered him calmly and with dignity; and when he cursed her for taking a beggar for her husband instead of a prince, she became almost as angry as he. Proudly she told him that her Posthumus was as far above the Queen's son as was an eagle above the ugly scavenging kite.

She spoke the truth; none could deny it; but Prince Cloten, in spite of his shortcomings as a man, was still a prince.

"O thou vile one!" raged the King, as his daughter continued to defy him; and God knew how it all would have ended had not the Queen herself appeared, and poured her soothing oil upon the sorely troubled waters.

Her power over the King was truly wonderful. He lowered the clenched hand that had been raised to strike his disobedient child, and, contenting himself with a last angry curse, departed, followed by his lords.

The Queen and Imogen were alone. "You must give way," began the Queen, when a servant approached. It was Pisanio, Posthumus's faithful attendant.

"What news?" demanded the Queen. The news was that Prince Cloten had drawn his sword upon Posthumus, whom he regarded as his unworthy rival in love.

The Queen frowned. "No harm, I trust, is done?" None. The combatants had been parted before royal blood was shed. The Prince had gone off to change his shirt, which stank more from fright than valour.

"Why came you from your master?" asked Imogen; and Pisanio told her that Posthumus had commanded him to remain behind and faithfully serve his wife.

Imogen sighed and smiled, while the Queen stared at Pisanio, and her eyes were sharp as needles . . .

Posthumus, with Imogen's love blazing from the diamond on his finger, and her image burning in his heart, sailed away into exile, and Pisanio watched him go. ("I would have broke my eye-strings, cracked them," whispered Imogen, picturing the dwindling vessel in her mind's eye, "till he had melted from the smallness of a gnat, to air.")

He found refuge in Rome, in the house of Philario, a friend of his father's, where the fame of his banishment for marrying King Cymbeline's daughter had gone before him. Wine and good company greeted him; but Posthumus had left better behind. He could think and talk only of his Imogen, who, in grace, beauty, wisdom and virtue excelled all other women in the world.

His listeners smiled indulgently; but one, a sleek-faced Italian gentleman by the name of Iachimo, saw fit to question such extravagant claims. "If she went before others I have seen," said he, with a cool, appraising glance at the boastful young man's finger, "as that diamond of yours outlustres many I have beheld, I could not but believe she excelled many; but I have not seen the most precious diamond that is, nor you the lady."

Posthumus frowned. To doubt that his wife was the best of women seemed, to him, to put her on a level with the worst. Passionately he insisted on her absolute perfection; but Iachimo, to whom all women were no more than flowers, to be plucked and worn for a day or two, then cast aside, was unconvinced. The lady's love, he was sure, might be stolen as easily as her husband's ring. "You may wear her in title yours," he said, with a mocking smile; "but you know strange fowl light upon neighbouring ponds."

Posthumus clenched his fists. Philario tried to intervene. He could see that both gentlemen, perhaps inflamed with wine, were becoming angry. But before he could prevent it, a wager had been proposed.

"I will lay you ten thousand ducats to your ring," cried Iachimo, "that, commend me to the court where your lady is, with no more advantage than the opportunity of a second conference, and I will bring from thence that honour of hers, which you imagine so reserved!"

"Let there be convenants drawn between us!" shouted Posthumus, enraged by the smooth Italian. "My mistress exceeds in goodness the hugeness of your unworthy thinking!" He banged his fist on the table so violently that the wine jumped out of the glasses, like a shower of blood. "I dare you to this match: here's my ring!"

In vain Philario protested that the wager was monstrous; but the gentlemen had shaken hands, and the harm was done. Next day, Iachimo sailed for Britain.

"Now, master doctor, have you brought those drugs?" demanded the Queen, her eyes fixed upon the little inlaid box that old Cornelius, the royal physician, was clutching in his thin white fingers.

They were alone together in the Queen's apartment, and the air seemed heavy with the scent of secrecy. The physician hesitated for a moment, then offered the box to the Queen. She took it eagerly. "I beseech your Grace," inquired Cornelius, humbly, "wherefore you have commanded of me these most poisonous compounds?"

The Queen looked up from the box in surprise. "I do wonder, doctor, thou ask'st me such a question. Have I not been thy pupil long?" she gently reminded him. Now that she had learned all he had to teach her, she wished to advance further, by her own efforts. She wanted the poisons to administer them to such lowly creatures as cats and dogs, so that she might discover their effects, and even find a cure. All was for the sake of beneficial knowledge.

But Cornelius shook his head. He doubted the wisdom of such a course. The Queen shrugged her shoulders and dismissed her old master's objections — "How now, Pisanio?" she exclaimed, as Posthumus's servant entered the apartment; then, turning back to Cornelius, she commanded, "Doctor, for this time your service is ended, take your own way."

Cornelius bowed and withdrew. He was deeply troubled. "I do not like her," he whispered to himself. "She doth think she has strange lingering poisons. I do know her spirit, and will not trust one of her malice with a drug of such damned nature." Instead of poison, he had given her a drug that would only stupefy the senses and give the appearance of death. It would not kill.

Cornelius nodded his long thin head. The pupil had been clever; but the master had been wise.

In her apartment, the Queen was urging Pisanio to persuade his mistress to forget her Posthumus and marry Prince Cloten. Earnestly she promised him all manner of honours and advantages if he should succeed; and in her eagerness to convince him, she leaned so far forward in her chair that the physician's box slipped from her lap and fell to the floor.

Pisanio knelt and picked it up. "Take it for thy labour," she said, as he offered it to her. "It is a thing I made, which hath the King five times redeemed from death. I do not know what is more cordial. Nay, I prithee take it," she insisted, as Pisanio seemed unwilling to accept her gift.

When Pisanio had departed with the box, the Queen smiled. She did not trust him. He was too faithful to his master. But she had given him that which would rid her of him for ever, and, she hoped, of his mistress Imogen, who stood between her son and the crown.

There was a visitor to the court of King Cymbeline, a gentleman from Rome. He came with a letter from Posthumus, commending him to the Princess Imogen. His name was Iachimo. Pisanio presented him to the lady. "You're kindly welcome," said she, and greeted him with a smile.

Iachimo caught his breath. Posthumus's claims for his wife had been no less than the truth. Of all women in the world, surely she was the loveliest! "If she be furnished with a mind so rare," he breathed, "I have lost the wager. Boldness be my friend!"

But Iachimo was not the man to admit defeat. It was not the ten thousand ducats that spurred him on, nor Posthumus's diamond ring; but pride in his own ability. Imogen, though wonderful beyond compare, was still a woman, and therefore must yield to his superior mastery in love. He bade Pisanio attend to his servant; then, having rid himself of the lady's protector, he set to work.

"Continues well my lord?" asked Imogen, eager for news of Posthumus. "His health, beseech you?"

"Well, madam," he answered, but in such a way, and with such a look as to suggest that much had been unsaid.

"Is he disposed to mirth?" pursued Imogen. "I hope he is."

"Exceeding pleasant," returned Iachimo, with downcast eyes; "none a stranger there so merry and so gamesome. He is called the Briton reveller."

Imogen expressed surprise. Her Posthumus had always been inclined to sadness. Iachimo shook his head. "I never saw him sad," he said; and then, as if it broke his heart to say so, he confided such a picture of Posthumus in exile as would have ruined any husband in the eyes of his wife. He talked of Posthumus's mocking the constancy of women, of his consorting with all the drunken whores of Rome— "Be revenged!" he urged, as he saw the lady shrink in horror from the vile image of her husband that he had presented.

"Revenged?" cried Imogen, in despair. "How should I be revenged?"

Iachimo smiled triumphantly in his heart, and told her. She should take him, Iachimo, into her heart and her bed—

Imogen stared at him. Her face was white; her eyes burned with anger and contempt. "Away!" she cried. "The King my father shall be made acquainted of thy assault! What ho, Pisanio!"

Iachimo's heart grew cold with dismay. He had overreached himself. This Imogen was a woman outside his experience. Her heart was true; her love was unassailable.

"Give me your pardon!" he begged; and before her servant could come, he exerted all his powers of persuasion to undo the harm he had done, not to Posthumus, but to himself. Most earnestly he assured her he had but been testing her loyalty to her husband, who was his dearest friend. Scarce pausing for breath, he set about elevating Posthumus from the depths of the infamy into which he had just plunged him, up to the skies! "He sits 'mongst men like a descended god!" he swore. "Be not angry, most mighty Princess, that I have adventured to try your taking of a false report. Pray, your pardon!"

Imogen, though proof against flattery of herself, was not armoured against praise for her beloved; nor was she unmoved by the gentleman's abject apologies. With all her heart, she forgave him: which gave Iachimo courage to beg a favour.

"Pray what is't?" she asked. Iachimo explained. He and his friends, among whom was Posthumus, had purchased some costly gifts for the Emperor in Rome. They were stowed away in a trunk, and he feared for their safety. "May it please you," he ventured hesitantly, as if fearing a refusal, "to take them in protection?"

Imogen smiled. "Willingly," she said. "Since my lord hath interest in them, I will keep them in my bedchamber."

Iachimo was overwhelmed with gratitude. "I will make bold," he said, "to send them to you for this night; I must aboard tomorrow."

It was midnight, and the taper beside Imogen's bed burned steadily, casting a soft radiance over the sleeper and, here and there, catching the furnishings of the bedchamber with little winks of gold. All was silent, save for the sleeper's gentle breathing; all was motionless, save for the rising and falling of her breast.

In a corner of the room crouched the black Italian trunk, wrapped up in shadow and secured with a silver clasp. Presently the steady flame of the taper was troubled, as if by some invisible motion in the air. The golden cherubs on the ceiling stirred uneasily, and the silver clasp of the trunk seemed to move.

A shadow deepened under the lid, like a thin black smile. Little by little, it grew deeper and wider, until it was a monstrous yawn. The trunk had opened. Silently, Iachimo crept out.

His heart was thunderous within his breast as he moved towards the bed. He gazed down upon the sleeper, and her beauty flooded his soul with longing. "But kiss, one kiss!" he breathed; and, bending low, touched her red lips with his own.

He drew back, fearfully; but her sleep was deep; she did not stir. He peered about him, at the furnishings, the painting on the ceiling, the pictures on the wall. His sharp eyes observed everything; and, taking out a little book, he noted down every last detail of the bedchamber. This done, he turned his attention back to the sleeping Imogen. There was a golden bracelet on her arm. With infinite care, he drew it off;

and in so doing, disturbed her covering sheet. His breathing quickened with excitement. "On her left breast a mole cinque-spotted," he whispered, "like the crimson drops i' the bottom of a cowslip. This secret will force him think I have picked the lock and ta'en the treasure of her honour!"

His task completed, he crept back inside the trunk and shut the lid. Crouching in the suffocating dark, he sweated with fear. "Though this a heavenly angel," he whispered, as the image of the sleeping Imogen lingered in his mind's eye, "hell is here!" But he comforted himself with the thought that he had learned enough to persuade Posthumus that he had been admitted, not only to his wife's bedchamber, but to her bed and her love. He would win the wager, if not by fair means, then by foul.

Outside Imogen's window, an admiring group was gathered.

> "Hark, hark, the lark at heaven's gate sings,
> And Phoebus 'gins arise . . ."

The voice was light and melodious, and the accompaniment sweet and true; but no Princess Imogen appeared at her window to smile upon the serenader. Prince Cloten scowled. He had gone to some expense to engage the musicians, having been advised that music in the morning would bring the lady to heel.

> "His steeds to water at those springs
> On chaliced flowers that lies . . ."

warbled the singer; but still no Imogen.

The two lords who waited on the Prince looked at one another. "That such a crafty devil as is his mother should yield the world this ass!" marvelled one; the other shrugged his shoulders; and the singer continued with his song.

> "And winking Mary-buds begin to ope their golden eyes;
> With every thing that pretty is, my lady sweet, arise:
> Arise, arise!"

She didn't. Angrily Prince Cloten dismissed the musicians and his attendants. He had wasted his time and his money. But he was not yet at the end of his resources. He had great faith in the power of gold. He knocked on the door. A lady answered. "What's your lordship's pleasure?" she asked.

"Your lady's person," said he, and gave her a golden coin. But his gift proved needless. Before the lady could depart, the Princess herself appeared. Once more Prince Cloten had wasted his money.

"Good morrow, sir," said Imogen, striving to keep her temper with the clumsy royal lout who kept pestering her with his hateful attentions. "You lay out too much pains for purchasing but trouble."

"Still I swear I love you!" cried the Prince, flinging wide his arms as if in expectation of the lady rushing into them. She did not. Nor did she give him any encouragement of any future rushing, save away from him.

"You sin against obedience, which you owe your father," he accused, changing the line of his attack. "For the contract you pretend with that base wretch, is no contract, none!" And he went on to abuse Posthumus in the vilest terms he could think of, concluding with, "The south-fog rot him!"

"Profane fellow!" cried Imogen in a fury. "His meanest garment is dearer in my respect than all the hairs above thee!"

Prince Cloten staggered back. "His garment?" he repeated, as if unable to believe his ears. He had never been so insulted in his life.

While the Prince stood brooding on the outrage of his pride, Imogen summoned Pisanio. She had lost the golden bracelet from her arm. "Shrew me if I should lose it for a revenue of any king's in Europe!" she said, with a troubled frown. It was Posthumus's gift; it was her manacle of love.

"'Twill not be lost," Pisanio assured her; and went away to search for it, while Imogen shut her door.

The sound of the door closing awoke Prince Cloten from his gloomy reverie. He looked up, saw the shut door, and scowled heavily.

"I'll be revenged!" he swore. Then the deadly insult returned to haunt him. "His meanest garment? Well!"

In Philario's house in Rome, the talk was of war. Britain, once conquered by Rome, had refused to pay her yearly tribute, and Rome threatened to send legions to demand it by force.

Staunchly, Posthumus declared that his countrymen would never yield to Roman arms; but scarcely had he uttered the words than Iachimo, fresh from King Cymbeline's court, entered the room to tell him that Britain, or the most precious part of it, had already yielded to a Roman conquest, and in a single night! The Italian had won the wager: Posthumus's much-praised wife had fallen at the very first assault!

Posthumus would not believe it. Iachimo was lying. He demanded proof. Iachimo shrugged his elegant shoulders. "First, her bed-chamber," he began; and went on to give so close an account of all its furnishings that Posthumus's faith began to falter. Then he recovered himself. All that Iachimo had told him might easily have been got by hearsay.

"Then if you can," said Iachimo, with a smile, "be pale, I beg but leave to air this jewel."

Posthumus did indeed grow pale: Iachimo was holding out the golden bracelet that he himself had put on Imogen's arm.

"She stripped it from her arm," murmured Iachimo, keenly observing the sudden anguish in Posthumus's eyes. "She gave it me, and said she prized it once."

A flood of bitterness and anger rose up in Posthumus's heart. "There, take thy hire," he cried, casting the diamond ring down on the table, "and all the fiends of hell divide themselves between you!"

"Have patience, sir," urged Philario, "and take your ring again, 'tis not yet won. It may be probable she lost it—"

"If you seek for further satisfying," interposed Iachimo, as Posthumus hesitated, "under her breast (worthy her pressing) lies a mole, right proud of that most delicate lodging. By my life, I kissed it. You do remember this stain upon her?"

"Ay," whispered Posthumus, "and it doth confirm another stain, as big as hell can hold!"

"Will you hear more?" asked Iachimo; but Posthumus had heard enough. Quietly, Iachimo slipped the diamond ring onto his finger and, together with Philario, left Posthumus seated at the table, with his head clutched in his hands, and tears running out and over his fingers, like silver rivers of despair.

Presently, Posthumus raised his head, and displayed a face ravaged with rage and dismay. All love was changed to hatred; all tenderness to an iron-hard resolve. Like Prince Cloten before him, all he desired was to seek vengeance upon Imogen.

There were writing materials on the table before him. Quickly, and with a trembling hand, he began to write two letters: one to his servant Pisanio, the other to his faithless wife.

Lucius, a Roman general, had been dispatched to the court of Cymbeline to make a last demand for the tribute that was owing. He was met with bold defiance; and the lords who attended on the King were amazed to see how the prospect of saving money inspired even the crafty Queen and her stupid son with noble patriotism. "Why should we pay tribute?" demanded Prince Cloten, thrusting out his big chest in opposition to the Roman. "If Caesar can hide the sun from us with a blanket, or put the moon in his pocket, we will pay him tribute for light; else, sir, no more tribute!"

The lords politely applauded him; but Lucius sighed and turned to

Lucius, a Roman general

the King. He was a courteous gentleman who had no personal quarrel with Cymbeline or his people; but it was his duty to speak for the Emperor, his master. Sadly he pronounced that, in consequence of Cymbeline's defiance, he must be prepared to face the fury of Rome's mighty legions; Rome and Britain were now at war.

The Emperor's stern decree was not the only threat of bloody vengeance that had come from Rome: there had also been the letters from Posthumus.

"O master, what a strange infection is fallen into thy ear!" whispered Pisanio, staring in horror and disbelief at what his master had written. Imogen was unfaithful! He, Pisanio, was ordered to murder her, and send a cloth, dipped in her blood, as proof that she was dead! The letter Posthumus had written to Imogen contained such news as would persuade her to give Pisanio the opportunity to kill her secretly.

"O damned paper, black as the ink that's on thee!" he cried in despair; and hastily concealed it as Imogen approached.

"Madam," he said, striving to hide his feelings, "here is a letter from my lord."

Eagerly she took the letter and broke the seal.

Posthumus had written to tell her that he was in Wales, near Milford-Haven, and he begged her come to him there. "O for a horse with wings!" she cried, looking up from her letter. "Hear'st thou, Pisanio? He is at Milford-Haven!" and, her words tumbling over one another with all the excitement of a birthday child, she demanded how far it was to Milford-Haven, how might she get there, when might she start—"Prithee speak, how many score of miles may we well ride 'twixt hour and hour?"

"One score 'twixt sun and sun, Madam's enough for you," answered Pisanio, "and too much too," he added under his breath. He turned aside, for he could no longer bear to see his mistress's ardent longing to set out for the wild mountains of Wales, where her husband had planned that she should be murdered.

"Thou told'st me, when we came from horse, the place was near at hand," complained Imogen, growing more and more impatient to be at Milford-Haven and meet with Posthumus. She and Pisanio had travelled far. Already they had reached the wild and mountainous land of Wales. They had left their horses behind, for the path was steep and rocky, and fit only for goats and eager lovers . . . and murderers, thought Pisanio, as he followed his mistress with an aching heart.

His master's terrible command weighed on him like lead. It was crushing him. He could scarcely lift his eyes to look at Imogen.

"Pisanio! man!" she demanded suddenly. "What is in thy mind that makes thee stare thus?"

He bowed his head. He could no longer hide the truth from her. Silently, he gave her the murderous letter. He watched her read it. He watched her cheeks grow pale as her heart turned to ashes within her. "What shall I need to draw my sword," he wondered wretchedly, "the paper hath cut her throat already!"

Imogen looked up. Her world had perished; nothing remained to her but death. She spoke quietly to Pisanio. "Come, fellow, be thou honest, do thy master's bidding." He did not move. She reached towards him, and quickly drew his sword from its scabbard. She offered it to him. "Do his bidding," she commanded, "strike!"

He shrank back. "Come," she urged him, "here's my heart—" She began to tug at her gown, to make her breast an easier target for Pisanio's sword. She frowned. There was a paper hidden there, a paper that she had treasured. It was Posthumus's letter, breathing love. She flung it from her, as if it had been a viper at her breast. Pisanio bent to pick it up.

"Where's thy knife?" demanded Imogen. "Thou art too slow to do thy master's bidding when I desire it too."

"O gracious lady!" wept the wretched Pisanio. "Since I received command to do this business I have not slept one wink."

"Do't, and to bed then."

Violently he shook his head. Nothing would persuade him to harm his mistress. "Good lady, hear me with patience," he pleaded, and unfolded a plan he had devised.

First, she must disguise herself as a man. He had brought clothing with him for that very purpose. Then she must make her way to Milford-Haven where Lucius, the Roman general, was expected, and offer herself to him as a page. It was likely that he would take her with him to Rome—

"Nay, be brief!" interrupted Imogen, her hopes reviving. "I see into thy end, and am almost a man already!" In Rome she would be able to discover how Posthumus had been deceived!

Pisanio, thankful to see his mistress recover her spirits, breathed more easily. He told her that he would send word that she was dead; and her absence from the court would seem to confirm it.

As he talked, and tried to tell her how to conduct herself as a man, he fumbled in his bag for the clothing. Suddenly his fingers encountered something he'd forgotten. It was the little box the Queen had given him. She'd told him it contained a drug that had many times saved the King's life. "If you are sick at sea," he said anxiously, thinking of the rolling, turbulent journey to Rome, "a dram of this will drive away distemper." He gave it to her; and, bidding her change her garments without delay, bade her farewell. "May the gods direct you to the best!" he prayed; and set off for the court as swiftly as he could.

He rode through day and night, fearful that his absence would be discovered and that he would be suspected of helping in Imogen's flight. At last, he reached the palace, and was instantly greeted with the red-faced fury of Prince Cloten.

"Villain, where is thy lady?" shouted the cheated lover, brandishing his fist before the alarmed Pisanio's face. "Is she with Posthumus?"

"Alas, my lord," cried Pisanio, "how can she be with him? When was she missed? He is in Rome."

But the Prince was not to be put off. He blustered and raged and threatened Pisanio with death unless he confessed all he knew. Trembling for his life, Pisanio drew out the letter that Imogen had cast away, the letter that told of a meeting-place at Milford-Haven, and gave it to the Prince.

While Cloten frowned and mouthed the words in his efforts to read—for he was an imperfect scholar—Pisanio reflected that by the time the fool would have reached Milford-Haven, Imogen would have gone.

At length, having mastered the contents of the letter, Prince Cloten smiled grimly. "Hast any of thy late master's garments in thy possession?" he asked. Pisanio nodded. He had the very suit that Posthumus had worn when last he'd taken leave of Imogen. "Fetch that suit hither," commanded the Prince; and his smile grew broader.

He had not forgotten the deadly insult that Imogen had offered him. She had said that Posthumus's meanest garment was worth more than his entire person. Now he would be revenged. In the very clothing that she had so praised, he would go to Milford-Haven, kill Posthumus, and ravish her in the sight of her husband's dead body.

When Pisanio brought him Posthumus's clothing, he straightway put it on and set out for Milford-Haven, and his revenge.

Imogen was weary. Before Pisanio had left her, they had stood upon a mountain top, and he had shown her Milford-Haven, sparkling in the distance. Now it had vanished, and the mountains crowded round her, like quiet giants in the gathering mists. "I see a man's life is a tedious one," she sighed; for her man's clothing had done less for her than her woman's gown. "Two beggars told me I could not miss my way," she remembered bitterly; and wondered how poor folk could tell such lies.

She stumbled on, talking to herself to keep up her spirits, which were in danger of sinking into her manly boots; for every crouching bush alarmed her, and hunger was gnawing her to the very bone. Suddenly she paused. The way ahead had divided: one path led upward, the other towards a patch of blackness in the rock which, on closer inspection, proved to be the entrance to a cave.

"Ho! who's here?" she called out in a voice that, despite her best efforts at boldness, trembled with fear. There was no answer. She approached nearer, for there was a smell of food proceeding from the cave that drew her as irresistibly as a lover's arms. "Best draw my sword," she counselled herself; and, drawing from its scabbard that fearsome weapon that Pisanio had left her with, and hoping it would frighten any possible enemy as much as it frightened her, she crept into the cave. "Such a foe!" she whispered, as she thought of her fearful, shaking self. "Good heavens!"

Once within, the black opening through which she'd entered, was transformed into a patch of fading light, which revealed, dimly, the interior of the cave. It was furnished like a humble cottage. There were three beds, three stools, and a rough table on which were three dishes and a joint of cold cooked meat. With a cry of delight, and a heartfelt prayer of thanks to the gods for what they had provided, she fell upon the meat and ate it all up.

She had scarcely swallowed down the last morsel, when terror seized her again. She heard voices outside, and the tramp of approaching feet! The inhabitants of the cave were coming home! From their talk, it was plain they were returning from hunting, and that they were hungry. "There is cold meat in the cave," said one, "we'll browse on that whilst what we have killed be cooked."

Miserably, Imogen looked at the table. She had finished their meal, right down to the bone. Suddenly, a shadow overwhelmed her. A head had appeared in the cave's opening, a shaggy, bearded head, with fierce,

astonished eyes. It vanished almost as abruptly as it had appeared, and she heard its owner tell his companions what he had seen: the empty dish, and herself.

There was no help for it. She summoned up what shreds of courage there remained to her, and went outside to face the hunters whose home she had invaded, and whose dinner she had eaten. They stood before her: an old man, and two youths. At first glance, they were wild and savage enough to have killed and eaten her in place of the meal they'd lost; but at second glance, she thought she spied some hope.

"Good masters, harm me not," she begged timidly, and, holding out her hand with money in it, offered payment for what she'd eaten.

They looked at her in astonishment. They wanted no money.

"Whither bound?" asked the old man.

"To Milford-Haven."

"What's your name?"

"Fidele, sir," she said, and trusted in her disguise to be believed.

To her relief, the old man nodded and smiled; and he and his sons— for surely he was their father—invited her to shelter for the night in their mountain dwelling. "Most welcome!" exclaimed one of the brothers, and clapped her warmly on the shoulder. "Be sprightly, for you fall 'mongst friends!" he laughed, as she staggered and he caught her in his arms.

The evening meal was over and the old man sighed with contentment. His two boys had shown their guest a kindness and courtesy that a king might have hoped for from his sons. And the beautiful youth they had taken into their home had proved as full of grace as his appearance had promised. He had cooked with rare skill; and like a fond nurse, he had even cut their vegetables into the shapes of letters that had spelled out their names: Morgan for the father, and Cadwal and Polydore for his sons.

The old man sighed again. There were other names that he alone knew, long-hidden names that, had they been discovered, would have meant his death. Once, he had been known as Belarius; and he was that very man who, long ago, King Cymbeline in one of his sudden rages had unjustly banished. He had fled from the court with the woman he loved, who had been nurse to the King's two sons, and had taken refuge in the wild and mountainous land of Wales. In revenge for Cymbeline's cruel sentence, they had carried off the infant princes and had brought them up in the mountains as their own sons.

Not long after, their supposed mother had died, and was buried near to the cave. Since that time, Belarius had been both father and mother to them; and now they were approaching manhood, he looked with pride upon what he and Nature had achieved. Their true names were Prince Guiderius and Prince Arviragus; but they needed no such grandness to be royal: they were princes by nature, and no court on earth could have bred a pair so courageous, so, upright and so fine.

Next morning they awoke, eager to go out hunting and show their guest the rare wonders of the forests and mountains and fast rushing rivers amid which they dwelt. But Fidele was unwell. "Remain here in the cave," advised Belarius, much concerned, "we'll come to you after hunting." Arviragus, no less concerned, gently urged her to follow the good advice, while Guiderius proposed that the others should go out hunting while he remained behind with the sick Fidele.

"So sick I am not," protested Imogen with a smile, "yet I am not well." Briefly Belarius and the brothers conferred, and decided that Fidele might safely be left untended.

"We'll not be long away," promised Arviragus, and Belarius added, "Pray, be not sick, for you must be our housewife."

"Well or ill," returned Imogen, "I am bound to you."

"And shalt be for ever!" called back Belarius, as the hunters left the cave. Though they had known each other for so short a time, a deep affection had sprung up between them.

Alone in the cave, Imogen remembered the little box that Pisanio had given her. "If you are sick," he'd said, "a dram of this will drive away distemper." She opened the box, took out the phial it contained, and drank some of its contents.

The hunters halted. Their way ahead was suddenly barred. A huge, brawny fellow had lumbered into view and stood astride the narrow path, fiercely brandishing his sword. Though he wore the garments of

a gentleman, Nature had provided him with nothing to match. His thick head came out of his shirt collar like a mad bull that had got among the washing.

It was Prince Cloten. Dressed in Posthumus's clothes, he had followed Pisanio's directions and believed that he had come at last to the very place where he would find his despised rival, cut off his head, and ravish his wife. He glared from side to side; then he spied three villainous mountain folk—an old man and two young ones—standing in his way. Even as he saw them, two—the old man and one of the young ones—made off, leaving the third to face him.

"Thou art a robber, a law-breaker, a villain!" shouted the Prince, advancing upon the wretch, who, from the savage skins he wore and the rough-hewn cudgel he carried, was plainly an outlaw. "Yield thee, thief!"

"To who? to thee? What art thou?" demanded Guiderius contemptuously. Though he asked, he knew quite well who the stranger was. Belarius had recognized him and, fearing an ambush, had gone with Arviragus to search for Cloten's attendants. "Have not I an arm as big as thine? a heart as big?" pursued Guiderius, calmly standing his ground. "Thy words I grant are bigger; for I wear not my dagger in my mouth."

The Prince's face grew red with anger. "Hear but my name, and tremble!"

"What's thy name?"

"Cloten, thou villain!"

Guiderius shook his head. "I cannot tremble at it. Were it Toad, or Adder, Spider, 'twould move me sooner."

"I am son to the Queen!" howled the Prince; and, beside himself with fury, fell upon the insolent wretch with a furious sword, meaning to dispatch him like a dog.

Belarius's fears had proved unfounded. No other men had been discovered, the Prince had been alone. He and Arviragus returned to the path. Guiderius and the warlike Cloten were nowhere to be seen. As they began to fear for his safety, Guiderius appeared. He was a little out of breath, but unharmed. "This Cloten was a fool," he declared, "an empty purse, there was no money in't," and, clutching it by its hair, he held up Cloten's dripping head!

"What hast thou done?" cried Belarius, in terror. This deed would surely bring the King's men howling about their ears for revenge!

But Guiderius was unmoved. "With his own sword, which he did wave against my neck, I have ta'en his head from him," he explained proudly. "I'll throw it into the creek behind our rock," he said; and off he went, swinging the glaring head like a schoolboy's satchel.

"I fear 'twill be revenged," muttered Belarius; but Arviragus was more concerned for Fidele, whom they'd left lying sick in the cave. He hastened away, leaving Belarius to wait for his brother.

Presently Guiderius returned. To Belarius's relief, he was empty-handed.

"I have sent Cloten's clotpoll down the stream," he began, when there was a strange interruption. They heard music. They stared at one another. It was Belarius's harp they heard; and it must have been Arviragus playing it. The music was slow and solemn, and it struck a chill into their hearts. "What does he mean?" wondered Guiderius uneasily. "Since death of my dearest mother, it did not speak."

They walked towards the cave. As they reached it, the music ceased. Arviragus came out. In his arms was Fidele.

"The bird is dead," he wept, "that we have made so much on!"

They stared at the lifeless body in frantic disbelief. It was as if the heart of their world had been torn out, leaving a black hole of grief.

"Let us bury him," murmured Guiderius at length.

"Where shall's lay him?" asked his brother.

"By good Euriphile, our mother."

"Be't so."

Slowly and sadly the brothers bore Fidele to the burial place. As they laid him gently down, Belarius remembered Prince Cloten, whose headless body had been left for flies to feed on. "He was a queen's son, boys," he reminded them, "and though he came our enemy, remember he was paid for that. Bury him as a prince."

"Pray you fetch him hither," said Guiderius, but more out of respect for his father than for the prince he'd killed.

When Belarius had gone, Arviragus said softly, "Let us sing him to the ground, as once to our mother." Guiderius nodded and they knelt beside the dead youth and began the song that Arviragus had been playing, the song they'd sung long ago, over their mother's grave:

> "Fear no more the heat o' the sun,
> Nor the furious winter's rages,
> Thou thy worldly task hast done,
> Home art gone and ta'en thy wages.
> Golden lads and girls all must,
> As chimney-sweepers, come to dust . . ."

When they'd finished their requiem, Belarius returned, bearing Cloten on his back. "Come lay him down," said Guiderius, with a touch of impatience; and while the brothers disposed the headless Prince's limbs into some semblance of dignity, Belarius gathered all the flowers he could find, to strew them over the dead. He tried, as best he could, to hide the bloody stump of Cloten's neck with primroses, harebells, and leaves . . .

When it was done, they went away. They would return at midnight to finish their melancholy task.

★

The light was fading, and the mist-wreathed mountains seemed to creep up round the burial place, like huge quiet children come to stare down at the pair who lay so still under a tattered coverlet of flowers. Then the coverlet stirred. One of the pair had begun to move!

Imogen opened her eyes. "Yes, sir, to Milford-Haven, which is the way?" she called out, still distracted by dreams and memories, and not knowing which was which. She stared about her. Where was she? She was lying on the earth and strewn all over with flowers. She turned her head. There was someone beside her. It was a man, and he too was lying under a scattering of flowers.

She looked more closely. She cried aloud in horror. The flowers that covered her bedfellow were speckled with blood! The man was dead! Fearfully she stretched out a hand to move away the honeysuckle and primroses and harebells that hid his face. He had none. His head had been severed at the neck!

But she did not fly from this horror. A greater one had overwhelmed her. The headless man was dressed in garments she recognized. It was Posthumus, her husband!

"Damned Pisanio! 'Tis he and Cloten!" she wept. In the madness of her grief, she could conceive only that the servant had forged the letters and murdered his master for money. "The drug he gave me, which he said was precious and cordial to me, have I not found it murderous to the senses? That confirms it home! O, my lord! my lord!" she wailed, and clung to the dead man in wild despair.

It was Lucius, the Roman general, on his way to Milford-Haven

with his officers, who found her, still clinging to her grim companion, and stained with his blood.

She told him she was a page and her master had been murdered by robbers who lived in the mountains.

"Thy name?" he asked.

"Fidele, sir."

"Thy name well fits thy faith," said Lucius, much moved by such fidelity to the dead. "Wilt take thy chance with me?"

"I'll follow, sir," sighed the still-weeping page. "But first, an't please the gods, I'll hide my master from the flies."

Lucius nodded, and gave orders that a grave should be dug and the dead man honourably buried. When this was done, he and his companions continued on their way to Milford-Haven, where legions from Gaul had landed, and a company from Rome was expected, to march against the rebellious Cymbeline.

Not far from Milford-Haven, a Roman soldier wandered alone in the countryside. He had crept away unnoticed from the camp. Once out of the sight of his fellows, he hid his Roman uniform under the ragged garment of a British peasant, and, to conceal his features, he smeared his face with earth. It was Posthumus. He had been brought from Rome in a company under the command of Iachimo, to fight against his native land.

He was clutching a piece of cloth, stained with blood. Pisanio had sent it to him to signify that his command had been obeyed, and Imogen was dead. Now he cursed the madness that had made him order her death: her life had been a thousand times more precious to him than her virtue. "O Pisanio," he groaned aloud, "every good servant does not all commands; no bond but to do just ones!" Wretchedly he stumbled on in search of the British forces, to fight with them against Rome, and die for Imogen.

"The noise is round about us!" cried Guiderius, his eyes shining with excitement. The uproar of battle filled the mountains as the advancing Romans met the fierce resistance of Cymbeline's army.

"Sons," urged Belarius, "we'll higher to the mountains, there secure us!" for they stood in as much danger from the King for the killing of Prince Cloten, as from Roman arms.

But the brothers scorned to hide. "What pleasure, sir, we find in life," demanded Guiderius, "to lock it from action and adventure?" They seized their swords and, with Belarius following, rushed down their mountain like avenging angels, to fight against the invaders.

Below, the battle raged among rocks and clefts and narrow ways, breaking up, like an interrupted torrent, into a thousand rattling skirmishes. Companies were scattered, captains cut off from their men. Iachimo, the glittering Roman commander, suddenly found himself alone upon a rocky path. He turned, seeking his followers. A wild-eyed British peasant, with a face to grow cabbages on, was at his heels. A pitiful opponent, scarcely worth the killing.

They fought, and in moments Iachimo was forced to retreat before the fury and unexpected skill of the peasant. With a violent blow, his sword was sent clattering from his grasp and, weeping with shame, he awaited death at the hands of the muddy lout who'd proved the better man. But he was spared. With a look

of contempt that pierced him as surely as a blade, his enemy left him in possession of his life.

Posthumus was seeking his own death, not Iachimo's. He'd heard a shout of triumph. Cymbeline had been taken! Desperately he ran to the defence of his king; but by the time he reached his object, the fortunes of war had most miraculously changed.

Three of the strangest warriors in the world had rescued Cymbeline, and were defending him against fifty times their number! Posthumus could scarce believe what he saw. In a narrow lane, the might of Rome was being beaten back by the supernatural strength and courage of an old man and two boys! He rushed to join them, and together they fought until the lane was choked with Roman dead.

The news of their heroic stand, flying from mouth to mouth, lifted up the spirits of Cymbeline's half-defeated army. Men near dead from weariness and fear, turned and began to fight like lions for their land. The Romans, amazed by the suddenness of the onslaught, fell back, and fled in terror and dismay. Lucius and his officers were made prisoner, and his fleeing soldiers were hunted down and put to death.

A search was made for the old man and his sons, to reward them for their great valour. Soon they were discovered; but the poor soldier who'd fought by their side, no less bravely than themselves, was nowhere to be found.

Posthumus was in prison. He'd stripped off his peasant's garment and given himself up to capture, as a soldier of Rome. The death he'd longed for had evaded him, even in the madness of battle; now he sought it at the end of a hangman's rope. "For Imogen's dear life take mine," he begged the gods, "and though 'tis not so dear, yet 'tis a life; you coined it." At last, worn out with hopeless repentance, he fell asleep.

As he slept on his straw bed, in the deepest pit of misery, with his limbs chained in iron and his conscience chained with guilt, he was visited by a strange and wonderful dream that flooded his darkened spirit with joy.

So real was this dream that it seemed to have the deeper truth of a

Three of the strangest warriors in the world

vision. When he awoke, and was told that the death he desired was still to be denied him, that instead of being hanged, his shackles were to be struck off and that he was to be taken before the King, he smiled and said to the messenger, "Thou bring'st good news, I am called to be made free!" almost as if he'd expected it.

He'd dreamed that the ghosts of his long-dead father and mother and his two brave brothers, moved by his despair, had dared to accuse the gods of afflicting men with needless suffering, out of spite; and Jupiter himself, in all his glory, complete with thunderbolt and glaring eagle, and shining like ten thousand candles, had come down into the prison cell to answer their charge. Angrily the god had told them that mortal suffering was no concern of theirs; then, in gentler tones, he had pronounced the impossible words that had kindled the impossible hope: "*Be content. He shall be lord of Lady Imogen, and happier much by his affliction made.*"

An extraordinary morning! an amazing morning! a morning that sent King Cymbeline's head spinning like a schoolboy's top; and every fresh blow sent it whirling the faster! Yet everything began calmly enough in the royal tent, with the brave old man and his sons kneeling before the King to be honoured and the King sighing that the poor soldier who'd fought with them had still not been found. He'd just had time to say, "Arise, my knights o' th' battle," when into the tent, like a black whirlwind, rushed old Cornelius, and all the Queen's ladies rushing after, with streaming eyes and tragedy mouths!

The Queen was dead! The King staggered, clutched his head in his hands. "How ended she?" he cried. "With horror, madly dying," said the physician; and before he could weep for her, he was told there was no need. She had been a monster of evil! She had always hated him and his daughter and had planned to poison them both. Her son, Prince Cloten, was to have been king. It had been Imogen's flight and her son's strange disappearance that had finished her off. Her wickedness had failed; she had killed herself in despair!

The King looked to the Queen's ladies. They nodded their heads. All that Cornelius had said was true. "O my daughter," he groaned, repenting of his folly towards her; but again he was cut off. In came the Roman prisoners and the father was forced to give way to the King. He put aside his distress and solemnly condemned them to death.

They bowed their heads, but did not falter; they were brave men. "Had it gone with us," said Lucius, their general, "we should not, when the blood was cool, have threatened our prisoners with the sword," and Cymbeline felt the sting of the reproach. But his blood was not cool. It was boiling with anger when he thought of his fiendish Queen. "But let it come," said Lucius. "This one thing only I will entreat: my boy, a Briton born, let him be ransomed," and out of the shuffling little crowd, he led a mud-stained youth.

There was a faint commotion among his attendants. Pisanio was muttering something, and the old man and his sons were staring at the youth as if he was a ghost; but Cymbeline's eyes were too full of tears, and his heart too full of tempests, for him to see more than a hazy lad with a hazy face.

Readily he granted the Roman's request, and, still smarting under Lucius's reproach, offered the boy any favour he might ask. He was sure he'd beg his master's life, and so spare the King the sorrow of having to execute a worthy gentleman and a friend.

"I do not beg thee my life, good lad, and yet I know thou wilt," said Lucius gently; and Cymbeline waited, confident that he would be able to be magnanimous and grand.

But the boy didn't answer. He was dreaming. He was staring, in the strangest way, at another prisoner. Dimly Cymbeline recognized him. He'd been at the court. Iachimo was his name . . .

"I see a thing bitter to me as death," the boy was muttering; "your life, good master, must shuffle for itself."

Cymbeline could scarce believe his ears. Nor, for that matter, could Lucius. It was intolerable! The wretched boy had abandoned his kind master for the sake of that slippery, serpent-like Italian! With difficulty, Cymbeline swallowed down his anger and disappointment. "What would'st thou, boy?" he asked.

"My boon is this," said the ungrateful page, "that this gentleman may render of whom he had this ring," and he pointed to a diamond that glittered showily on the Italian's finger.

Worse and worse! The lad cared more for a trumpery jewel than for

a good man's life! But the King had given his word. Scowling heavily, he demanded of the Italian, "That diamond on your finger, say how came it yours."

Iachimo stepped forward; and, to Cymbeline's irritation, he heard the ladies of the court sigh for the dark-eyed, red-lipped Italian gallant, who wore his chains like graceful ornaments, and, with a melodious jangle of iron, sank to his knees.

At first falteringly, like an actor in an unfamiliar part, and then with increasing eloquence, Iachimo confessed how he'd deceived the noble Posthumus, maligned the virtuous Imogen, and falsely won the wager that had gained him the ring. It was a story so monstrous in its wickedness that the page's eyes burned with fury and the King would have struck Iachimo dead, had not his remorse been so splendidly displayed. He wept, he groaned, he tore at his hair in a manner most abandoned, and might have done himself an injury had he not been violently interrupted.

A figure, bursting out from among the prisoners, rushed fiercely towards him. "Methinks I see him now!" cried Iachimo in alarm; and skipped nimbly aside.

It was Posthumus! He was dressed as a Roman soldier, and looked half mad with rage. "Italian fiend!" he howled at Iachimo; but his rage seemed more against himself than against the villain who'd tricked him. "O Imogen, my queen, my wife, my life!" he cried out in anguish. "O Imogen, Imogen, Imogen!" and he struck himself again and again upon the breast.

Then the boy did something foolhardy. He ran to the side of the demented man and tried to hold back his arm. "Peace, my lord," he begged, "hear, hear—" He got no further. With a furious blow, Posthumus struck the interfering page to the ground.

There was uproar in the tent; and, a moment later, a greater uproar in Cymbeline's head. Pisanio had rushed to the fallen boy. He was shouting, "O gentlemen, help! Mine and your mistress! O, my lord Posthumus, you never killed Imogen till now! Help, help! Mine honoured lady!" He pulled off the page's cap—and out rushed Imogen's golden hair! Merciful heavens! the boy was his beloved daughter!

She was reviving! She was accusing Pisanio strangely. "Thou gavest me poison!" Frantically he denied it. The drug he'd given her he'd had from the Queen. She'd sworn it was a cordial; and old Cornelius, who knew everything, confirmed that, although the Queen had asked him for poison, he'd given her a drug that would bring about only a semblance of death. "Have you ta'en of it?" She nodded. "Most like I did, for I was dead."

The Queen again! Was there no end to her wickedness? But now it was over, and she had paid for her villainy. Fondly Cymbeline watched his daughter approach her husband. He, poor young man, still stood, as dazed with wonderment as Cymbeline himself. "Why did you throw your wedded lady from you?" she asked him softly. "Think that you are upon a lock, and now throw me again." She held out her arms. For an answer, he clasped her to his heart as if he would never let her go. "Hang there like fruit, my soul, till the tree die."

They had embraced long enough. Cymbeline wiped the tears from his eyes, and broke the news to Imogen that the Queen was dead. "I am sorry for't, my lord," said she, putting her hand upon her father's, as if to comfort him in his loss. He shook his head. "O, she was naught," he said bitterly. "But her son is gone, we know not how, nor where."

"My lord," said Pisanio, "now fear is from me, I'll speak truth," and he told how Prince Cloten, mad at the flight of Imogen, had put on her husband's garments and followed her to Milford-Haven, swearing to murder Posthumus and ravish his wife. "What became of him," he concluded, "I further know not."

"Let me end the story." It was the elder of the old man's two sons who spoke: a fine-looking youth who, though poorly dressed, bore himself like a prince. "I slew him there."

This was a blow, a terrible blow. "He was a prince," said the King. "The wrongs he did me were nothing prince-like," returned the youth, as if he made no distinction between one man and another save his quality as a man. "I cut off's head."

"That headless man I thought had been my lord!" cried Imogen; but Cymbeline's heart was too heavy to ask his daughter what she meant. The youth had killed a royal prince. It was a crime against the state. The penalty must be death. "Stay, sir King!" cried the old man. "This man is better than the man he slew—" But no pleading could alter the King's decree. "Take him hence," he commanded his guards. "The whole world shall not save him."

"Not too hot!" cried the old man warningly, as if he knew Cymbeline's sudden angers only too well. With his arms tightly about his two dear sons, he gave up his rights as their father. "Here are your sons again," he wept, "and I must lose two of the sweetest companions in the world!" and he confessed that he was that Belarius who had been unjustly punished long ago, and the two youths were the royal infants he'd stolen away!

There was silence. Cymbeline stared unbelievingly at his sons and daughter, now so marvellously restored to him. It seemed as if all his misfortunes, brought about by his blindness and folly, had, like a tightly coiled spring, suddenly unwound; and that Jupiter had given him a second chance. He held out his hands to his splendid princes, and smiled at his daughter. "O Imogen, thou hast lost by this a kingdom!"

"No, my lord," she answered; "I have got two worlds by it," and sister and brothers embraced. It seemed they were already known to one another, though how, and when, and why, remained for Cymbeline to discover. Only one thing still lingered, like a shadow on his happiness. "The forlorn soldier that so nobly fought," he sighed, "he would have well becomed this place, and graced the thankings of a king."

But Jupiter, if indeed it was the god who had made the morning, did not spoil perfection for lack of one detail. "I am, sir, the soldier that did company these three!" cried Posthumus, coming forward; and he called upon Iachimo, whom he had defeated in single combat, to confirm that he had been that very man, in the ragged garment of a peasant.

"I am down again!" cried Iachimo, once more sinking gracefully to his knees; and, with woeful looks and gallant gestures, that wrung the hearts of all the ladies present, he gave back the ring and the golden bracelet he'd stolen from the sleeping Imogen's arm. "Take that life," he begged earnestly of the man he'd wronged, confident that it would not be demanded of him.

He was not disappointed. Posthumus shook his head. "Live," he said, "and deal with others better."

Cymbeline rejoiced. His daughter's husband had proved himself a prince not by blood, but most surely by nature. He turned to Lucius and the Roman prisoners. "We'll learn our freeness of a son-in-law," he declared: "pardon's the word to all!"

So peace was made, honourably, between Britain and Rome; and there was peace in King Cymbeline's once-turbulent heart. With those he loved about him, he knelt to give thanks for the forgiveness he'd been shown: "Laud we the gods," he prayed, "and let our crooked smokes climb to their nostrils from our blest altars . . ."

King Richard the Third

George, Duke of Clarence, had been arrested! Heavily guarded, he was hurried along the dark, stony passages deep in the Palace of Westminster, on his way to the Tower. He was pale and bewildered, and stumbled as he walked. So sudden had been his arrest, that he was still clutching a glass of wine from the dining-table at which he'd been seized. Foolishly, he was trying not to spill it—as if it was as precious as his life's blood—

"Brother, good day; what means this armed guard?"

The party halted. Out of the shadows and into the leaping torchlight limped a queer, misshapen figure: a hunchback in black velvet. Instinctively, the guards shrank back. Although he was short in stature, and a pitiable object, there was an air of danger about him; and his restless right hand went continually to his dagger.

But the prisoner sighed with relief. The hunchback was his brother, Richard, Duke of Gloucester. Hastily—for the guards were plainly restive—Clarence told him that he had been arrested by order of their brother, the King.

"Upon what cause?"

"Because my name is George," came the reply.

The hunchback stared, uncomprehendingly; but as his brother explained, his lean, sinewy face grew hard with anger and indignation.

199

The King, it seemed, had grown as sick in mind as he was in body. He was swayed by dreams and prophecies. Some wizard had told him that the letter G was dangerous to him, that 'G' would steal his throne. "And for my name of George begins with G," said Clarence, as if still unable to believe it, "it follows in his thought that I am he."

The hunchback scowled, and his hand hovered menacingly above his dagger. "Why, this it is, when men are ruled by women!" he exclaimed furiously. He blamed the Queen. It was she and her kindred who were making trouble. It was she and her brother who had sent the great Lord Hastings to the Tower, from where, thank God! he had just been released.

"We are not safe, Clarence, we are not safe!"

Clarence nodded. The times were indeed dangerous. Richard, seeing his troubled look, clasped him by the hand. "Well, your imprisonment shall not be long," he promised. "I will deliver you, or else lie for you."

There never was such a brother as Richard! Though he was shrunk and twisted in his body, his heart was straight and true.

"Have patience," Richard urged; and Clarence smiled. "I must, per-force," he murmured ruefully. "Farewell."

Impulsively, Richard embraced his brother, and there were tears in his eyes. Thoughtfully, he relieved him of the inconvenience of the wineglass, and stood, a little figure with a mighty shadow, watching with a sorrowful gaze as Clarence was taken off to the Tower.

Presently, the footsteps of the grim procession died away. The hunchback remained unmoving; but the expression on his face had changed. He was smiling; and his shadow, cast upon the stony wall by the leaping torchlight, jumped and danced as if with glee. "Go," he whispered after Clarence, "tread the path that thou shalt ne'er return; simple, plain Clarence, I do love thee so that I will shortly send thy soul to Heaven—"

It had not been the Queen or her kindred who had poisoned the King's mind against Clarence; it had been the hunchbacked Duke of Gloucester himself.

His smile broadened. So . . . the King was sick. "He cannot live," he murmured, "I hope, and must not die till George be packed with post-horse up to Heaven." His hand touched his dagger. "Clarence hath not another day to live: which done, God take King Edward to his mercy, and leave the world for me to bustle in!"

He laughed; and, raising the glass of wine he'd had off Clarence to his monstrous shadow, the pair of them drank a silent toast to the ill-health of all who stood between Richard and his huge ambition: the throne itself!

Already the hunchback's hands were rich with royal blood. He'd stabbed to death the mild and foolish King Henry in the Tower, and murdered his son at Tewkesbury. The removal from this world of his brother Clarence was but another rung on the bloody ladder he'd begun to mount. Clarence was a fool, and Richard had no time for fools . . .

But now his busy thoughts turned to softer matters. He needed a wife, and one who would make him royal in his bed. "I'll marry Warwick's youngest daughter," he decided; then, recollecting that he had killed her husband and her father, which might, on the lady's side, prove some impediment to the match, he shrugged his shoulders and grinned: "The readiest way to make the wench amends is to become her husband, and her father . . ."

He gave a little hop and a skip, and concluded by sweeping a gallant bow to his shadow. The pair of them would go a-courting, smelling like a bridegroom, of roses . . .

Down a steep street from St Paul's to Blackfriars, a dead, forgotten king was being carried, on his way to burial. His following was meagre: no muffled drums or solemn trumpets, no stately, black-draped carriage; only a weeping lady and a little shuffling of mourners, and four weary gentlemen bearing his coffin, open to a leaden sky.

The way was uneven and from time to time the bearers, despite their best endeavours, stumbled and jerked the coffin, so that the silent form within seemed to toss and turn, as if, even in his sleep of death, the murdered King Henry was being plagued with bad dreams of his troublesome reign, and its bloody end.

Presently, the mourning lady, who followed first after the coffin, begged the bearers halt awhile. Gently, the coffin was lowered to the ground, and the bearers stood back respectfully. The lady knelt, and gazed sadly at the crumbling face of murdered majesty.

"Poor, key-cold figure of a holy king," she sighed, "hear the lamentations of poor Anne, wife to thy Edward, to thy slaughtered son, stabbed by the self-same hand that made these wounds . . ." Bitterly, she cursed the monster who had orphaned and widowed her. Then, rising to her feet, bade the bearers take up the coffin again—

"Stay, you that bear the corse, and set it down!"

From out of the ground, it seemed, the devil himself had sprung forth!

"Set down the corse!" It was the velvet hunchback. He crouched in the coffin's path. He drew his sword—

"What, do you tremble? Are you all afraid?" cried the Lady Anne as the bearers set the coffin down and shrank away from the murderous Duke. "Foul devil, for God's sake hence, and trouble us not!"

Those who watched were indeed trembling: not for themselves, but for the lady. Heedless of the hunchback's drawn sword, his savage temper and reputation for quick murder, she cursed him, pleaded for Heaven's vengeance on his head, called him 'hedgehog', 'toad', 'lump of foul deformity'—

But far from silencing her with a thrust of his sword, he stood, half-crouching, his head twisted up on his misshapen shoulders, and gazing almost mildly at his accuser. "Lady," said he, reproachfully, "you know no rules of charity, which renders good for bad, blessings for curses."

The softness of the reply served only to drive the Lady Anne to wilder expressions of grief and loathing, even to spitting in the hunchback's face, to which he responded with silken compliments and amorous smiles; and when she drew back the covering of the dead king's body and displayed his wounds to the monster who had made them, he laughed and, resting his foot on the coffin's edge, declared, "The better for the King of Heaven that hath him."

"He is in Heaven, where thou shalt never come," she cried.

"Let him thank me that holp to send him hither," returned the hunchback, "for he was fitter for that place than earth."

"And thou unfit for any place but hell!"

"Yes, one place else, if you will hear me name it."

"Some dungeon?"

"Your bedchamber."

The watchers held their breath. What was happening was extraordinary, unbelievable! Over the body of her murdered husband's murdered father, the murderer was courting the lady! He pleaded, he coaxed, he cajoled, he skipped and danced around her; while she, poor soul! like a caught fly, struggled in vain. "If thy revengeful heart cannot forgive," he cried, every inch the lover, "lo here I lend thee this sharp-pointed sword—" He gave her the weapon and, kneeling before her, begged her to kill him if she would not take him to her bed! She took the sword; she hesitated—

"Nay, do not pause," he urged, "for I did kill King Henry—

but 'twas thy beauty that provoked me! Nay, now dispatch: 'twas I that stabbed young Edward—but 'twas thy heavenly face that set me on!"

In an instant, she might have rid the world of a monster; but the hunchback had judged shrewdly. She shook her head and let the sword fall. Richard's eyes glittered with triumph. He lifted her unresisting hand and, taking a ring from his own finger, placed it upon hers. "Vouchsafe to wear this ring."

"To take is not to give," she whispered feebly; but it was all too plain that the dragon had conquered the lady . . .

Courteously, the twisted Duke stood aside, and suffered the dead King and his attendants to pass on. When the procession had gone, he shook his head as if amazed by his own unsuspected powers as a lover. "Was ever woman in this humour woo'd?" he marvelled. "Was ever woman in this humour won? I'll have her," he laughed; and his hand went to his dagger, "but I will not keep her long . . ."

Then, setting his feathered cap at a gallant angle, he and his leaping shadow went on their merry, murderous way back to the palace . . .

The King's sickness was deepening. The Queen and her muttering, pale-faced kindred were greatly distressed: not so much for the King as for themselves. If he should die, what would become of them? The King's two sons—the little Princes—were too young to rule; and it had been decided that, should the King die, his youngest brother, the hunchbacked Duke of Gloucester, would be Protector. And the Duke hated the Queen and her family—

"They do me wrong, and I will not endure it!"

Even as they stood, whispering and murmuring uneasily, the hunchbacked Duke burst in among them, raging like the boar that was painted on his shield! "Who is it that complains unto the King—?" he demanded, limping and hobbling round the room and glaring into every frightened face. They were all against him! They had poisoned the King's mind with tales of his harshness. All lies! "Cannot a plain man live and think no harm, but thus his simple truth must be abused—?" he shouted, blazing with indignation. "A plague upon you all!"

In vain the Queen and her kindred tried to defend themselves against the furious accusations of the hunchback, whose hand was never far from his dagger. Their voices grew shrill; they began to turn upon each other, like snapping dogs.

"Hear me, you wrangling pirates!"

All unnoticed, there had crept into the room, a living dead woman. Thin as a twist of smoke, she had drifted among the quarrelling lords, with her wild white hair hanging about her wild white face, and muttering hate. At length, she could bear it no longer. "Hear me, you wrangling pirates!" she screamed, staring about her at those who had robbed her of husband and crown. She was Queen Margaret, the half-mad widow of murdered King Henry.

One and all, she cursed them for their crimes against her; for they were of the House of York, and she, of Lancaster: the two mighty families whose bloody quarrel had caused the kingdom to groan and bleed with civil war.

"Have done thy charm, thou hateful withered hag!" cried Richard, with a menacing gesture towards her.

"And leave out thee?" she shouted. "Thou elvish-marked, abortive, rooting hog!"

Then, turning to the others, she warned them of the monster in their midst. "The day will come," she prophesied, "that thou shalt wish for me to help thee curse this poisonous bunch-backed toad!"

At last she was done with them: "Live, each of you, the subjects to his hate," she pronounced, pointing a finger, sharp as a quill, at the hunchback, "and he to yours, and all of you to God's."

But no sooner was she gone from the room than news came that caused her curses and grim prophesies to be forgotten. The King was calling for them; and by the grave looks of the messenger, he was nearing his end. At once, all their old fears were brought back; and anxiously the Queen and her kindred hastened to the King's side.

The hunchback was alone. So, one of his brothers was dying, and the other, on the edge, awaiting only the final push. He smiled, and hobbled off to his own apartment, where two good lads were ready for him, two excellent fellows, well-skilled in the trade of private murder . . .

The Duke of Clarence, a prisoner in the Tower, awoke in terror. He had had a bad dream. He had dreamed that he was walking on board a ship, beside his brother Richard; when Richard had stumbled, fallen against him and tumbled him into the all-engulfing sea. "O Lord!" he confided in trembling tones, to the Keeper of the Tower, "methought what pain it was to drown: what dreadful noise of water in my ears; what sights of ugly death within my eyes!"

Priest-like, the Keeper sat beside the bed and listened as the prisoner confessed how, in his dream of death, the shrieking ghosts of all he had wronged had come to drag him away to the torments of hell . . . "My soul is heavy," he sighed, at length, "and I fain would sleep . . ."

"God give your Grace good rest," murmured the Keeper, pityingly; and kept watch over the prisoner until his eyes closed in sleep.

He rose to go. He stopped. Two men stood in the doorway. One was bearded, the other, dirty-shaven; otherwise there was little to be seen: they wore caps pulled down over their eyes.

"What would'st thou?" he whispered, uneasily.

"I would speak with Clarence," answered the bearded one; and produced a warrant, bidding the Keeper deliver the Duke of Clarence into the bearers' hands.

Silently, the Keeper pointed to the sleeping Duke, and then withdrew. He wanted no part in the dark business that was afoot.

The hunchback's two good lads stared down at the quiet, helpless prisoner.

"Shall I stab him as he sleeps?" whispered the bearded one, drawing a knife.

The other shook his head. To kill a sleeping man was cowardly; and they would answer for it on the Day of Judgement. At the mention of Judgement, the bearded one frowned. Some stirrings of conscience troubled him—

"Remember our reward, when the deed's done!" murmured his companion.

At once, conscience perished. "He dies! I had forgot the reward!"

While they were debating the sleeper's death, Clarence awoke. He stared with sudden dread at the two figures beside him.

"In God's name, what art thou?"

"A man, as you are."

"Who sent you hither? Wherefore do you come?"

They looked at one another; and their looks were plain. They had come to murder him. In terror, he fled from his bed. He rushed about the room for escape. There was none. Frantically, he pleaded with his murderers, turning from one to the other for some spark of pity in their stony eyes. There was none. They were merely tradesmen, about their business . . .

"I will send you to my brother Gloucester, who shall reward you better for my life than Edward will for tidings of my death!" he promised desperately; for he believed that it was the King who had ordered his murder.

Then came the hammer blow. "You are deceived," said the bearded one grimly: "your brother Gloucester hates you. 'Tis he that sends us to destroy you here."

Clarence faltered. He grew icy cold as, for the first and last time he saw into the devilish villainy of his brother's heart. Horror, disbelief and despair were so plain in Clarence's face that the bearded murderer scowled and bit his lip.

"My friend," cried Clarence eagerly, falling to his knees and lifting his arms in supplication, "I spy some pity in thy looks!"

But the other fellow was more resolute.

"Look behind you, my lord!" cried out the bearded one. Too late. His companion had already thrust his knife into the prisoner's back.

He went down like a sack of meat. But not dead. Angrily, the murderer struck again and again; but the man still clung on to his life. And worse, there was no help from the murderer's friend: he just stood there, his bushy face all tangled up with pity. So, mindful of his employment, he heaved the dying Duke up onto his broad shoulders and, with grunts and curses, thrust him, head foremost, into a barrel of malmsey wine that stood in a corner of the room.

When the commotion subsided, some few dark bubbles arose, and then no more. True to his dream, Clarence was dead by drowning.

"By heavens," panted the murderer to his feeble friend, "the Duke shall know how slack you have been!"

"I would he knew that I had saved his brother," whispered the bearded one. "Take thou the fee!" and he fled.

"Go, coward as thou art!" muttered the other, contemptuously; and, with a shrug of his shoulders, went off to collect his pay for a task well done.

Richard was well-pleased. He had judged shrewdly and had butchered his brother Clarence in excellent good time. King Edward was dead. Now all that lay between himself and the throne were Edward's unnecessary brats, the two little Princes. But there was still much to be done. The Princes must be removed from the influence of their mother, the Queen; and the power of that wretched woman and her ambitious family must be destroyed.

The elder of the children, the Prince of Wales, was at Ludlow; and the Queen's brothers set off in haste to bring him back to London for his coronation. But they were too late. The hunchback had a clever friend, a proud and greedy man who saw much to gain from Richard's success: the mighty Duke of Buckingham. Said he to Richard, privately: "My lord, whoever journeys to the Prince, for God's sake let not us two stay at home."

Richard nodded. They were of one mind. "My dear cousin," he

Clarence was dead by drowning

murmured, "I as a child will go by thy direction. Toward Ludlow then, for we'll not stay behind."

When the Queen's brothers reached Ludlow, in happy expectation of being greeted by their royal nephew with shouts of childish delight, they were met instead with sudden disaster! By order of the great Dukes of Gloucester and Buckingham, they were instantly arrested for having plotted the murder of the Duke of Clarence in the Tower! Bewildered, they denied the monstrous charge. In vain. They were dragged away to Pomfret Castle, to be executed without delay. Now the young Prince had only one uncle left to look after him: the uncle with the crooked back and the crooked smile . . .

"Ay me!" cried the Queen in terror, when she learned of the fate of her brothers and her eldest child. "I see the ruin of my House: the tiger now hath seized the gentle hind!"

In fearful haste, she fled to the Abbey for holy sanctuary, taking with her her remaining child, the pretty little Duke of York.

But there was no sanctuary for one so near the throne. The Duke of Buckingham, fighting holiness with holiness, despatched the Lord Cardinal to fetch the child from his mother's arms, if needs be, by force . . .

The little Princes met in a London street, with dukes and lords and fat old bishops and God knows what else besides, smiling their welcomes, while trumpets shouted loud hurrahs. And beyond, crowded the people, their faces like heaped-up apples, some red, some yellow, some wrinkled and pecked by birds, and some half-eaten by worms . . .

"O my lord!" cried the Duke of York, to his comical, hopping, hump-backed Uncle Richard, "the Prince my brother hath outgrown me far!" and he pointed to his brother, who was soon to be King.

"He hath, my lord," agreed Uncle Richard; and his hand stroked his dagger.

"I pray you, uncle," begged the little Duke, "give me this dagger," and he held out an eager, childish hand for the glittering toy.

"My dagger, little cousin?" laughed Uncle Richard. "With all my heart!"

But the Prince of Wales, proud of his coming dignity, saw fit to spoil his brother's pleasure. "A beggar, brother?" he said with a frown.

But Uncle Richard was all good humour; and when the child asked for his sword as well, he laughed again: "What, would you have my weapon, little lord?"

"I would, that I might thank you as you call me."

"How?"

"Little!"

"My lord of York will still be cross in talk," interrupted the Prince of Wales severely; "Uncle, your Grace knows how to bear with him."

"Uncle," pleaded little York, "my brother mocks both you and me: because that I am little like an ape, he thinks that you should bear me on your shoulders!" and he pointed, mischievously, to his uncle's hump!

There was silence. The Duke of Buckingham put on a school-masterish face, and wagged a reproachful finger. But Uncle Richard took it in good part. Laughing, he bade the Princes pass along, and said he would bring their mother to meet them at the Tower.

"What," cried York, to his brother, "will you go unto the Tower, my lord?"

"My Lord Protector needs will have it so," said the Prince of Wales.

"I shall not sleep in quiet at the Tower."

"Why," asked Uncle Richard, much surprised, "what should you fear?"

"My uncle Clarence' angry ghost: my grandam told me he was murdered there."

"I fear no uncles dead," said the Prince of Wales, with an odd look at Uncle Richard.

Uncle Richard smiled. "Nor none that live, I hope," he said gently.

"And if they live, I hope I need not fear," said the Prince of Wales, and took his brother, York, tightly by the hand. "But come, my lord," he said: and, hand in hand, the two little Princes walked on towards the Tower.

The Dukes of Gloucester and Buckingham stared after them. "Think you, my lord," murmured the Duke of Buckingham, "this little prating York was not incensed by his subtle mother?"

Richard nodded. "No doubt, no doubt. O, 'tis a parlous boy, bold, quick, ingenious, forward, capable: he is all the mother's, from the top to toe."

"Well, let them rest," said the Duke of Buckingham, with a meaning smile; and turned to more pressing matters. If Richard was to become King, he needed more support. Accordingly, he told Sir William Catesby, a trusted follower of Richard, to sound out Lord Hastings, the Lord Chamberlain, and discover if he could be won over to their cause. "Shall we hear from you, Catesby, ere we sleep?" Richard asked.

"You shall, my lord," said Catesby with a smile, and away he went.

"Now, my lord," murmured the Duke of Buckingham to his royal friend, "what shall we do if we perceive Lord Hastings will not yield to our complots?"

"Chop off his head, man!" answered Richard, as if surprised his clever friend should ask so foolish a question. Then, linking his arm affectionately with Buckingham's, he promised, "When I am king, claim thou of me the earldom of Hereford, and all the moveables whereof the King my brother was possessed."

"I'll claim that promise at your Grace's hand."

"And look to have it yielded with all kindness," Richard assured him. They smiled fondly at one another: they were the best of friends.

"Good morrow, Catesby, you are early stirring," said Lord Hastings in some surprise. It was four o'clock in the morning, and he had been roused from a pleasant sleep in the loving arms of the merry Mistress Shore. While King Edward had lived she had shared the royal bed; and now she comforted the Lord Chamberlain's. "What news, what news in this our tottering state?"

"It is a reeling world indeed, my lord," said Catesby gravely, "and I believe will never stand upright till Richard wear the garland of the realm."

"How, wear the garland?" demanded Hastings, with a frown. "Dost thou mean the crown?"

"Ay, my good lord," murmured Catesby; upon which Hastings grew red in the face with anger. "I'll have this crown of mine cut from my shoulders before I'll see the crown so foul misplaced!" he cried, outraged by the idea of the rightful heir to King Edward's throne being pushed aside.

Catesby bowed his head. "God keep your lordship in that gracious mind," he said; and averted his eyes . . .

When Catesby had gone, Lord Hastings was satisfied that he had, by his firmness, put a stop to the Duke of Gloucester's ambition. None but the young Prince of Wales must be king; and the sooner he was crowned, the better. It was with this fixed resolve, that he attended, that very morning, a meeting of the High Council in the Tower . . .

"Now, noble peers," said he, taking his place at the table in the rich dining-apartment of the Tower, "the cause why we are met is to determine of the coronation." He gazed inquiringly at the assembled lords. Some toyed with their wineglasses, some studied their fingernails. None answered. "In God's name, speak," he demanded impatiently: "when is the royal day?"

There was a general murmuring, and the fat Bishop of Ely proposed that it should be tomorrow; but the Duke of Buckingham was doubtful. "Who knows the Lord Protector's mind herein?" he very properly observed.

"Your Grace, we think, should soonest know his mind," said the Bishop; but Buckingham shook his head. He turned to Lord Hastings, and smiled: "Lord Hastings, you and he are near in love."

This was very true. Though others might speak against the hunchback Duke, he, Hastings, had always found him to be a good and true friend. "I have not sounded him," he admitted, "but you, my honourable lords, may name the time, and in the Duke's behalf I'll give my voice, which—"

"—In happy time, here comes the Duke himself!" cried the Bishop, as, into the chamber, limped the Lord Protector of the Realm.

He was, thank God, in excellent spirits. All smiles, and with his hand, as was his habit, touching his little jewelled dagger, he hobbled round the room, apologizing for his lateness: he had overslept.

"Had you not come upon your cue, my lord," said Buckingham, also in high good humour, "William, Lord Hastings had pronounced your part—I mean your voice for crowning of the King."

At once, the merry hunchback, catching the reference to the stage, imitated the actor. "Than my Lord Hastings," he declaimed with a

sweeping bow, "no man might be bolder! His lordship knows me well, and loves me well." Then, glancing at the laden table, he addressed the fat Bishop. "My Lord of Ely, when I was last in Holborn," he confided with a knowing smile, "I saw good strawberries in your garden there; I do beseech you, send for some of them!"

"Marry, and will, my lord, with all my heart!" cried the Bishop, and left the table, quivering with eagerness to oblige the Duke. When he was gone, the Duke of Gloucester and the Duke of Buckingham murmured together on some private matter; then they, too, withdrew . . .

Briefly, talk was resumed about the coronation day, when the Bishop of Ely returned. He peered round the table. "Where is my lord the Duke of Gloucester?" he asked anxiously. "I have sent for these strawberries."

"His Grace looks cheerfully and smooth today," said Lord Hastings, with a happy smile. He had every reason to feel pleased. It was plain that all foolish idea of being king had been banished from the Duke of Gloucester's mind, and, like a little boy, his desire had turned to strawberries! "I think," said he to the company, "there's never a man in Christendom can lesser hide his love or hate than he, for by his face straight shall you know his heart—"

213

He stopped. The easy faces round the table had changed. They were staring at him intently, almost fearfully. He looked up. The Dukes of Gloucester and Buckingham had returned. Their looks were grim.

"I pray you all, tell me what they deserve," Richard demanded harshly, "that do conspire my death by devilish plots of damned witch-craft, and that have prevailed upon my body with their hellish charms?" He fixed his stare upon Lord Hastings.

"I say, my lord," muttered Hastings, his happiness freezing on his face, "they have deserved death."

"Then be your eyes the witness of their evil!" shouted the hunchback; and, dragging up his sleeve, displayed his arm, all shrunken, withered and brown. "See how I am bewitched! And this is Edward's wife, that monstrous witch, consorted with that harlot, strumpet Shore, that by their witchcraft thus have marked me!"

"If they have done this deed, my noble lord—" whispered Hastings, in sudden terror.

"If?" screamed Richard. "Thou protector of this damned strumpet, talks thou to me of ifs! Thou art a traitor! Off with his head! Now by Saint Paul I will not dine until I see the same!" He turned to two gentlemen who were plainly eager to please him: "Lovell and Ratcliffe, look that it be done; the rest that love me, rise and follow me."

With one accord, the company rose and followed the furious little hunchback, leaving the dazed and broken Hastings with his executioners.

"Come, come, dispatch," said one impatiently: "the Duke would be at dinner; make a short shrift: he longs to see your head."

With a groan of despair, Lord Hastings suffered himself to be led away. When he had gone, the Bishop of Ely's servant, sweating from haste, came in with a bowl of bright red strawberries for his Grace, the Duke.

The Lord Mayor of London, his shining chain of office jingling and dancing on his portly bosom, and accompanied by no less a gentleman than Sir William Catesby, hastened to the Tower. His attendance had been requested by the highest in the land: the noble Dukes of Gloucester and Buckingham.

Little pearls of anxiety trickled down the Lord Mayor's crimson cheeks, brought on by both the heat of the day and the worry of the times. Since the death of the King, there was a great uneasiness about a land being governed by a child; and citizens had been speaking out against the Queen's party and against the Duke of Gloucester. There was a general fear of tyranny, oppression and ruinous war; and now, the sudden execution of Lord Hastings, without examination or trial, was a great scandal, and cause for concern.

The two Dukes were waiting by the draw-bridge of the Tower. They both looked weary, like soldiers after a battle; but it was only to be expected, for they carried on their shoulders the heavy burdens of state. Before the Lord Mayor could speak, they told him about Lord Hastings. They were free and open; they held nothing back. Lord Hastings had been a dangerous traitor. The safety of the realm had been threatened.

"The peace of England," confided the Duke of Gloucester, clasping the Lord Mayor's hand warmly between his own, "enforced us to this execution!"

People said harsh things about the Duke of Gloucester, but the Lord Mayor, having met him, found all the talk to be quite mistaken. Though small and unfortunate in his bodily appearance, the Duke was a most excellent, true-hearted gentleman, not in the least high and mighty, and with no trace of deceit or guile about him. He took the Duke's word for it about Lord Hastings without question; and when the Duke of Buckingham, drawing him to one side, murmured that it might be no bad thing for England if a man like the Duke of Gloucester were to be king, the good Mayor nodded his fat head in whole-hearted agreement.

The Duke looked pleased; and then, to the Mayor's great pride, the noble gentleman linked arms with him and confided something not generally known. There were doubts about the little Prince's right to the throne. It was suspected (and strongly suspected!) that King Edward, the child's father, was himself a bastard and should never have worn the crown! The Mayor was shocked, amazed; and when the Duke suggested he should gather the aldermen and leading citizens and persuade them to beg the Duke of Gloucester to become England's rightful king, he readily agreed. He had never felt more important in his life.

Away he went, propelled into haste by the Duke of Buckingham, who filled his trembling ears with the Duke of Gloucester's many virtues. As quickly as he could, he gathered together the aldermen and as many leading citizens as he could lay hands on; and, in hasty procession, led them to Baynard's Castle. There, he had been informed, the good Duke of Gloucester would be found at prayer.

"Ah, ha, my lord," cried the Duke of Buckingham, as they reached Baynard's Castle, "this prince is not an Edward: he is not lolling on a lewd love-bed, but on his knees in meditation!" and sure enough, the good Duke of Gloucester was to be seen at a window with a holy clergyman on either side of him. And one of them, the Mayor was honoured to see, was his own brother, Doctor Shaa! He was overcome. Never had he seen a prince displaying such modesty, such humility, and such downright holiness!

"Long live Richard, England's worthy King!" shouted the Duke of Buckingham, and threw his cap into the air.

"Amen!" cried the Lord Mayor, and, with vigorous wavings of his arms, encouraged the aldermen and citizens to shout likewise: "Amen! Long live Richard, England's worthy King!"

Three women, all in black, stood before the Tower. One was the Queen, another was the Lady Anne, now the hunchback's wretched wife, and the third was the old Duchess of York, his unlucky mother. The day was dying and the Tower loomed darkly against the bloody sky. Somewhere within its grim bulk were the two little Princes; but by order of the Duke of Gloucester, they were not to be seen, even by their mother.

"O my accursed womb," wept the old Duchess, striking at her belly with frail, despairing fists, "the bed of death! A cockatrice hast thou hatched to the world whose unavoided eye is murderous!"

As the women stood, staring up at the ancient fortress, a gentleman approached the Lady Anne. "Come, madam," he murmured, "you must straight to Westminster, there to be crowned Richard's royal queen."

"Go, go, poor soul," said the Queen, to her unwilling successor, "I envy not thy glory."

The Lady Anne sighed. Since her wedding to the crooked Duke, her life had been a misery to her. "For never yet one hour in his bed did I enjoy the golden dew of sleep, but with his timorous dreams was still awaked," she whispered. "He hates me . . ."

"Come, madam, come," urged the gentleman. "I in all haste was sent."

Sadly, the women parted. The Queen was last to leave. She looked back to the Tower, where her children were imprisoned. "Pity, you ancient stones, those tender babes," she pleaded. "Rough cradle for such pretty little ones, rude ragged nurse, old sullen playfellow for tender princes, use my babies well."

King Richard in glory. Trailing a vast velvet robe, like heavy scarlet wings, he hopped and hobbled across the royal chamber, as if he would fly up the steps to the throne. Awkwardly, he mounted, and seated himself in the sacred place. Dukes and lords stood watching him; and he watched them. He was frowning. Though he wore the crown there was something still gnawing at his soul. He beckoned to his friend, Buckingham, who came and knelt beside him.

"Shall we wear these glories for a day," he asked softly, "or shall they last . . . ?"

"For ever let them last!" answered his friend.

But Richard shook his head. "Young Edward lives—think now what I would speak."

"Say on, my loving lord," murmured Buckingham, unwilling to commit himself.

"Why, Buckingham, I say I would be king."

"Why so you are, my thrice-renowned lord."

"But Edward lives."

"True, noble Prince."

"Cousin, thou wast not wont to be so dull. Shall I be plain? I wish the bastards dead. What say'st thou now?"

"Your Grace may do your pleasure."

"Tut, tut, thou art all ice. Say, have I thy consent that they shall die?"

Buckingham looked about him. Was it possible they had been overheard? "Give me some little breath, some pause," he muttered uncertainly, "before I positively speak in this." He rose, bowed and withdrew. His face was pale. Even he shrank from the murder of children.

Richard stared after him. "High-reaching Buckingham grows circumspect," he murmured thoughtfully. He summoned a page. Did the boy know, he inquired, almost idly, of any gentleman who might be bought for money. The page knew of just such a gentleman. His name was Tyrrel. Quietly, Richard bade the boy call him hither.

Before he was king, he had been consumed only with a desire for the crown; now it was his, he was filled with a dread of losing it. He must be secure. His wife, Anne, was in his way. He needed a better marriage . . .

Lord Stanley, a man he did not trust, approached the throne. He bowed, but not low enough. He had news. The Marquess of Dorset, the Queen's kinsman, had fled to France and joined forces with the Earl of Richmond, of the hated House of Lancaster, who was in exile there.

Richard brushed the news aside. He had other matters on his mind. He summoned Sir William Catesby. Catesby came and knelt before his master. Richard beckoned him close. "Rumour it abroad," he murmured in Catesby's ready ear, "that Anne my wife is very grievous sick; I will take order for her keeping close." Catesby stared. "Look how thou dream'st!" muttered Richard angrily. "I say again that Anne, my Queen, is sick and like to die. About it!" Catesby stumbled away.

It was in Richard's mind to marry Elizabeth, his niece and daughter of King Edward. It was a bold plan. "Murder her brothers, and then marry her—uncertain way of gain!" He shrugged his shoulders and peered about him. There was a fellow who had slipped in among the throng, a restless-looking gentleman who was plainly trying to catch his eye. Beside him, hovered the page. Richard looked at him inquiringly. The page nodded. This was the man. The page whispered to his companion; and the man came quickly forward and crouched beside the King.

"Is thy name Tyrrel?"

"James Tyrrel, and your most obedient subject."

"Art thou indeed?"

"Prove me, my gracious lord."

"Dare'st thou resolve to kill," murmured Richard, "a friend of mine?"

"Please you; but I had rather kill two enemies," answered the loyal fellow.

"Why then thou hast it; two deep enemies," whispered the King. "Tyrrel, I mean those bastards in the Tower."

The page had chosen well. Tyrrel was a fellow after Richard's own heart. No hesitations, no doubts; he nodded eagerly, and hurried away.

Back came the Duke of Buckingham, all smiles. It seemed he had thought better of his previous evasiveness. But he was too late. Richard was no longer interested. Instead, he spoke of Dorset's flight to the Earl of Richmond.

"I hear the news, my lord," said Buckingham; and then that arrogant and greedy gentleman presumed to remind the King of his promise. "I claim the gift," he said, bringing his face so close that the King could smell his sickly breath. "The earldom of Hereford, and the moveables which you have promised I shall possess."

"I do remember me," said Richard, as if Buckingham had not spoken, "Henry the Sixth did prophesy that Richmond should be King, when Richmond was a little peevish boy."

"My lord!" muttered Buckingham, growing red in the face.

"How chance the prophet," mused Richard, almost to himself, "could not, at that time, have told me—I being by—that I should kill him?"

"My lord, your promise for the earldom—"

Richard looked at him coldly. "I am not in the giving vein today. Thou troublest me. I am not in the vein."

With that, he rose, and, followed by his court, left the chamber.

"And is it thus?" whispered Buckingham, trembling with anger. "Repays he my deep service with such contempt?" Then he remembered the fate of Hastings. He grew cold. He left the chamber, and with all the haste he could command, fled from London while his head was still on his shoulders.

Good news and bad. Tyrrel had proved an honest fellow. King Edward's two brats were dead. Pillows had been pressed on their sleeping faces, and forced down till their little strugglings had finished. Then their sweet little bodies had been buried . . .

Now the bad. The foolhardy Buckingham had raised an army in Wales; and much worse, the fat Bishop of Ely had abandoned his strawberries in Holborn and gone over to the dangerous Earl of Richmond.

But good again. He was a widower. Anne, his Queen, was dead. Her life had been a misery to her; it was a kindness to have helped her out of it.

The good outweighed the bad. The way to marry his brother's daughter, Elizabeth, was now free from all impediment. He rubbed his hands together. "To her go I, a jolly thriving wooer," said he cheerfully. He scented himself with roses and put on his gorgeous velvet gown that flowed after him, like a sea of blood. Then, in royal splendour, he set out from the palace, accompanied by the warlike music of trumpets and drums.

Suddenly the music ceased. Two shouting women had stopped it. One was the Queen, the other was that tedious old crone, his mother, the Duchess of York. They had learned of the deaths of the little Princes.

"Tell me, thou villain-slave, where are my children?" shrieked the Queen.

"Thou toad, thou toad, where is thy brother, Clarence?" screamed his mother, and much else besides. Furiously the King commanded the music to strike up and drown the accusing voices. The trumpets blazed, and the howling women were reduced to frantic white faces with mouths like empty black Os, shouting nothings!

They gave up their useless clamour, and the King signalled the music to cease.

"Be patient and entreat me fair," he warned; and his mother bowed her head.

"I will be mild and gentle in my words," she promised.

"And brief, good mother, for I am in haste."

"Art thou so hasty?" she asked bitterly. "I have stayed for thee, God knows, in torment and in agony."

"And came I not at last to comfort you?" said he, and mockingly opened his royal arms as if to embrace her.

She shrank back in horror. "Thou cam'st on earth to make the earth my hell!" she cried; and all her hatred for her murderous, misshapen son burst out in a flood of bitterness. "A grievous burden was thy birth to me: tetchy and wayward was thy infancy; thy schooldays frightful, desperate, wild, and furious; thy age confirmed, subtle, sly and bloody—"

Richard scowled. He'd had enough of his mother's disagreeable screechings. He raised his hand for the trumpets to drown her out—

"Hear me a word," she demanded, "for I shall never speak to thee again!"

Richard shrugged his shoulders; and in gratitude for his forbearance, his mother cursed him, and prayed that he should fall in battle. "Bloody thou art; bloody will be thy end!" she prophesied; and, turning away, she departed, her black gown flapping like a harpy's wings.

The Queen was about to follow, when Richard detained her. "Stay, madam: I must talk a word with you." He had not forgotten the purpose of his expedition: to secure the Lady Elizabeth as his wife. This meeting with her mother might prove advantageous. True, he had just murdered her little sons, but he was confident that with a little flattery, a little show of repentance, and a few worthless promises, her frantic outpourings of grief would soon be cut down to . . . sighs.

"I have no more sons of the royal blood for thee to slaughter!" cried she.

"You have a daughter—"

"And must she die for this? O let her live!" pleaded the Queen wildly. "I'll corrupt her manners, stain her beauty, slander myself as false to Edward's bed—"

"Wrong not her birth; she is a royal princess."

"To save her life I'll say she is not so!"

"Her life is safest only in her birth," said Richard gently. "I love thy daughter, and do intend to make her Queen of England."

She stared at him. His shameless villainy was beyond belief! She began to rail and rage against him, crying out the bloody catalogue of all his misdeeds—

"Look what is done cannot be now amended," said Richard, when she paused for breath. "If I did take the kingdom from your sons, I'll give it to your daughter . . ."

It was a fair and reasonable offer, but the wretched woman would not have it: she was still distraught over the loss of her sons.

"Harp not on that string, madam," said Richard, losing patience; "that is past."

"Harp on it still shall I, till heart-strings break!" she wept. Wearily, Richard sighed; and put forward all the excellent reasons for the marriage: the Queen's family would be secure, England would be at peace—

"Yet thou didst kill my children."

"But in your daughter's womb I bury them," murmured Richard, "where, in that nest of spicery, they will breed selves of themselves to your recomforture."

The Queen shook her head. All her fire and fury was spent. "Shall I be tempted of the devil thus?" she whispered.

"Ay, if the devil tempt you to do good."

"Shall I go win my daughter to thy will?"

"And be a happy mother by the deed." He opened his arms. "Bear her my true love's kiss," said he, and, enfolding her in his embrace, kissed her cold lips tenderly, like a son.

"Relenting fool, and shallow, changing woman!" he murmured, as the beaten Queen departed, dazed and forlorn.

The marriage would undoubtedly secure him; but before it could take place, other matters began to clamour for his attention. Suddenly the land had begun to stir and heave with the maggots of rebellion. News came in of uprisings in Kent, and armed men gathering in the west. As he crouched on the throne, Richard's looks were fierce and his thoughts were bloody. It seemed as if his mother's curse was being visited upon him—

"Richmond is on the seas!"

It was that slippery gentleman, Lord Stanley, who brought the news.

"There let him sink, and be the seas on him!" said Richard contemptuously. "What doth he there?"

"He makes for England, here to claim the crown."

Richard's hand went to his dagger. He half drew it from its sheath, as if he would bury it in Stanley's throat. "Is the chair empty? Is the sword unswayed? Is the King dead? Where is thy power then to beat him back?"

Fearfully Stanley confessed that his power was in the north. He begged leave to go and gather his friends. But Richard did not trust him. "Go then, and muster men," he bade him, "but leave behind your son, George Stanley," and his hand returned to his dagger.

No sooner had Stanley scuttled away, than yet another messenger of doom approached.

"My lord, the army of great Buckingham—"

"Out on you, owls! Nothing but songs of death!" shouted Richard in a fury, and struck the messenger so that the wretch stumbled and fell. But he had been over-hasty. This time the news was good. Buckingham's army had been scattered by storm and flood, and their leader had wandered away like a beggar.

"I cry thee mercy!" laughed Richard, and flung the fellow a purse of money to heal his unjust blow. Then he turned to Sir William Catesby, whose news was even better: Buckingham had been taken!

It gladdened Richard's heart to hear it. He smiled in rare delight. Very soon, now, that ambitious gentleman's smooth, sleek, nodding head would be nodded off his shoulders.

But Catesby carried other news that was not so welcome. The Earl of Richmond, with a mighty army, had landed in Wales! At once, a fierce energy seized Richard. "While we reason here a royal battle might be won and lost!" he cried; and gave orders to march against the invader without delay. Then a little smile flickered across his face, like a fleeting ray of sunshine. He commanded that the Duke of Buckingham be brought to Salisbury, and put to death. Even in the turmoil of approaching war, Richard was not the man to forget his friends.

★

"Fight, gentlemen of England!"

The sun was setting in fiery glory as King Richard's army pitched camp. In the nearby village of Bosworth, frightened inhabitants dragged in their inquisitive children, bolted their doors, and prayed for their lives and property. War had come to them: the Earl of Richmond and his forces were close at hand.

Richard bustled to and fro. His soldier's eye was everywhere, approving strengths, spying out weaknesses . . . "My Lord of Surrey, why look you so sad?" he asked reproachfully.

The young man blushed. "My heart is ten times lighter than my looks!" he assured his king.

With a laugh, Richard turned to the young man's father. "My lord of Norfolk, we must have knocks—ha, must we not?"

"We must both give and take, my loving lord."

Richard nodded; and turned to watch as soldiers raised his tent. With a cheer, it went up, like a great gold and scarlet flower, blossoming on the green. He hobbled round it, examining the silken ropes and iron pegs, satisfying himself that all was well done. "Here will I lie tonight," he declared at length, "but where tomorrow?" He shrugged his shoulders. "Well, all's one for that! Come, noble gentlemen," he invited the lords and officers who accompanied him, "let us survey the vantage of the ground. Let's lack no discipline, make no delay," he warned: "for, lords, tomorrow is a busy day!" and he rubbed his hands together, in the manner of a sturdy workman approaching his task. War was his natural element, and he thrived in it. A man in armour has no hump. "Weak piping time of peace," as he contemptuously called it, he had always despised . . .

By nine o'clock, Richard and his nobles returned to the royal tent. The ground had been surveyed and the plan of battle decided upon. He called for ink and paper to draw up orders for his captains, and dispatched Catesby to bid Lord Stanley bring in his power before sunrise. If he failed, his son George would pay for it with his life. He turned to the Duke of Norfolk. "Hie thee to thy charge; use careful watch, choose trusty sentinels."

"I go, my lord."

"Stir with the lark tomorrow, gentle Norfolk," he called after him;

and then, ordering that his favourite horse, Surrey, be saddled for him in the morning, he retired within his tent.

A single lamp burned on his table, making of the tent's interior, a smoky, golden nest. The air was heavy, oppressive, and hard to breathe. Beside his couch, his armour had been set out. It lay there, gleaming dully, like a dead and empty King. He remembered that the visor of his helmet had been stiff; but the effort of going to make sure it had been eased was too great. A strange weariness had come over him. His limbs felt dull and heavy, as if they were already incased in armour, invisible and of immense weight.

Someone had entered the tent. It was Ratcliffe, with ink and paper. He set them on the table and was about to leave. "Give me a bowl of wine," said Richard, and frowned. "I have not that alacrity of spirit nor cheer of mind that I was wont to have." Obediently, Ratcliffe poured out the wine, and, with a faintly troubled look at his master, withdrew.

The wine did not refresh him. It failed to lighten either his spirits or his limbs. He tried to settle down to composing the morrow's orders; but his thoughts were sluggish, and his pen like lead. He rose from the table and lay on his couch. Ordinarily, sleep avoided him, but now it seemed to be dragging him down, down into blackness . . .

The tent-flap shifted as a sudden cold wind arose. The lamp flickered wildly; then the wind died and the flame burned steadily again. But its colour had changed, from yellow to a curious pale blue. The sleeper stirred. He was troubled. He had become aware that ghosts had entered the tent.

They were clustering round the lamp, like weird, tall grey moths. They were a strange company, huge-eyed and bloodless: an old king and his son, lords and dukes in their prime, a weeping flimsy lady, and even two children, hand in hand. They were not unfamiliar to the sleeper. He had murdered them all to gain the crown.

He struggled vainly to avoid them as they advanced upon him. One by one, they bent over him and, whispering their deaths in his ear, bade him, "Despair and die . . . Despair and die . . . Tomorrow in the battle think on me . . . Despair and die . . ."

★

The sunset had given promise of fair weather; but the morning sky was thick and sunless. Many an uneasy glance was cast upward; but Richard, in armour and mounted up on Surrey, his beloved horse, was in high spirits. To be among steel and soldiers revived him wonderfully. "The sun will not be seen today!" said he to Ratcliffe. "Why, what is that to me more than to Richmond? For the self-same heaven that frowns on me looks sadly upon him!"

Norfolk came riding up with news that the enemy had begun to advance. At once, Richard was all energy, all action: "Come, bustle, bustle! Call up Lord Stanley; bid him bring his power! March on! Join bravely. Let us to it pell-mell—if not to Heaven, then hand in hand to hell!"

With a wave of his mailed hand, he galloped off to the hillside, where his forces were drawn up in line of battle. Up and down the ranks he rode, stirring his soldiers into warlike fury. "Let's whip these stragglers o'er the seas again," he shouted, "these famished beggars weary of their lives! Fight, gentlemen of England! Fight, bold yeomen! Draw, archers, draw your arrows to the head! Spur your proud horses hard, and ride in blood!"

A horseman approached. Norfolk was back. "What says Lord Stanley?" demanded Richard. "Will he bring his power?"

But even as he asked, he knew the answer. Norfolk's face was pale, his looks were grim. Stanley had deserted and gone over to the enemy! "Off with his son George's head!" screamed Richard, mad with rage. But even this satisfaction was denied him. "My lord," warned Norfolk, "the enemy is past the marsh! After the battle let George Stanley die."

Richard stared at him. He grew cold. For a moment, it was no longer Norfolk there beside him. It was Buckingham, smiling and nodding his sleek, smooth, chopped-off head. "Despair and die!"

The King's forces met the rapidly advancing enemy on the lower slopes of the hill; and in an instant the morning was hideous with screams and shouts and raging steel, as a surging torrent of swords and axes set about hacking off arms and legs and heads, and scattering brains like bloody flowers in the trampled grass.

For a while, the contest seemed equal: the tide of conflict flowed to and fro, with neither side gaining an advantage. Then Lord Stanley, with all his great power, struck at the flank of the King's army, and split it into a thousand warring fragments, of dying horses and leaderless men! The battle was won, and lost—

"A horse! A horse! My kingdom for a horse!"

The hunchback was fighting for his life. His horse had been slain beneath him; but he fought on like a madman. Hopping and staggering in his heavy armour, he killed and killed and killed. He was searching for Richmond—

"Withdraw, my lord!" pleaded Catesby, desperate to save his master; but the hunchback was past all hearing, past all reason!

"Slave!" he shouted wildly, "I have set my life upon a cast, and I will stand the hazard of the die! I think there be six Richmonds in the field: five have I slain today instead of him!" and, thrusting Catesby aside, he stumbled rapidly away, like a huge iron insect, blindly seeking

more Richmonds to kill. The last Catesby saw of him was as he vanished into the dark storm of war, madly shouting, "A horse! A horse! My kingdom for a horse!"

Another Richmond! Thin, milky, awkward fellow, more like a cautious girl than a prince of war! With a savage grunt, the hunchback lifted up his dripping sword— He cried out in rage and bewilderment. Richmond was no longer there. Suddenly, the whirling air was full of whispers: "Despair and die . . . despair and die . . ."

Grim and dreadful shapes were advancing upon him: the old king and his son, bleeding from their wounds, murdered Clarence, Hastings and sleek Buckingham . . . even the two dead children and the gaunt, suffocating Anne! Wildly, he tried to strike at them, to kill them again! But he could scarcely move! The heaviness had returned: his limbs were like lead. "Despair and die!" whispered the ghosts. "Despair and die!"

With a single blow, Richmond struck him to the ground; and his blood and brains rushed out of his splintered head. His mother's prophecy had been fulfilled: "Bloody thou art; bloody will be thy end." Richard was dead.

It was evening. Cautiously, the inhabitants of the village of Bosworth came out of their cottages and began to wander over the deserted battlefield. So it was all over, and there would be a new King: Henry Tudor, Earl of Richmond, of the House of Lancaster. It was said he was to marry the Lady Elizabeth of York, and so bury for ever the bloody rivalry of their Houses in a marriage bed. At last, there would be peace. The villagers sighed with relief, and began to gather up the spent arrows and broken lances, for staking out next year's peas and beans.

The Comedy of Errors

Early one summer's morning, in sunny Ephesus, the old gentleman who stood in the market-place under guard, told the strangest, saddest story in the world. Even though he came from hated Syracuse, women wept, grown men sniffed, and children left off picking their noses as he told of the cruel events that had brought him from happy prosperity to his present despair.

It happened once, when he was a young merchant, that business took him to a distant town, far across the sea. He left behind in Syracuse, a young and loving wife. After six long months, she grew wearied of waiting; and though she was heavy with child, she packed up her possessions, said farewell to her friends, and sailed away to join her love.

She reached him only just in time. No sooner had she arrived, than she gave birth to a pair of babes, sons, as alike as reflections in a glass. *At the very same time, and in the very same inn*, another woman, a poor simple peasant, gave birth likewise to twins, both alike!

Surely it was the working of Providence! Straightway, the merchant offered the poor woman money, to take her sons and bring them up as servants to his. She, thankful to be relieved of her double burden, readily agreed; so he, together with his wife, their infant sons and infant servants, embarked on a ship bound for Syracuse. Then disaster struck!

They were scarce a league out of harbour when a terrible storm arose! In terror of their lives, the sailors took to their boat, leaving the husband and wife, with the four little babes, to perish in the sinking ship. All blasted and shiny from the flying sea, the poor passengers did what they could to save themselves. Not wanting to put all their chicks into one basket, each took a pair of babes and lashed them, together with themselves, to either end of a broken mast; and prayed to heaven to be spared.

Their prayers were answered: the ship sank, but the mast with its precious burden floated free! The storm abated and, presently, two ships were seen approaching, one from the east, and one from the west. Oh, how the parents' hearts rose! and even the babes seemed to set up a tiny cheer! But Fate was not yet done with them.

Before the vessels could draw near, the mast struck upon a rock, and split in two! Helplessly, the merchant watched as his wife and her two babes drifted away. He saw them being taken up by one of the vessels, which then turned and sped off. By the time that he and his two little ones were rescued by the other ship, the first had vanished across the wide sea, never to be seen again.

Sadly, the merchant returned to Syracuse. There he brought up the two infants. His son Antipholus, and the other, Dromio; for that was the pair he thought he'd got.

Often, of a night-time, he would talk to the boys of their brothers. Antipholus grew misty-eyed; but Dromio, who was too thick-witted to take in much more than his own name, only scratched his head and grinned.

By the time he was eighteen, Antipholus's curiosity about his lost brother knew no bounds, and be begged leave of his father to go out into the world to seek for him. Most unwillingly, that leave had been granted, and the two youths had set out upon their quest.

From that day until this, the old gentleman had never seen them more. For five long years he had been searching for them, until at last he had come to Ephesus . . .

His tale was done. A great sigh went up from the market-place, and every eye was a spoon of tears. Even the Duke was moved. But war was war, and business was business. Either the old gentleman, who was plainly as poor as a mouse, must find a thousand marks to ransom himself, or his head was to be cut off.

But the Duke was a kindly man. He granted the old gentleman until nightfall to find the money to save himself. "Try all the friends thou hast in Ephesus," he urged him, "beg thou or borrow to make up the sum, and live."

The old gentleman smiled sadly. Then, with the gaoler's hand upon his frail shoulder, and chains upon his shrunken legs, he trudged forlornly away. Where should he find a friend in Ephesus . . . ?

The market-place was busy again. Merchants bargained, women gossiped, and children went back to picking their noses and thieving from the stalls. Among the bustling throng, two young men had appeared. Their eyes were everywhere, as they took in the sights of the town. Plainly, they were strangers in Ephesus. One was of a thoughtful gentlemanly appearance: the other was not. He was as round-faced as an apple, and his only response to the wonders about him, was to scratch his head and grin.

They were the long-lost Antipholus and Dromio; and they had

missed the old gentleman by inches!

Said Antipholus to his servant, giving him a purse of money, "Go, bear it to the Centaur and stay there, Dromio, till I come to thee." He had heard strange tales of Ephesus, and he was too seasoned a traveller to risk being robbed in the street. "They say," he warned Dromio, "this town is full of cozenage, as nimble jugglers that deceive the eye, dark-working sorcerers that change the mind, soul-killing witches that deform the body . . ."

Dromio scratched his head and grinned. Frowning, Antipholus watched him as he hurried off towards the Centaur Inn. Presently he turned a corner and was lost from view. Antipholus sighed, and gazed about him at the ever-shifting crowds. As in many another town, he was searching among strange faces for one that he would know. "I to the world am like a drop of water," he whispered, "that in the ocean seeks another drop." He shook his head. Strangers . . . strangers all—

Suddenly his eyes widened and his heart beat fast! He could scarce believe it: his quest was ended! At last, in Ephesus, he had found the brother he had never seen since they'd both been babes in the sea! Deep in a doorway, staring at him with incredulous joy, was the long-lost other half of himself! As his father had told him, they were exactly alike!

He held out his arms in greeting. So did his brother. He advanced towards him. So did his brother. He rushed forward to embrace him. So did his brother. Then, in an instant, his cry of joy turned to a howl of pain! To the shrieks of laughter of little children, he staggered back, leaving the bloody imprint of his nose upon the mirror he'd collided with!

He should have remembered that he was in Ephesus. It was a con-juror's shop, and the mirror had been set up to deceive. Angrily he wiped the tears from his eyes. When he opened them again, Dromio was back before him. He was amazed. "How chance thou art returned so soon?"

Dromio stared at him. "Returned so soon? Rather approached too late," he said and then, all in one breath, came out with: "The capon burns, the pig falls from the spit. The clock hath strucken twelve upon the bell; my mistress made it one upon my cheek. She is so hot because the meat is cold. The meat is cold because you come not home. You come not home because—"

"Stop in your wind, sir!" cried Antipholus, furiously. He was in no mood for Dromio's stupid jests. "Where have you left the money that I gave you?" he demanded, for there had been no time for Dromio to have gone to the Centaur and returned.

Dromio scratched his head; then he grinned. "O, sixpence that I had o'Wednesday last to pay the saddler for my mistress' crupper. The saddler had it, sir, I kept it not."

This was too much. A crowd of children had gathered, and they were all pointing at his bloody nose and laughing at him. "What, will thou flout me thus unto my face?" he shouted at Dromio. "There, take you that, sir knave!" and, with both fists, Antipholus set about the villain's head.

"For God's sake, hold your hands!" shrieked Dromio, his ears singing the anthems of a service he knew only too well. "I'll take my heels!"

He fled. Breathing heavily, Antipholus watched him go; and the little children, fearful for the safety of their own ears, vanished away. Antipholus thought of his money. Fear seized his heart. Uneasily he stared about him. "Dark-working sorcerers that change the mind!" he whispered. His servant had been bewitched and had stolen his purse! "I greatly fear my money is not safe!"

Away he rushed like a madman, to the Centaur Inn. Violently out of breath, he inquired for his purse. It was with the landlord, safe and sound! Vastly relieved, he returned to the market-place, where he found Dromio looking for him as if nothing had happened. "You received no gold? Your mistress sent to have me home to dinner?" Antipholus accused him.

Dromio scratched his head. "When spake I such a word?"

The villain's impudence knew no bounds! Antipholus lost his temper. Once more he began pummelling Dromio's head.

"Hold, sir, for God's sake!" howled Dromio. To his astonishment, his master held. The blows ceased; Antipholus's furious face had turned gentlemanly.

Gratefully, Dromio lifted up his head, and saw the cause of his salvation. Like gorgeous vessels, a pair of silken ladies had come sailing down the street, flying the flags of friendship. Antipholus frowned in puzzlement.

"Ay, ay, Antipholus," greeted one, the senior in dignity of the pair, approaching with a brisk rustle, "look strange and frown," and before he could utter a word, she began heaping on his startled head all the reproaches of an injured wife! "Some other mistress hath thy sweet aspects. I am not Adriana, nor thy wife. The time was once when thou unurged wouldst vow that never words were music to thine ear, that never objects pleasing in thine eye, that never touch well welcome to thy hand, that never meat sweet-savoured in thy taste, unless I spake, or looked, or touched, or carved to thee. How comes it now, my husband, O how comes it that thou art then estranged from thyself?"

"Plead you to me, fair dame?" inquired Antipholus, his head beginning to spin. "I know you not."

"Fie, brother, when were you wont to use my sister thus?" Now the other one sailed into the attack. "She sent for you by Dromio home to dinner!"

"By Dromio?" Suddenly the waves of madness that had begun to engulf him, fell back. Dromio had indeed come to him with a tale of a wife and dinner. It was a plot; and Dromio was in it! How else did the women know their names?

"I, sir? I never saw her till this time!" cried Dromio, seeing his master's hands turn to fists. "I never spake with her in all my life!"

But before Antipholus could answer Dromio in the only language the villain knew, his raised arm was drawn down, and softly linked with Adriana's. "Come," murmured she, with all the tenderness of sorrowful wifehood, "I will fasten on this sleeve of thine. Thou art an elm, my husband, I a vine . . ."

She drew him towards a prosperous-looking house, above which hung the sign of the Phoenix. Plainly, it was hers. She was smiling; so was her sister, and so, it seemed, was the bird on the sign.

As they approached the door, he looked again at Adriana. She was a handsome woman, though lacking a little of her sister's bloom. "What, was I married to her in my dream?" wondered Antipholus. "Or sleep I now . . . ?" Once more he remembered that he was in

Ephesus, that town of soul-killing witches. He shivered, and heard Dromio, moaning in terror behind his back: "This is the fairy land . . . we talk with goblins, owls and sprites . . ."

"Dromio, go bid the servants spread for dinner!" commanded the sister.

"Dromio, keep the gate!" commanded the lady herself. "And let none enter lest I break your pate!" and with a loving smile, she drew the bewildered Antipholus into the house.

"Am I in earth, in heaven, or in hell?" he wondered. He shrugged his shoulders and left off resisting. The ladies were fair; it was a strange adventure, to be sure, but the very stuff of a young man's dream.

No sooner had the door closed upon the four, than four more appeared in the street: a merchant, tall and stately; a goldsmith, merry and stout; and *Antipholus and Dromio*! Down to the last whisker, they were the pair who had just entered the house!

But they were not. Wonderful to relate, they were the very babes who, lashed to the other half of the broken mast, had been borne away by the wild sea, never to be seen again!

Their history was a strange one. Before the vessel that had saved them could make port, it was boarded by cruel fishermen of Corinth who seized the babes, supposedly hoping for a ransom. The weeping mother, robbed of her dear one and his companion, had only time to tell their names: Antipholus and Dromio—for, like her husband, that was the pair she thought she'd got—and which was the little master and which his little man. Then the mother and babes were parted for ever.

The wailing little ones were carried off to Corinth, and it was from there that a kindly nobleman, taking pity on them, had brought them to Ephesus, where they had lived and prospered ever since. Antipholus was now the proud possessor of a handsome house and a handsome wife; and Dromio was his man.

"Good Signior Angelo," said this new Antipholus to the goldsmith, "you must excuse us all. My wife is shrewish when I keep not hours." He was late home for dinner and he asked the goldsmith to support him in saying that he had lingered in his shop to watch the making of a necklace he meant to give his wife.

The goldsmith readily agreed, but the merchant, who did not care for deceit, gravely shook his head. "You're sad, Signior Balthasar," said Antipholus, clapping him on the shoulder; and promised him a splendid dinner in his house.

He went to open the door. It was locked. A little puzzled, he turned to his Dromio: "Go bid them let us in."

His Dromio approached the door, bent down and roared through the key-hole to the servants within: "Maud, Bridget, Marian, Cicely, Gillian, Ginn!"

"Mome, malthorse, capon, coxcomb, idiot, patch!" a voice roared back. "Either get thee from the door or sit down at the hatch!"

He jumped back, amazed. His master, feeling the curious eyes of his companions upon him, strode forward and, banging on the door, demanded to know who it was who dared keep him out of his own house.

"The porter for this time, sir," came the reply, "and my name is Dromio!"

"O villain!" cried Dromio, outraged, "thou hast stolen both mine office and my name!" and he, too, began thumping and kicking at the door like a madman, to get at the invisible thief.

"Let him knock till it ache!" cried an angry female voice within; upon which Antipholus, beside himself with anger, shouted: "You'll cry for this, minion, if I beat the door down!" and attacked the door with his fists till the house began to shake.

At length, from the shuttered window above, came the voice of Adriana, shrill with annoyance: "Who is that at the door that keeps all this noise?"

Antipholus sighed with relief. "Are you there, wife?" he called. "You might have come before!"

He waited; but instead of the door being opened, he received a further blow.

"Your wife, sir knave?" came his wife's voice, coldly. "Go get you from the door!"

Antipholus grew red in the face. Even a saint would have been roused to anger at being so shamed before his companions; and Antipholus

was a man. Furiously he bade Dromio go fetch him an iron crowbar to break in the door; but the merchant, not wishing to become embroiled in a vulgar domestic brawl, counselled otherwise. Gravely he pointed out that violence in the public street would bring dishonour on the husband no less than on his wife. "Depart in patience," he advised Antipholus, "and about evening, come yourself alone to know the reason of this strange restraint."

Antipholus breathed deeply; then, seeing the wisdom of the merchant's words, he yielded to the gentleman's persuasion. But he had promised his companions a dinner, and a dinner they should have. "I know a wench of excellent discourse," he said, casting a bitter look towards the shuttered window of his mutinous wife, "pretty and witty, wild, and yet, too, gentle. There will we dine." He turned to the goldsmith. "Get you home and fetch the chain," he bade him. "Bring it, I pray you, to the Porpentine, for there's the house. That chain will I bestow—be it for nothing but to spite my wife—upon mine hostess there."

The goldsmith shrugged his shoulders; the merchant looked disapproving; but Antipholus was resolute, even though, as he admitted to himself, "This jest shall cost me some expense."

They had gone. A moment later, as if by design, the door of Antipholus's house opened. Out came the other Antipholus, together with the sister of she with whom he'd dined. Her name was Luciana, and, to Antipholus, she did indeed seem a being made all of light. "And may it be," she was gently accusing, "that you have quite forgot a husband's office? If you did wed my sister for her wealth, then for her wealth's sake, use her with more kindness."

Her reproaches were justified: while he had been consuming Adriana's dinner with his jaws, he had been consuming Luciana's beauty with his eyes. And Adriana had wept.

"Or if you like elsewhere," Luciana advised him, with a sad, wise smile, "do it by stealth. Let not my sister read it in your eye. Be secret-false; what need she be acquainted? Alas, poor women," she sighed, "make us but believe, being compact of credit, that you love us; though others have the arm, show us the sleeve."

"Sweet mistress," protested Antipholus, desperate to be believed, 'your weeping sister is no wife of mine, nor to her bed no homage do I owe! Far more, far more to you do I decline!" and, suiting his action to his words, he knelt before the lovely Luciana, who had gone a fair way to enslaving his heart. "O train me not, sweet mermaid, with thy note to drown me in thy sister's flood of tears!" he pleaded. "Sing, siren, for thyself, and I will dote. Spread o'er the silver waves thy golden hairs and as a bed I'll take thee, and there lie—"

"What, are you mad?" cried Luciana, skipping back with a little scream.

"Sweet love—"

"Why call you me 'love'?" wailed Luciana. "Call my sister so—"

"It is thyself, mine own self's better part, mine eye's clear eye, my dear heart's dearer heart—"

"—All this my sister is, or else should be!" begged Luciana; but Antipholus was not to be silenced. "Thee will I love," he cried. "Give me thy hand!"

. . . attacked the door with his fists

"O soft, sir, hold you still!" she pleaded, avoiding his eager grasp. "I'll fetch my sister to get her good will!" With that, she fled, fearing as much for her reason as for her virtue. Antipholus was mad—

The door had no sooner shut upon her than out rushed Dromio. His eyes were wild, his cheeks were pale, and he trembled in every limb. He had a fearful tale to tell.

His situation had turned out to be the same as his master's. A strange woman had claimed him as her husband! A fearsome woman, and monstrous fat! "She's the kitchen wench," moaned Dromio, "and all grease, and I know not what use to put her to but to make a lamp of her and run from her by her own light! If she lives till doomsday she'll burn a week longer than the whole world!" But the worst thing of all was that, not only did she know Dromio's name, she knew everything about him, even to his very birthmarks! It was witchcraft!

Antipholus gazed at the house. It was indeed a house of witches. He himself had been ensnared, to be lured, maybe, to his destruction. He shivered. The wisest course was to be gone. He bade Dromio go at once to the harbour and secure passage on any vessel leaving Ephesus that night, and then to meet him in the market-place.

Joyfully, Dromio hastened away; but Antipholus lingered. Time and again he looked back at the house of his strange adventure. He smiled, he frowned, he shook his head. He had made up his mind. "I'll stop mine ears against the mermaid's song," he decided firmly; but it was more in hope than conviction.

"Master Antipholus!"

A gentleman, short, stout and merry, was hastening after him. He stopped.

"Ay, that's my name."

"I know it well, sir," confessed the gentleman. Then, smiling a goldsmith's smile, which displayed a gorgeous tooth or two winking among the white, he drew a glittering chain from his purse and offered it to Antipholus. He would have brought it to the Porpentine, he said, only it had not been finished in time.

Once more, Antipholus's head began to spin. "What is your will that I shall do with this?"

"Go home with it, and please your wife withal," the goldsmith

241

advised, "and soon at supper-time I'll visit you, and then receive my money for the chain."

"I pray you, sir, receive the money now," protested Antipholus, "for fear you ne'er see chain nor money more—"

"You are a merry man, sir!" laughed the goldsmith. "Fare you well!" and deftly hanging the chain about Antipholus's neck, trotted away, smiling his Midas smile.

Antipholus stared after the goldsmith, then down at the chain. Plainly, it was valuable. Like all fairy tales, his adventure had led him to gold. Only a fool would refuse it. At a rapid pace, he set off for the market-place, where Dromio would be waiting for him with news of a ship . . .

In another part of the town, the door of the Porpentine Inn opened, and out came Antipholus and Dromio. The other ones. Antipholus had not recovered his temper: the dinner with the fair hostess had not gone well. He'd thought better of giving the costly gold chain to the wench for nothing, merely to spite his wife. So to spare himself some of the expense, he'd offered to exchange it for a ring she'd been wearing, that had taken his eye. Readily, she'd agreed; but the goldsmith and the promised chain had failed to arrive. Consequently, his anger against the cause of all his present troubles burned fiercely in his breast.

"Go thou and buy a rope's end," he commanded Dromio; "that will I bestow among my wife and her confederates for locking me out of my doors by day!" He would have used his fists, but they were still bruised from banging on the door.

Away rushed Dromio, and Antipholus set off for the market-place to call at the goldsmith's shop. But he was spared the journey. The goldsmith was in the street, and coming towards him. He was accompanied by a merchant and an officer of the law. Antipholus ignored them and, addressing himself to the goldsmith, bitterly reproached him for his failure to bring the chain.

The goldsmith looked briefly surprised; then, smiling his irritating smile, he presented Antipholus with the bill for the chain. He needed the money, he said. He owed it to the merchant, who had brought the officer to make sure it was paid.

"I am not furnished with the present money," said Antipholus, and told the goldsmith to take the chain to his house, where his wife would pay for it.

The goldsmith shrugged his shoulders. "Well, sir, I will. Have you the chain about you?" He held out his hand.

Antipholus stared at it; blankly. He waved it away, as a man might dismiss a troublesome fly.

The hand returned. "Nay, come, I pray you, sir, give me the chain."

Antipholus, already sorely beset by the misfortunes that had befallen him that day, was in no mood to bandy words with the goldsmith, who was plainly trying to excuse himself for not having come to the Porpentine. As patiently as he could, he explained that he did not have the chain. He had never had the chain. It was the goldsmith who had the chain; and once more he thrust the hand aside.

The goldsmith's habitual good humour began to desert him. The merchant by his side was growing impatient; the officer was shuffling his feet. A crowd had begun to gather; reputations were at stake. As Antipholus was plainly not going to give up the chain, the goldsmith loudly demanded his money.

"I owe you none till I receive the chain!" shouted Antipholus, losing his temper entirely.

"You know I gave it you half an hour since!" shouted the goldsmith, losing his.

Furiously, Antipholus denied it, and clenched his fists. The goldsmith had had enough. Never in his life before had he met with so bare-faced an attempt to cheat him! "Arrest him!" he demanded of the officer, and pointed a trembling finger at Antipholus. "I would not spare my brother in this case if he should scorn me so apparently!"

Even as the officer clapped his hand upon Antipholus's shoulder, his servant, Dromio, appeared. Eagerly, he told his master that he had secured passage on a vessel bound for Epidamnum, and sailing with the tide. Doubtless, thought the goldsmith grimly, with the chain. "Sir, sir," he said to the speechless Antipholus, "I shall have law in Ephesus to your notorious shame!"

Antipholus glared at Dromio. "What ship of Epidamnum?" he demanded.

"A ship you sent me to," returned the villain, with his stupid grin.

"Thou drunken slave!" roared Antipholus. "I sent thee for a rope!"

With difficulty, he mastered himself, and took stock of his position. Somehow or other, the world had gone mad and he, Antipholus of Ephesus, beloved husband and respected citizen, had been arrested for debt! He needed money, urgently. He took a key from his pocket. "To Adriana, villain, hie thee straight," he commanded Dromio. "Give her this key, and tell her in the desk that's covered o'er with Turkish tapestry there is a purse of ducats. Let her send it." Then, as Dromio showed signs of bewilderment, he shouted, "Hie thee, slave! Be gone!" and raised his fists.

Away rushed Dromio like the wind. Though he dreaded returning to the house of witches, and, in particular, to the fat witch in the kitchen, his master stood in need of help, and he was his master's man.

When he reached the house, Adriana and Luciana were grieving over the strangeness that had come over Antipholus. Like a true sister, Luciana had told Adriana of Antipholus's mad love for her; and Adriana, while abusing her faithless husband, had grieved afresh. It was in the midst of these tearful complainings that Dromio arrived.

"Here, go!" he panted, breathless from running, and holding out the key. "The desk, the purse, sweat now, make haste!"

At once, fear clutched at Adriana's heart. "Where is thy master, Dromio? Is he well?"

For answer—and with his words tumbling over one another in his frantic hurry to get them out—Dromio told how his master had been arrested for debt and needed the money to deliver himself.

As soon as she understood, Adriana ran to fetch the purse and thrust it into Dromio's hands. "Go, Dromio, there's the money!" she cried. "Bear it straight and bring thy master home immediately!"

All anger against her husband was gone. Instead, she felt horribly frightened. Antipholus's strange behaviour, and now his strange arrest made her dread that his brain had turned and his reason was undermined.

★

Back rushed Dromio, to discover, to his relief and joy, that his master was walking in the market-place, free of all restraint. It was the other Antipholus.

"Master, here's the gold you sent me for!" he cried; and gave him the purse.

Wonderingly, Antipholus received the purse. He opened it. There was gold inside. He was surprised; but then he reflected that, if a perfect stranger had given him a gold chain, why should his servant not bring him ducats as well? He smiled. Surely he was a golden youth, blessed by all!

"Is there any ship puts forth tonight?" he asked Dromio. "May we be gone?"

Dromio scratched his head. His master's memory was short. He reminded him that, within the hour, he had told him of a vessel bound for Epidamnum—

"The fellow is distract," sighed Antipholus, shaking his head, "and so am I, and here we wander in illusions. Some blessed power deliver us from hence!"

No sooner had he called upon a blessed power than the door of an inn, bearing the sign of the Porpentine, flew open, and out stepped a damsel all in red! Her gown was red, her hair was red, and red as strawberries were her smiling lips!

"Well met, well met, Master Antipholus," she greeted him. "Is that the chain you promised me today?" and she pointed at the chain he was wearing round his neck.

Like a bad fairy, the scarlet damsel had appeared to snatch away his fairy-tale gold! He had lingered in Ephesus too long. Already she was advancing upon him, swaying, holding out her hand—

"Satan, avoid!" cried Antipholus in terror. "I charge thee, tempt me not!" and Dromio quaked and moaned behind his back.

"Your man and you are marvellous merry, sir," said the damsel, with a smile like strawberries and cream. "Will you go with me? We'll mend our dinner here." She pointed back to the inn.

Violently Antipholus shook his head. "What tell'st thou me of supping? Thou art as you are all, a sorceress! I conjure thee to leave me and be gone!"

The damsel frowned. "Give me the ring of mine you had at dinner," she demanded, "and I'll be gone, sir."

"Avaunt, thou witch!" cried Antipholus; and master and man fled for their lives.

The hostess of the Porpentine—for she it was—stared after the vanished pair in some alarm. The gentleman must have lost his wits! Why else should he try to cheat her out of her ring? It was worth forty ducats—too much for her to lose! Although she was never a one to run to wives, she could see no other way. She would have to go to Adriana and tell her that her husband was mad.

So away she went, in a burst of scarlet worry, even as, in the very next street, Adriana's husband, still in the grip of the officer, was on his way to gaol.

Where was his Dromio? Adriana's husband, followed by a crowd of jeering children, joyful at the fall of the mighty and delighting in the shame of the respectable, glared about him in mounting desperation. Where was his servant with the money that would save him? The money that was in his desk that was covered over with Turkish tapestry—he could see it in his mind's eye. At last, he was rewarded. His troubles were over: Dromio was hurrying towards him, all smiles!

"How now, sir," he demanded eagerly, "have you that I sent you for?" and he held out his hand for his purse.

"Here's that, I warrant you, will pay them all!" said Dromio proudly, and gave his master a short length of rope.

Antipholus looked at it. He frowned. "But where's the money?"

"Why, sir," returned Dromio, surprised, "I gave the money for the rope."

"Five hundred ducats, villain, for a rope?" shrieked Antipholus; and, beside himself with rage, hurled himself upon Dromio, with rope, fist and boot!

"Good sir, be patient!" cried the officer, attempting to restrain him; but it was hopeless. "Thou whoreson, senseless villain!" howled Antipholus, and continued to lay about him like a madman!

It was at this unlucky moment that the hostess returned. She had fetched Adriana and her sister to witness Antipholus's distraction for

themselves.

"How say you now?" said the hostess triumphantly. "Is not your husband mad?"

There could be no doubt about it; and Adriana thanked heaven that she'd had the forethought to bring Doctor Pinch with her; for he was a physician skilled in lunacy and troubles of the mind.

"Good Doctor Pinch," she begged tearfully, "establish him in his true sense again!"

The good doctor, a hungry-looking gentleman, smiled in his scanty beard. "Give me your hand," he said, approaching his patient with practised ease, "and let me feel your pulse."

"There is my hand, and let it feel your ear!" responded Antipholus, and fetched the doctor a mighty thump on the side of his head.

With a cry, the good doctor fell back, straight into Adriana's startled arms.

'Dissembling harlot!" roared Antipholus, seeing all in a flash: the locked doors, the deceiving wife, and now his rival in her embrace! "Thou art false in all," and he rushed upon her, shouting that he'd

247

pluck out her traitorous eyes!

"O bind him, bind him!" shrieked Adriana, skipping behind Doctor Pinch. "Let him not come near me!"

At once, half a dozen stout citizens came forward, and Antipholus was swiftly bound hand and foot. "Go bind this man," cried Doctor Pinch anxiously, "for he is frantic too!" and Dromio, who had valiantly come to his master's aid, now suffered his master's fate.

"Good Master Doctor," wept Adriana, deeply distressed, "see him safely conveyed home to my house. O most unhappy day! Go bear him hence," she pleaded, and willing hands lifted the struggling, shouting pair aloft, and bore them away; and the crowd of jeering children followed after, dancing and screaming with glee.

"Say now, whose suit is he arrested at?" asked Adriana, when the street was quiet again.

"One Angelo, a goldsmith," returned the officer. "Do you know him?"

"I know the man," said she; but before she could utter another word, she was struck dumb with terror!

Round a corner, with fearful, bloody looks and rapiers drawn, had appeared Antipholus and Dromio! The other ones.

"God for thy mercy!" screamed Luciana. "They are loose again!" and with one accord, she and her sister, the hostess, the officer and good Doctor Pinch, shrieked and fled!

Antipholus and Dromio gazed after them. "I see these witches are afraid of swords," said Antipholus with satisfaction; and Dromio agreed. They put up their weapons and set off for the Centaur Inn, to collect their possessions and board the ship that was to carry them away.

"Signior Antipholus!" It was the goldsmith who had accosted him, the generous gentleman who had given him the chain. But gone were his gorgeous smiles, and there was a grim-faced merchant by his side, with money in his eyes. "I wonder much that you would put me to this shame and trouble," said the goldsmith, and pointed an accusing finger at the chain. "This chain you had of me. Can you deny it?"

"I never did deny it!" said Antipholus indignantly.

"Yes, that you did, sir!"

"Who heard me deny it?"

"These ears of mine!" It was the merchant who spoke, his money-bag eyes pursed up in anger. "Fie on thee, wretch! 'Tis pity that thou liv'st to walk where any honest men resort!"

Never had Antipholus been so insulted in all his life! He challenged the merchant. The merchant called him 'Villain!' He drew his sword. The merchant drew his. Their blades crossed; but before they could murder each other, back came the witches at the head of a furious crowd!

"Run, master, run!" shouted Dromio. "For God's sake, take a house!"

Hither and thither they rushed, like a pair of hunted deer! Doors here, doors there, all shut against them—save one! "This is some priory! In, or we are spoiled!" and into the holy place they fled, desperate for sanctuary!

The crowd halted. There was silence. It was as if all Ephesus, suddenly empty of Antipholuses and Dromios, had paused to draw breath and wipe its distracted brow. All eyes were upon the dark doorway; eager hands gripped ropes, ready to bind the madmen within—

The crowd fell back. A figure had appeared, a stately dame in white. It was the Lady Abbess. A murmuring arose—

"Be quiet, people," commanded the stately dame. "Wherefore throng you hither?"

"To fetch my poor distracted husband hence," cried Adriana, stepping forward with her sister close behind. "Let us come in, that we may bind him fast and bear him home for his recovery."

The Abbess frowned. "How long hath this possession held the man?"

"This week he hath been heavy, sour, sad . . ."

"Hath he not lost much wealth by wrack of sea?" inquired the Abbess. "Buried some dear friend? Hath not else his eye strayed his affection in unlawful love—? Which of these sorrows is he subject to?"

Sadly, Adriana confessed that she feared it was the last, that some other love had caught her husband's roving eye; and she cast a bitter glance upon the hostess of the Porpentine.

"You should for that have reprehended him," said the Abbess sternly.

"Why, so I did!"

"Ay, but not rough enough."

"As roughly as my modesty would let me," protested Adriana with dignity; and her sister nodded by her side.

"Haply, in private?" suggested the Abbess.

"And in assemblies too!" cried Adriana eagerly. "In bed he slept not for my urging it; at board he fed not for my urging it. Alone, it was the subject of my theme; in company I often glanced at it; still did I tell him it was vile and bad."

The Abbess held up her hand. "And therefore came it," said she, with a look that chilled Adriana to the heart, "that the man was mad. The venom clamours of a jealous woman poisons more deadly than a mad dog's tooth. Thy jealous fits have scared thy husband from the use of wits."

"She never reprehended him but mildly!" cried Luciana, quick to her sister's defence. "Why bear you these rebukes," she muttered, pushing the humbled Adriana forward, "and answer not?"

But Adriana knew she had defended herself only to her own defeat. "I will attend my husband," she promised, with tears in her eyes, "be his nurse, diet his sickness, for it is my office . . . let me have him home with me."

The stately Abbess shook her head. She herself would minister to the sick man's needs.

"I will not hence and leave my husband here!" wept Adriana. "And ill it doth beseem your holiness to separate the husband and the wife!"

"Be quiet, and depart. Thou shalt not have him," pronounced the Abbess, and vanished within the priory.

"Complain unto the Duke of this indignity!" cried Luciana, outraged by the high-handed behaviour of the holy dame. Adriana nodded and turned to go; when, with a loud and solemn roar, the priory bell began to toll. The sun was setting, and it was five o'clock.

The crowd grew still; and a chill fell upon the air. To the sound of muffled drumbeats, a dreadful procession had come slowly into view. At its head, all in black, walked the Duke, followed by his officers and guards. Then came the old gentleman of Syracuse, still in chains, and close behind, the hooded executioner, whose shouldered axe shone blood-red in the setting sun. The tragic old man had found no friend in Ephesus, and the time for his death had come.

"Yet once again proclaim it publicly," loudly announced the Duke as the procession drew near the abbey. "If any friend will pay the sum for him, he shall not die!"

No friend came forward and the procession was moving on. "Kneel to the Duke!" whispered Luciana, and, with a sisterly push, sent Adriana stumbling into the royal path.

"Justice, most sacred Duke," cried Adriana, as the Duke looked sternly down, "against the Abbess!"

"She is a virtuous and a reverend lady," said the Duke with a frown. "It cannot be that she hath done thee wrong."

Oh yes she had! Adriana nodded vigorously; and all her pent-up anger, grief and bewilderment burst out in a flood! Without pausing for breath, she told the Duke the wild history of Antipholus's madness: how he and his man (as mad as he!) had rushed into houses, snatching away rings and jewels; how they'd broken loose from restraint; how they'd threatened citizens with drawn swords; and how, at last, they'd fled into the priory—"and here," she concluded tearfully, "the Abbess shuts the gates on us, and will not suffer us to fetch him out!"

The Duke hesitated. Adriana reminded him that Antipholus had served him well, and that he himself had promoted their marriage.

"Go," said the Duke to his attendants, "some of you knock at the abbey gate and bid the Lady Abbess come to me."

But before they could stir, there was an interruption. A servant from Adriana's house came running, wild-eyed! "O mistress, mistress, shift and save yourself!" he panted. "My master and his man are both broke loose, beaten the maids a-row, and bound the Doctor, whose beard they have singed off with brands of fire!"

"Peace, fool, thy master and his man are here!" cried Adriana angrily, and pointed to the priory.

But the servant was not to be denied: "Mistress, upon my life I tell you true! He cries for you, and vows, if he can take you, to scorch your face and to disfigure you!" Suddenly, there came a sound of shouting, a roaring as of lions or bulls! "Hark, hark, I hear him, mistress! Fly, be gone!" and there burst upon the scene, wild and disordered, furious and amazed, Antipholus and Dromio!

"Ay me!" shrieked Adriana, thinking she was going mad, "It is my husband! Witness you that he is borne about invisible! Even now we housed him in the abbey here, and now he's there, past thought of human reason!"

Antipholus, disregarding the terror his appearance had caused, turned to the Duke. "Justice, most gracious Duke, O grant me justice," he cried, "against that woman there!" and pointed a furious sooty finger at the near-fainting authoress of all his misfortunes: his wife! In a voice that shook with anger, he told the Duke of all the outrageous disasters and fearful indignities that had befallen him that day, until he came to the last of all, of which he could scarcely speak. "My wife, her sister and a rabble more of vile confederates," he sobbed, "brought one Pinch, a hungry, lean-faced villain, a mere anatomy, a mountebank, a threadbare juggler, and a fortune-teller, a needy, hollow-eyed, sharp-looking wretch, a living dead man! Then all together they fell upon me, bound me, bore me thence, and in a dark and dankish vault at home there left me and my man—"

He could utter no more. He stood, with outstretched arms before the Duke, a suppliant for justice, a man much wronged.

The goldsmith began to speak, then the merchant, then the hostess of the Porpentine, then all together—of dinners and locked doors, of rings and chains and swords, until the Duke's head began to spin. "Go call the Abbess!" he cried, raising his hand for silence. "I think you are all stark mad!"

"Most mighty Duke!" Suddenly another voice was heard, a voice that had last been heard in the market-place, telling a strange and tragic tale of wandering and loss. It was the old man from Syracuse. His eyes were shining brightly with tears of relief and joy! "I see a friend who will save my life!"

"Speak freely, Syracusian," said the Duke, encouragingly.

The old man shuffled forward until he stood before Antipholus and Dromio.

"I am sure you both of you remember me," he said, and held out his shackled arms in welcome to his son!

Antipholus retreated hastily. "I never saw you in my life till now," he said. He was the other one.

The old man faltered. "O grief hath changed me since you saw me last. Dost thou not know my voice?" he pleaded, stumbling forward another step, and peering with anxious, screwed-up eyes. "I cannot err. Tell me thou art my son Antipholus!"

"I never saw my father in my life," said Antipholus, forgetful of that sea-drenched figure shouting and waving, as the broken mast he was lashed to, drifted away for ever.

Sadly the Duke shook his head. It was plain that grief and age had robbed the old man of his wits.

"Most mighty Duke, behold a man much wronged!"

In the doorway of the priory stood the Lady Abbess; and beside her, another Antipholus and Dromio!

There was silence; and then it seemed that all Ephesus breathed "*Ah!*" as the cause of the day's distractions was revealed!

The two Antipholuses stared at one another; likewise the Dromios. It was as if the vision that each beheld in his morning mirror had stepped from the glass and come to life!

"I see two husbands," whispered Adriana, "or mine eyes deceive me!"

"Which is the natural man," wondered the Duke, "and which the spirit?"

Then Antipholus of Syracuse, recognizing his father, rushed to embrace him; and the old man wept happy tears. The day that had begun in sorrow and darkness, was ending in brightness and joy. He was saved—

But there was a still greater wonder to come. While all had been exclaiming and wondering over the doubled pair, the Lady Abbess had been silent. She had eyes only for the old gentleman of Syracuse. At last, she spoke: "Speak, old Egeon, if thou be'st the man that hadst a wife once called Emilia, that bore thee at a burden two fair sons. O, if thou be'st the same Egeon, speak, and speak unto the same Emilia!"

"If I dream not," whispered Egeon, for that indeed was his name, "thou art Emilia!" and he gazed in wonderment at his restored wife! "If thou art she, tell me, where is that son that floated with thee on the fatal raft?"

She sighed; and, between the tender embracings of husband, wife and sons, she told of how she and the babes had been cruelly parted, and how she had come to Ephesus, where, dwelling in holy seclusion, she had never seen them again until this very day.

At last, the sea-storm that had parted them so long ago, had blown itself out in a tempest of madness, and washed them all together again.

"Which of you two did dine with me today?" asked Adriana, uneasily, of her two husbands.

"I, gentle mistress," answered one.

"And are you not my husband?"

He shook his head. He had been the wrong Antipholus in the right one's place. He turned to Luciana, and renewed his declaration of love; and she, with a glance at her sister, smiled and held out her hand. Now she would have a husband as handsome as Adriana's.

"This is the chain, sir, which you had of me," said the goldsmith, pointing to one of the Antipholuses.

"And you, sir," said the other, "for this chain arrested me." He had been the right Antipholus, in the wrong one's place.

So at last all debts were paid and all property restored. The Duke, much moved, released Egeon from his ransom and chains. At the Lady Abbess's invitation, the rejoicing company went into the priory to partake of a feast. But two remained behind. The brothers Dromio.

Said one: "There is a fat friend at your master's house that kitchened me for you today at dinner. She now shall be my sister, not my wife."

Said the other: "Methinks you are my glass, and not my brother. I see by you I am a sweet-faced youth. Will you walk in to see their gossiping?" He offered the way. His brother held back.

"Not I, sir. You are my elder."

"That's a question. How shall we try it?"

They scratched their heads and grinned.

"We'll draw cuts for the senior," said one. "Till then, lead thou first."

"Nay," said the other. "We came into the world like brother and brother, and now let's go hand in hand, not one before the other."

And in they went.

The Winter's Tale

King Leontes of Sicilia was angry. A time of happiness was at an end. Polixenes, the friend of his boyhood, was leaving him. For nine carefree months Polixenes had been his guest, and it had seemed that time had stepped backward and he had lived again amid the golden recollections of childhood. But now it was over. Polixenes was resolved to return to his faraway kingdom of Bohemia, and not all Leontes' pleadings could make him change his mind.

"One seve'night longer!" Leontes begged; but Polixenes shook his head, so Leontes, in despair, turned to Hermione, his queen, and demanded that she should try where he had failed. "Speak you!" he urged; and, leaving his wife to persuade his friend, he retreated, with quick, impatient steps, to the far end of the hall where his little son, Mamillius, was playing by the fire with ladies from the court.

Anxiously he watched as his wife, bulky with her unborn child, conversed with his handsome friend. They were smiling and laughing. All seemed to be going well. Plainly Polixenes was quite captivated by the beautiful Hermione. Already Polixenes was nodding . . .

Eagerly Leontes walked back. Hermione was saying, "If you first sinned with us," when she looked up and saw her husband approach.

"Is he won yet?" Leontes demanded.

Hermione smiled triumphantly. "He'll stay, my lord."

255

Leontes turned to Polixenes, who bowed gallantly to the lady who had conquered his resolve. Leontes frowned. "At my request he would not," he muttered; then he recollected himself and, after paying tribute to his wife's success, he returned to his little son and the fire.

He looked back. Hermione had linked her arm with Polixenes. Leontes bit his lip. "Too hot, too hot!" he whispered; and little Mamillius, hearing him, tried to tug him away from the fire. His wife and friend were approaching. Their heads were almost kissing-close together. "To mingle friendship far is mingling bloods!" There was a painful leaping in his breast. "I have *tremor cordis* on me; my heart dances, but not for joy—not joy."

Hermione and Polixenes were smiling at him. He looked down to his son. "What! hast smutched thy nose?" he exclaimed. There was a speck of soot on his son's face, like a badge of dishonour. "Come, captain, we must be neat—" He tried to repair the damage, but only made it worse—

"Are you moved, my lord?"

Hermione was speaking to him. Both she and Polixenes were looking concerned. At once he realized that his face was betraying his inmost thoughts. Leontes struggled to smile, and was surprised by how calm his voice sounded as he bade Hermione entertain his friend, while he remained with his son.

"If you would seek us, we're yours i' the garden," said she, leading Polixenes away. "You'll be found," murmured Leontes, "be you beneath the sky," and he watched them go.

Mamillius was staring at him. "Go play, boy, play," he urged; and then began to mutter, "Thy mother plays, and I play too—but so disgraced a part . . . Many a man . . . holds his wife by th'arm, that little thinks she has been sluiced in's absence, and his pond fished by his next neighbour, by Sir Smile, his neighbour . . ."

A dark suspicion had entered his head; and once there, everything he saw, everything he heard, had conspired to feed it. Now it was no longer a suspicion; it was a hideous certainty! His friend was his wife's lover, and the father of the child she was carrying!

"How now, boy!" Mamillius was still staring at him. The boy looked almost frightened. "Go play, Mamillius!" he bade him, and, with an

Their heads were almost kissing-close

impatient wave of his hand, despatched the boy and his attendants from the room.

One man remained. It was old Camillo, his shrewd councillor. Leontes beckoned him close. "Ha' you not seen," he asked him quietly, "my wife is slippery?"

Camillo stared at his master in amazement. Then amazement turned to indignation and, to Leontes' fury, his servant dared to reproach him for so foully slandering the Queen! "Good my lord, be cured of this diseased opinion, for 'tis most dangerous!" the fellow begged.

"You lie, you lie!" shouted the King. He seized Camillo by the chain of office he wore round his neck. He twisted it like a halter and, half strangling the man, forced him to admit the justice of the suspicion that Polixenes was the Queen's lover.

"I must believe you sir!" cried the old man, helplessly, and Leontes released him.

Trembling, Camillo stood before his master. "Might'st bespice a cup, to give mine enemy a lasting wink?" Leontes asked him. The old councillor grew pale as he understood what was asked of him: that he should murder Polixenes with poison, "Do't, and thou hast the one half of my heart," continued Leontes softly; "do't not, thou splitt'st thine own."

"I'll do't, my lord," said Camillo. Leontes nodded, and left him.

Never was a man more frightened and more wretched than Camillo. He was bound, by solemn oaths of loyalty, to a king who had been struck down by madness! Either he must obey his master and become a murderer, or break his oath and lose his life.

He shook his head. Better to break his oath and lose all than to obey a wicked command. He would warn Polixenes and, that very night, they would fly from dangerous Sicilia!

The Queen was in her parlour with her ladies and her little son. "Take the boy to you!" she begged, for the boy was as restless as the fire that burned fitfully in the hearth. "He so troubles me, 'tis past enduring!"

"Come, my gracious lord!" offered one fair pearly lady, holding out her velvet arms. "Shall I be your playfellow?"

"No!" cried Mamillius, shaking his head till his bright curls flew.

"You'll kiss me hard and speak to me as if I was a baby still! I love you better," he declared, turning to another; but before he could plague her, his mother took pity on her women and called her son back to her side.

"Sit by us," she commanded, "and tell's a tale."

Mamillius frowned. "Merry or sad, shall't be?"

"As merry as you will," said his mother with a smile.

The child thought deeply. "A sad tale's best for winter," he decided. "I have one of sprites and goblins."

His mother looked properly alarmed. "Come on, sit down," she pleaded, "and do your best to fright me with your sprites; you're powerful at it!"

Mamillius settled himself down beside his mother, and, with a scornful look at the laughing ladies, began his tale in a fearful, horrible, ghostly whisper: "There was a man dwelt by a churchyard—"

But what became of that man who dwelt by the churchyard was never to be told. The door burst open and the King, followed by his lords and armed guards, entered the room! His eyes blazed with anger, and the veins in his temples were swollen and seemed to writhe like serpents.

Leontes had discovered a plot against his life! He knew it as soon as he'd heard that Polixenes and Camillo had fled from Sicilia. Their flight confirmed their guilt. Together with his faithless Queen they had conspired to kill him! But now his thoughts were for Mamillius, his true-born son. The child must be taken away from its unclean mother!

He stared at the child who was crouching beside the adulteress. "Bear the boy hence!" he commanded harshly; and when the frightened child had been dragged from the arms of the amazed Queen, Leontes turned to his followers. "You, my lords," he cried, "look on her, mark her well!" and, pointing a trembling finger at his wife, hurled her vile treachery into her white face. "Away with her to prison!" he shouted.

Hermione bore all with quiet dignity. She bowed her head and, praying that her husband's sickness—for surely a sickness it must be!— would pass as suddenly as it had struck, she begged leave to take her women with her, for the birth of her child was near. "Adieu, my lord," she bade him sadly, as she was led away. "I never wished to see you sorry; now I trust I shall."

No sooner had the adulteress, her belly all swollen with her guilty brat, departed, than his lords dared to plead with Leontes to think again.

"Be certain what you do, sir," warned Antigonus, a man old enough to know better.

Leontes stared at him contemptuously. "Cease, no more," he commanded. "You smell this business with a sense as cold as is a dead man's nose!"

They were fools, all of them, to be so blind to the Queen's guilt; but he, the King, had foreseen their tender feelings for the Queen. He had taken steps to allay all doubts. He had sent messengers to the temple of Apollo to question the sacred Oracle, so that the god himself might confirm the treachery of Polixenes and Camillo and the guilt of the Queen. "Have I done well?" he demanded, when he had revealed what he had done. The courtiers sighed, and nodded.

"Nor night, nor day, no rest!" The King was in his bedchamber, pacing to and fro. Since he had discovered his wife's crime, he had not slept. The fierceness in his brain would give him no relief. Polixenes and Camillo were beyond his vengeance, but the Queen was not. She must be tried, condemned and put to death by burning; then he would have peace.

"My lord!" a servant had entered. He had come from the bedside of little Mamillius. The boy had fallen sick. His mother's disgrace had brought it on.

"How does the boy?"

"He took good rest tonight," the servant answered. Leontes dismissed him, and resumed his troubled pacing.

Suddenly there was a commotion outside the room. He heard Antigonus' quavering voice cry out: "You must not enter!" A moment later the door was thrust open and into the room stumbled Antigonus, vainly trying to hold back a rushing lady, whose gown flowed and billowed like an angry sea. It was his wife, Paulina, and he might as well have tried to stop the weather. Several lords followed cautiously in her wake.

"Away with that audacious lady!" commanded the King, retreating as Paulina advanced towards him with an embroidered bundle clutched in her arms. "Antigonus, I charged thee that she should not come about me. I knew she would!"

"I told her so, my lord," protested the feeble husband.

"What! can'st not rule her? Force her hence!"

"Let him that makes but trifles of his eyes first hand me!" warned the lady, raising a threatening hand; and not a man dared encounter her.

Suddenly Paulina knelt before the King. "The good Queen (for she is good) hath brought you forth a daughter," she told him; "here 'tis; commends it to your blessing." And she laid the bundle at Leontes' feet.

He looked down and saw that the bundle contained a creased and crumpled infant, foul as dirty washing. "This brat is none of mine," he swore, and turned away with a shudder. "It is the issue of Polixenes. Hence with it, and together with the dam commit them to the fire!"

"It is yours!" cried Paulina; "and so like you, 'tis the worse!"

He tried to silence her, but she would not be silenced, and set about abusing him as no subject should have dared, while Antigonus, her pitiful husband, stood by and did nothing to control his outrageous wife. "Thou art worthy to be hanged that will not stay her tongue!" Leontes raged at him; to which the wretch replied, "Hang all the husbands that cannot do that feat, you'll leave yourself hardly one subject!"

"Once more," cried Leontes, "take her hence!"

"A most unworthy and unnatural lord—" accused Paulina.

"I'll ha' thee burnt!" shouted the King.

"I care not!" she shouted back. "It is an heretic that makes the fire, not she which burns in't!"

"Away with her!" screamed the King; and at last his lords made a move to obey him.

"I pray you, do not push me," said Paulina with dignity, as nervous hands sought to escort her. "I'll be gone. Look to your babe, my lord," she called back defiantly, "'tis yours!" Then she was gone.

The babe was crying. Leontes could not endure the noise. "Take it hence," he commanded, "and see it instantly consumed with fire!" He looked at Antigonus. "Even thou and none but thou!" The fellow grew pale. He was trembling. "Go, take it to the fire, for thou sett'st on thy wife!"

"I did not, sir!" wailed Antigonus, and appealed to his companions to confirm his innocence.

They all supported him, fools and liars that they were; and then, with one accord, they knelt and begged Leontes to recall his terrible command. He stared at them, and then at the crying babe. "What will you adventure to save this brat's life?" he asked Antigonus.

"Anything, my lord!"

"Mark and perform it: seest thou? for the fail of any point in't shall not only be death to thyself but to thy lewd-tongued wife." Antigonus nodded eagerly; and the King went on: "We enjoin thee, that thou carry this female bastard hence; and that thou bear it to some remote and desert place, quite out of our dominions; and that there thou leave it, without more mercy, to its own protection. Take it up!"

Leontes breathed deeply as Antigonus gathered up the howling brat and bore it away. "No!" he muttered. "I'll not raise another's issue!" Even as he said it, the gods themselves seemed to approve his action. A servant came in, all smiles. The messengers who had been sent to the temple of Apollo had returned. They were on their way to the palace with the words of the sacred Oracle. "Prepare you, lords!" cried Leontes triumphantly. "Summon a session, that we may arraign our most disloyal lady!" Very soon now, all the world would hear that Apollo himself had justified the King!

The court was in session, and all the lords of Sicilia had crowded into the courtroom in a vast murmuring throng. The King sat in the place of Justice and behind him, like solemn black volumes on a shelf, sat the judges who were to try the Queen. Leontes spoke.

"Produce the prisoner."

The murmuring ceased. All heads turned, like a field of corn in a wind. It was not every day that a queen came to her trial. There was a great sigh as she entered, very upright, with her head held high; but before the day was out, that proud, insolent head would be bowed in shame!

Leontes waited until she stood before him, attended by the noisy hag Paulina, and her foolish weeping women; then he spoke again:

"Read the indictment."

The clerk of the court stood up and, reading from his scroll, uttered the solemn words: "Hermione, Queen to the worthy Leontes, King of Sicilia, thou art here accused and arraigned of high treason, in committing adultery with Polixenes, King of Bohemia, and conspiring with Camillo to take away the life of our sovereign lord, the King . . ."

There was a moment's silence, then the prisoner answered the charge. She spoke loud and clear, and denied everything. Her shamelessness knew no bounds; and Leontes, to his mounting anger, could see that her dignified bearing was gaining the sympathy of all. But not for long! Furiously he accused her again.

"Sir," she answered, gazing almost sadly straight at him, "you speak a language I understand not. My life stands in the level of your dreams, which I'll lay down."

"Your actions are my dreams! You had a bastard by Polixenes. Look for no less than death!"

"Sir," said she, unmoved, "spare your threats: the bug which you would fright me with, I seek." She looked up to the judges. "Your honours all, I do refer me to the Oracle: Apollo be my judge!"

The judges nodded and straightway the two messengers who had returned from the sacred temple of Apollo, entered the court. Anxiously Leontes searched their faces for any sign that would betray that they knew the contents of the sealed scroll they carried. There was none.

Solemnly the clerk of the court required them to swear, upon the sword of Justice, that they had received the scroll from the hands of the high priest of the temple and that the seals had not been broken.

"All this we swear," said they, laying their hands upon the sword.

Leontes breathed deeply. "Break up the seals, and read."

The fellow's thick fingers began to fumble with the seals. Crack! Crack! Crack! He broke them, one by one. He began to unroll the scroll. The Queen was watching him. Her face was calm. But her women were looking fearful. And Paulina's eyes were enormous!

The scroll was open. The fellow was staring at it. His lips were moving, but no words came. Then the words came, it seemed in a shout:

"HERMIONE IS CHASTE; POLIXENES BLAMELESS; CAMILLO A TRUE SUBJECT; LEONTES A JEALOUS TYRANT: HIS INNOCENT BABE TRULY BEGOTTEN: AND THE KING SHALL LIVE WITHOUT AN HEIR IF THAT WHICH IS LOST BE NOT FOUND."

The fellow was smiling. He heard voices crying out: "Blessed be the great Apollo!" Everyone was smiling, laughing. Her women were looking joyful—

"Hast thou read the truth?"

"Ay, my lord," said the fellow, and offered him the scroll; "even so as it is here set down."

He took it, glanced at it; but his hand was trembling too violently for him to read. He could see Paulina staring at him triumphantly. He did not look at the Queen. "There is no truth at all i' the Oracle," he said, "the sessions shall proceed." Carefully, he tore the sacred scroll into fragments and flung them down. "This is mere falsehood."

Even as he uttered the words, there came a violent clap of thunder!

"My lord the King! the King!"

A servant from the palace had come rushing into the court. His looks were desperate—

"What is the business?"

"O sir, the Prince, your son, is gone!"

"How! gone?"

"Is dead."

There was a roaring in his ears. The courtroom seemed to sway and topple. He heard a loud cry of grief and dismay. It was a howl, such as a stricken animal might have uttered. Yet it was his own voice.

He had blasphemed against the god, and his punishment had been swift and terrible!

"Look down and see what death is doing!"

Paulina was shouting at him, frantically. Hermione had fallen to the ground. The death of her son had struck her down. Her women were kneeling by her. She did not move.

"Take her hence!" Leontes pleaded desperately. "She will recover . . ."

They carried her away; and Leontes stared after her, half blind with misery. There was a stillness inside his head, like a house that had been blasted by storm and all its furnishings in ruins. Over and over again, he swore he'd undo all the wickedness his madness had brought about.

Paulina returned: her face was white, her eyes were pools of tears. Hermione was dead! Wildly she cursed him for his savage tyranny.

"Go on, go on," he groaned; "thou canst not speak too much; I have deserved all tongues to talk their bitterest!"

At last she took pity on him; but he could not take pity on himself. His madness had cost the lives of his wife and son, and the loss of his infant daughter. "Prithee," he begged Paulina, "bring me to the dead bodies of my queen and son. Once a day I'll visit the chapel where they lie, and tears shed there shall be my recreation. Come, and lead me to these sorrows."

Then, leaning on Paulina's comforting arm, he left the court. When he had gone, the clerk of the court carefully gathered up the fragments of the torn-up sacred scroll. He found HERMIONE IS—and searched for CHASTE, which he found, much trampled upon. Then a larger piece caught his eye. THE KING SHALL LIVE WITHOUT

AN HEIR IF THAT WHICH IS LOST BE NOT FOUND.
He sighed and shook his head.

Far, far away, on the wild sea-coast of Bohemia, under a dreadful sky, two figures staggered ashore from a vessel that heaved at anchor nearby. One was a sailor, bearing a chest; the other was Antigonus. He had kept his oath of obedience to his king, even though the command had been harsh and unnatural. Under his cloak he bore Hermione's babe. Reaching the shelter of some rocks, Antigonus and his companion huddled down together. "Go, get aboard," Antigonus bade the man. "I'll not be long . . ." The sailor nodded and, warning Antigonus of the worsening weather, and of the wild beasts that roamed thereabouts, he stumbled back to the vessel.

Antigonus watched him out of sight; then, opening his cloak, he laid the sleeping babe tenderly beside the chest. "Blossom, speed thee well,"

he whispered, and made a little pillow for it, of a bundle of clothing to which was fastened a jewel of its mother's, and its name, by which it had come most strangely.

Antigonus had dreamed that the ghost of Hermione had visited him on board the ship and, weeping, had begged him bear her child to Bohemia. "And for the babe is counted lost for ever," the poor ghost had wailed, "Perdita, I prithee call't . . ." So 'Perdita' it was.

He looked up. The sky was black, and sharp lightnings had begun to race across it. The storm was almost upon them. Hastily he wrapped up the child as best he could; then, bidding it a last farewell, he rose to go.

But something was waiting for him. A huge darkness. A sudden glare lit up the sky and land, and Antigonus shrieked in terror! Rearing above him, with savage claws outstretched, was a monstrous bear! "I am gone for ever!" he howled as he fled away with the bear pursuing him. Then the storm, or the bear, or both together, swallowed him up.

The infant Perdita was not the only lost one on the wild sea-coast of Bohemia that day. Two sheep, frightened by huntsmen, had strayed away, and their shepherd was searching and calling, and cursing the young fools who had cost him so dear. "I would there were no age between ten and three-and-twenty, or that youth would sleep out the rest," he grumbled as he trudged along. "Would any but these boiled brains, hunt this weather?"

He came to some rocks. He peered among them. He saw a chest; he saw a bundle. Inquisitively he poked it with his crook. A tiny wail broke forth. He grunted in surprise. He knelt down; he opened the bundle. "Mercy on's!" he cried aloud, "a bairn, a very pretty bairn!" and he gave the infant his little finger to suck, to stop its noise.

He scratched his head; then, noting the fineness of the cloth in which the babe was wrapped, he nodded knowingly. "I can read waiting gentlewoman in the scape," he murmured. "They were warmer that got this than the poor thing is here." Gently he lifted the babe and sheltered it under his cloak. Then he called out for his son, who was still searching for their sheep.

Quickly the boy came. He was all wet and wild with amazement. He had just seen two fearful sights. At sea, he had seen a ship being swallowed up by the waves, and on land he had seen a gentleman being swallowed up by a bear!

"Name of mercy, when was this, boy?"

"Now, now!" cried the son. "The men are not yet cold under water, nor the bear half dined on the gentleman: he's at it now!" and he told his father how the bear's dinner had cried out that his name was Antigonus and that he was a nobleman.

"Heavy matters! heavy matters!" sighed the shepherd. "But look thee here, boy!" He opened his cloak. "Now bless thyself! Thou met'st with things dying, I with things new-born!"

The father and son stared at one another; then the shepherd remembered that it had once been prophesied that the fairies would make him rich. He nodded towards the chest. "Open't!" he breathed. The boy hesitated; then, very cautiously, he lifted the lid. "What's within, boy?" The boy looked up. His face was a moon of wonderment. "You're a made old man!" he whispered. "Gold, all gold!"

"This is fairy gold," declared the shepherd solemnly; and, while his son went off to bury whatever the bear had left of the gentleman, he set about carrying his wonderful gifts back to his cottage, leaving his lost sheep to find for themselves. "'Tis a lucky day, boy," he puffed, dividing his labours between the fairy gold and the fairy babe, "and we'll do good deeds on't!"

All this was in a wintertime, long, long ago; but now it was a summer's day in Bohemia, and two elderly gentlemen were talking together in the royal palace. They had been friends for sixteen years; and though their backs were not as straight as they once had been, nor their beards as crisp and black, a kindly eye would still have known them for Camillo and King Polixenes.

Their talk was of Prince Florizel, Polixenes' son, who had been absent from the court for many days. It was rumoured that he spent his time at the house of a humble shepherd who, sixteen years before, had become mysteriously rich. But it was not the shepherd's gold that drew the Prince: the old man had another treasure, richer by far. He had a daughter, the fame of whose beauty had spread far beyond the humble cottage where she dwelt.

Polixenes was troubled. Both as a father and a king, he must go and see for himself how matters stood between his son and the lowly maid. He begged Camillo to accompany him. Camillo sighed. He longed to return to Sicilia and to his old master, who, from all accounts, had become a most gentle and saintly king. But he could not refuse his friend. "My best Camillo!" cried Polixenes gratefully. "We must disguise ourselves!"

There was a song in the air. Along the lane it floated, like a melodious breeze:

> "When the daffodils begin to peer,
> With a heigh, the doxy over the dale—"

The singer was a merry fellow, with a skip in his step and a roving twinkle in his eye. His clothes were ragged and poor, but he wore them with an air; indeed, in places, he seemed to be wearing more air than clothes. He had once been a courtier who had fallen, like a rotten apple, on hard times. But he had bounced. A man must live, so he had become, as he modestly put it, "a snapper-up of unconsidered trifles." His name, like the famous thief of old, was Autolycus . . .

Suddenly his song died on his lips. Hastily he skipped out of the lane and crouched down in the ditch. His eyes were sharp as pins: someone was coming—

The shepherd's son marched along on his way to market. Sixteen years had filled out every part of him, except for his head. He had been a little fool; now he was a big one. "Three pound of sugar; five pound of currants," he chanted, his nose in a list of good things his sister had given him to bring back for their sheep-shearing feast; "rice—what will this sister of mine do with rice?"

But before he could unravel this mystery, an extraordinary thing happened. A poor ragged wretch rose up from the ditch and, staggering, fell at his feet! "O that ever I was born!" groaned the wretch. "O! help me, help me!" and, beating the ground with despairing hands,

poured out a tale of such cruel beatings and heartless robbery that the shepherd's son was overcome with pity.

"Alack, poor soul!" he cried; "lend me thy hand; I'll help thee!" and, bending down, he offered a sturdy arm.

"Softly, good sir," moaned the poor soul, "I fear, sir, my shoulder-blade is out."

"Canst stand?" tenderly inquired the shepherd's son, and tried to help him to his feet.

"Softly, dear sir," murmured Autolycus, and, with quick, darting fingers, emptied his helper's pocket. "You ha' done me a charitable office."

"Dost lack any money?"

"No, good sweet sir!" protested Autolycus, quickly preventing the fool's hand from discovering his loss. "Offer me no money, I pray you! That kills my heart!" and he explained that he had a kinsman nearby who would gladly supply all his needs.

"Then fare thee well," said the shepherd's son, "I must go buy spices for our sheep-shearing," and off he went.

Autolycus watched him go. "I'll be with you at your sheep-shearing too!" he murmured, and his nimble fingers itched at the prospect of fleecing all the shearers.

★

269

The old shepherd stood at the gate of his cottage and contemplated, with beaming satisfaction, the holiday throng of lads and lasses who had come to his sheep-shearing feast to enjoy themselves. Time had dealt kindly with him, and prosperity had lent his weathered countenance an air of happy importance, which increased as he watched Perdita, the daughter he had come by so strangely, long ago. Every day she grew in grace and beauty, and now she stood, Queen of the Feast, and outshining the summer's day!

But she was neglecting her duty. Two new guests, old gentlemen with long white beards and hats pulled down to shelter their eyes, had arrived and were standing by. Where was the Queen of the Feast to bid them welcome and give them herbs and flowers? As always, she was with Doricles, the lad who seemed to have set up home in their cottage and in the lass's heart.

"Fie, daughter," reproached the old shepherd, beckoning her to his side, "when my old wife lived, upon this day, she was both pantler, butler, cook, both dame and servant; welcomed all, served all. You are retired, as if you were a feasted one and not the hostess of the meeting. Come on, and bid us welcome to your sheep-shearing!"

She blushed, and curtsied to the strangers. "Reverend sirs," she said, giving them posies from her basket, "for you, there's rosemary and rue; these keep seeming and savour all the winter long: grace and remembrance be to you both, and welcome to our shearing!"

"Shepherdess," said one, a trifle sadly, "well you fit our ages with flowers of winter."

At once she made amends: "Here's flowers for you!" she cried, ransacking her basket. "Hot lavender, mints, savory, marjoram, the marigold that goes to bed wi' the sun, and with him rises weeping: these are flowers of middle summer, and I think they are given to men of middle age! Y'are very welcome!" Then, with another curtsey, off she went, hand in hand with her lad, to join in the dancing that had just begun.

The strangers gazed after her. "This is the prettiest low-born lass that ever ran on the greensward!" murmured the taller of the pair, admiringly; and the other agreed. "Good sooth, she is the queen of curds and cream!" and the old shepherd's heart swelled with pleasure and pride in the lass the fairies had brought him.

"Pray, good shepherd," asked the tall one, "what fair swain is this which dances with your daughter?"

"They call him Doricles," replied the shepherd, pleased to hear the lad praised, for he and Perdita made a handsome pair. "He says he loves my daughter; I think so too; and to be plain, I think there is not half a kiss to choose who loves another best!"

The tall one sighed, as if he wished he was young again, and continued to gaze at the dancers from under his low-brimmed hat.

Presently the dancing ended and a merry voice came swinging along:

"Will you buy any tape,
Or lace for your cape,
My dainty duck, my dear-a?"

A pedlar had come, a ragged fellow with a bright red beard and pin-bright eyes. He was hung all over with baskets and boxes, brimming over with everything a lass's heart could wish for.

"Any silk, any thread,
Any toys for your head,
Of the new'st and fin'st, fin'st wear-a?"

In a moment, all the lads and lasses were after him, all save Perdita and her Doricles. It was plain they saw more treasures in each other than in the pedlar's wares. Nonetheless, the strangers were surprised. "When I was young," said the tall one to Doricles, who was still flushed and breathless from dancing, "I was wont to load my she with knacks. I would have ransacked the pedlar's silken treasury, and have poured it to her acceptance; you have let him go."

"Old sir," answered the lad, with his arm round Perdita's waist, "I know she prizes not such trifles as these are. The gifts she looks from me are packed and locked up in my heart, which I have given already . . ."

"This shows a sound affection," observed the shorter of the strangers; and the old shepherd agreed. But love should not be all on one side.

"Say you the like to him?" he asked his daughter.

271

She looked up into her lad's eyes. "I cannot speak so well," she said gravely, "nothing so well; no, nor mean better; by th' pattern of mine own thoughts I cut out the purity of his."

"Take hands; a bargain!" cried the shepherd; "and, friends unknown, you shall be witness to't: I give my daughter to him, and will make her portion equal his!"

"O, that must be i' th' virtue of your daughter!" declared the lad, gallantly. "One being dead, I shall have more than you can dream of yet! But come on, contract us 'fore these witnesses!"

"Soft, swain, awhile, beseech you. Have you a father?" It was the tall stranger who spoke. His voice trembled.

"I have; but what of him?"

"Knows he of this?"

"He neither does, nor shall," said the lad, impatiently.

"Methinks a father," said the stranger, "is at the nuptial of his son a guest that best becomes the table. Let him know it."

"Let him, my son," urged the shepherd. "He shall not need to grieve at knowing of thy choice."

But the lad was determined that his father should know nothing of his betrothal. He took Perdita by the hand and together they knelt before the old shepherd. "Mark our contract!" he begged.

Then a terrible thing happened. The tall stranger shouted out, in a voice of thunder, "Mark your divorce, young sir!" He tore off his hat, and clawed away his false white beard. It was the King!

He was mad with rage; for he was the very father whose rights had just been so impudently denied! Doricles was not Doricles. He was Prince Florizel, the King's son! And worse! It was plain that Perdita had known all along! She had deceived her father, and ruined him!

Furiously, the King cursed the old shepherd and his daughter for daring to ensnare the Prince. Then, swearing he'd cast off his son for ever if he dared lay eyes on his low-born lass again, he stormed away, shouting for the Prince to follow.

To do the lad justice, he stayed by his lass; and to do the lass justice, she bore herself bravely. "I was not much afeared," she said, "for once or twice I was about to speak, and tell him plainly the self-same sun that shines upon his court, hides not his visage from our cottage, but

It was the King!

looks on alike. Will't please you, sir, be gone?" she begged the Prince. "I told you what would come of this. This dream of mine, being now awake, I'll queen it no inch farther, but milk my ewes and weep."

The old shepherd felt a hand upon his shoulder. The second stranger was trying to comfort him. But it was no use. Bitterly the father stared at his daughter. "O cursed wretch!" he groaned. "Thou knew'st this was the Prince. Undone, undone!" and he stumbled back to his cottage to mourn over the ruins of the day.

Camillo gazed sadly at the Prince and his shepherdess. The wildness of Polixenes' rage had brought to mind the madness that had struck down Leontes, long ago . . .

The young Prince was striding back and forth, swearing he'd give up his kingdom and all the treasures of the world rather than be parted from his shepherdess, and nothing Camillo could say would alter his resolve. He had a vessel prepared. He would sail away with his Perdita, to the ends of the earth, if need be.

Camillo sighed. "If you will not change your purpose," he said, "make for Sicilia." The Prince halted in his pacing and looked at the old councillor with interest. Much encouraged, Camillo went on: "Present yourself and your fair princess (for so I see she must be) 'fore Leontes." The Prince frowned. What reason should he give for his visit? He should say, advised Camillo, that he brought greetings from his father, Polixenes; for Camillo had heard that Leontes longed to be reconciled with his friend. "Methinks I see," Camillo murmured, "Leontes opening his free arms, and weeping his welcomes forth . . ."

To Camillo's relief, the lovers saw the good sense of his advice. Suddenly he became aware they were not alone. The red-bearded pedlar from the feast was standing by, and observing them with his pin-bright eyes. Camillo beckoned to him. The fellow approached. He was visibly shaking with fright, as if he had more on his conscience than he had on his back. "Fear not, man," said Camillo, kindly; "here's no harm intended to thee."

"I am a poor fellow, sir," protested the pedlar piteously; but when he was offered gold to exchange his rags for the young gentleman's fine clothes, his eyes glittered with greed. In moments, it was done:

the pedlar became the Prince, and the Prince became the pedlar.

Camillo smiled. Not even the Prince's father would have recognized his son. Bidding farewell to the translated pedlar, the three departed, the lovers to their ship, and Camillo to the court.

Once alone, Camillo breathed deeply. There was more to his plan than he'd revealed. He would tell the King of the lovers' flight. He and Polixenes would follow the pair to Sicilia; and there, Camillo devoutly hoped, with the help of Leontes, father would be reconciled with son, and friend with friend. And, what was more, he, Camillo, would be home again.

Autolycus, the pedlar, scratched his head. He'd overheard enough to discover that the Prince was meaning to run away with his shepherdess. He frowned, and wondered how best he might profit by his knowledge. As he stood outside the shepherd's cottage, wondering where his best interests lay, with the King or with the Prince, the cottage door opened and out came the old shepherd and his son. The son was carrying a chest, and the old man, a bundle.

"There is no other way but to tell the King she's a changeling, and none of your flesh and blood," the son was saying; and the old man was nodding. "I will tell the King all," he said, "every word, yea, and his son's pranks too! Let us to the King!" He tapped the bundle he was carrying and said, very knowingly, "There is that in this fardel will make him scratch his beard!"

Autolycus' heart beat fast. Here was something for the Prince! He pulled off his red beard and hastened after the old shepherd and his son.

"How now, rustics," he greeted them, "wither are you bound?"

"To th' palace, an it like your worship," answered the old shepherd, taking the stranger to be a great gentleman, by his courtly attire.

Sternly Autolycus demanded to know what was in the chest and the bundle.

"Sir," answered the shepherd, "there lies such secrets in this fardel and box which none must know but the King."

Autolycus shook his head. The King was not in his palace. He had gone aboard a new vessel in the harbour to take the sea air. However, as they seemed to be an honest pair, and he liked the look of them, he would conduct them to the ship and himself present them to the King.

The simple souls were delighted. They even offered him money for his pains! "Walk before toward the sea-side," he bade them; and there was a skip in his step as he shepherded the foolish shepherds away from the palace and towards the Prince. He had once served the Prince, and if the secrets proved of value, he might serve the Prince again!

There was a ghostly queen in the royal palace of Sicilia. She walked the shadowy passages, she stirred among the hangings on the walls. Sometimes she gazed out of mirrors; sometimes she fled into silvery nothingness, out of the corner of an eye. Leontes, bowed down with years and sorrows, saw his lost wife everywhere, and nowhere. Even after sixteen grieving years, she still haunted his waking hours and visited his dreams. Vainly his courtiers begged him to marry again and beget an heir; but always the Lady Paulina reminded him of the words

of Apollo: "The King shall live without an heir if that which is lost be not found."

"Will you swear," she demanded, "never to marry, but by my free leave?"

"My true Paulina," he promised, "we shall not marry till thou bid'st us."

"That shall be when your first queen's again in breath; never till then."

A servant entered. He had strange news. "One that gives out himself Prince Florizel, son of Polixenes, with his princess (she the fairest I have yet beheld)," he informed the King, "desires access to your high presence."

"His princess, you say, with him?" asked Leontes, surprised by the suddenness and lack of ceremony of the Prince's arrival.

"Ay; the most peerless piece of earth, I think, that e'er the sun shone bright on!"

"O Hermione!" cried Paulina, and indignantly rebuked the servant for daring to suggest that the newcomer was fairer than the lost Queen.

"Go," Leontes bade the servant. "Bring them to our embracement."

While they waited, Paulina took the opportunity to remind Leontes that he, too, might have had a son of just Florizel's age—"Prithee, no more," begged the King. "They are come!"

Leontes' eyes filled with tears. The Prince was the very image of the youth Polixenes had been, and the sight of him renewed all Leontes' grief for what he had lost. "Most dearly welcome!" he cried. "And your fair princess—goddess! Welcome hither, as is the spring to th' earth!" He shook his head, and wondered that Florizel should have exposed so rare and wondrous a princess to the dangers of the sea.

"Good my lord," explained Florizel, with a smile, "she came from Libya," and added that she was the daughter of the King of that land, whose royal father had shed many tears on parting with his treasure.

Leontes never doubted it; she had a truly royal air; but even as he held out his arms in love and greeting to the pair, a lord came in and approached with a grave and troubled air.

"Please you, great sir," said this gentleman, "Bohemia greets you from himself, by me; desires you to attach his son, who has (his dignity and duty both cast off) fled from his father, from his hopes, and with a shepherd's daughter!"

"Where's Bohemia? speak!'

Polixenes and Camillo were in Sicilia. The lord informed the astonished King. They had seized the humble father and brother of the shepherdess and were threatening the unlucky wretches with instant death—

"O my poor father!" cried the shepherdess. "The heaven sets spies upon us, will not have our contract celebrated!"

Her voice was sweet, but her accent was as rustic as the fields where she tended her sheep!

Leontes frowned. "Is this the daughter of a King?"

"She is, when once she is my wife!" cried Florizel defiantly; and Leontes had to turn away to hide a smile. The young Prince's wit and ardour were hard to resist. "That 'once', I see, by your good father's speed, will come on very slowly," he said, and reproached the young

man for disobeying his father.

But Florizel was unrepentant. He reminded Leontes of his own youth, and begged him plead their cause. "At your request," he assured the King, "my father will grant precious things as trifles!"

"Would he do so," smiled Leontes, "I'd beg your precious mistress, which he counts but a trifle!"

"Sir," murmured Paulina warningly, "your eye hath too much youth in't. Not a month before your Queen died, she was more worth such gazes than what you look on now."

Leontes shook his head. "I thought of her, even in these looks I made," he said sadly; then, bidding the lovers follow him, he set out to meet with Polixenes and plead their cause.

All the bells of Sicilia were ringing! The two Kings had met and something wonderful had happened! But what? "Beseech you, sir," begged Autolycus, plucking a hurrying courtier by the sleeve, "were you present at this relation?"

"Nothing but bonfires!" cried the courtier in high excitement. "The oracle is fulfilled; the King's daughter is found!"

Another gentleman of the court joined them, then another, and another, and they all fell to gossiping and chattering at once of the marvels they had seen. It was like an old tale! The shepherd had opened his bundle and there, for all the world to see, was the proof that the infant he'd found on the sea-shore was the lost princess! Everything was there: the mantle of Hermione and her jewel, and letters from Antigonus—

"What, pray you, became of Antigonus, that carried hence the child?" asked one. "Like an old tale still," came the reply: "he was torn to pieces with a bear!"

There was a moment's silence out of respect for the memory of old Antigonus, then it was back to the joyful scene. Then one remembered how the Princess had wept when she learned of her mother's death, and a sadness fell upon all as the memory of the lost Queen, like a faint, forgotten perfume, filled the air . . .

"Are they returned to the court?" inquired one of the gentlemen. No, he was told, they had all gone to see the newly-finished statue of

Queen Hermione that Lady Paulina had been keeping in a house some distance away. It was rumoured to be so exact a likeness that one might speak to it and expect an answer. "I thought she had some great matter there in hand," observed another gentleman, "for she hath privately, twice or thrice a day, ever since the death of Hermione, visited that removed house. Shall we thither?"

"Let's along," they all agreed, and hastened away, leaving Autolycus alone.

Gloomily he regarded his shadow, which was all hunched and dejected, like a crow at a feast that had been picked clean. If only the Prince and Princess hadn't been so wretchedly sea-sick for all the voyage and kept to their beds, the great discovery might have been made on board the ship, and he, Autolycus, might have got some benefit from it. But now he had nothing. He scowled. "Here come those I

have done good to against my will," he muttered, as the old shepherd and his son approached.

They had prospered horribly: the Kings had made them gentlemen. But Autolycus was never the man to hold another's good fortune against him. "I humbly beseech you, sir," he cried, flinging himself, for a second time, at the feet of the shepherd's son, "to pardon me all the faults I have committed to your worship, and to give me your good report to the Prince, my master!"

"Prithee, son, do," advised the old shepherd solemnly, "for we must be gentle, now we are gentlemen."

His son pondered. "Wilt thou amend thy life?" he demanded of the prostrated Autolycus.

"Ay, an it like your good worship!"

"Give me thy hand," said the son. "I will swear to the Prince thou art as honest a true fellow as any is in Bohemia."

He raised Autolycus to his feet; and then, as recollection stirred, he clapped his hand to his pocket to make sure all was well within it. He laughed. "Hark! the kings and the princes, our kindred, are going to see the Queen's picture. Come, follow us; we'll be thy good masters!" Then off they went, the two new-made gentlemen with their new-made man.

Paulina's house was filled with kings and lords and ladies. They had crowded in to behold the wonder that Paulina had been so long in preparing. Already they had seen much to admire, but nothing yet to marvel at. "O Paulina," murmured Leontes, "your gallery we have passed through, but we saw not that which my daughter came to look upon, the statue of her mother."

Gently Paulina answered him: "As she lived peerless, so her dead likeness, I do well believe, excels whatever yet you looked upon, or hand of man hath done; therefore I keep it lonely, apart."

She beckoned, and led her royal guests into a smaller room, that was furnished like a chapel. She approached a heavy velvet curtain, and stretched out her hand. For a moment she paused. She stared at Leontes in a manner that made his heart falter. "Here it is," she said. "Behold, and say 'tis well!" She drew back the curtain.

Leontes cried aloud, and tears filled his eyes. Raised upon a dais, in royal robes and royal in her gentle beauty, stood Hermione herself!

"I like your silence," said Paulina proudly, for the room was breathless before this marvel of the sculptor's art. "Comes it not something near?"

"Her natural posture," whispered Leontes; and his heart ached as he gazed at the semblance of his lost Queen. He sighed, and shook his head. Wonderful as the statue was, it was not quite the Hermione he remembered. "But yet, Paulina," he sighed, "Hermione was not so much wrinkled, nothing so aged as this seems."

"O, not by much!" protested Polixenes, gallantly; and Paulina

281

explained, "So much the more our carver's excellence, which lets go by some sixteen years and makes her as she lived now!"

But Perdita, who had never seen her mother in the bloom of her youth, was overcome with love and admiration. "Lady," she wept, kneeling before the statue, "dear Queen, that ended when I but began, give me that hand of yours to kiss!"

She reached up, but Paulina stopped her. "O patience! The statue is but newly fixed; the colour's not dry!"

She reached to close the curtain. "Let be, let be!" begged Leontes. He turned to Polixenes, "See, my lord, would you not deem it breathed? and that those veins did verily bear blood?"

"Masterly done!" nodded Polixenes.

"I'll draw the curtain," said Paulina anxiously; "my lord's almost so far transported, that he'll think anon it lives!"

"Let't alone!" Leontes pleaded. "Let no man mock me, for I will kiss her." He drew near and stood beside his daughter; and the statue, motionless, breathless, gazed down.

Then Paulina spoke. "Either forbear, quit presently the chapel, or resolve you for more amazement. If you can behold it, I'll make the statue move indeed, descend, and take you by the hand."

"What you can make her do," whispered Leontes, "I am content to look on."

Paulina nodded. "It is required you do awake your faith. Then all stand still," she commanded. "Music, awake her: strike!"

She clapped her hands and unseen musicians began a solemn music. She turned to the statue. "'Tis time; descend; be stone no more!"

The stone began to stir; her breast began to rise and fall. Slowly, slowly, Hermione descended from her dais, holding out her arms to her husband and her daughter.

"Nay, present your hand," Paulina urged the amazed and trembling Leontes. "When she was young, you woo'd her; now, in age, is she become the suitor?"

"O, she's warm!" wept Leontes, his arms about his marvellously restored wife. "If this be magic, let it be an art lawful as eating!" The long dark winter of his life was over, and it was spring again.

"If she pertain to life," wondered Camillo, "let her speak too!"

Paulina laughed at the doubter. "That she is living, were it but told you, should be hooted at like an old tale; but it appears she lives, though yet she speak not. Mark a little while." She turned to Perdita. "Please you to interpose, fair madam, kneel, and pray your mother's blessing. Turn, good lady," she bade the Queen, "our Perdita is found!"

At last Hermione spoke. "You gods, look down, and from your sacred vials pour your graces upon my daughter's head!"

It was ended; but how it all came about was yet to be told, by cradle and fireside, and wherever an ear was open to listen to the wonderful tale: how Paulina had kept Hermione hidden, and how Perdita had been found!

"Go together, you precious winners all!" cried Paulina, weeping half with joy, and half with a sadness that lingered in her heart. "I, an old turtle, will wing me to some withered bough, and there my mate (that's never to be found again) lament, till I am lost."

But Leontes had other thoughts. "Thou shouldst a husband take by my consent," he told her, "as I by thine a wife." There was one he knew who had long admired her, and, he believed, she had looked not unkindly on him. "Come, Camillo," he said, "and take her by the hand."

With a smile, Camillo obeyed his master, for this was a just command; and Paulina was not displeased. Then, as the lovers, old and young, left the chapel, Leontes reflected that there was justice in the match he had made: Antigonus had borne his child away, and Camillo had been the instrument of bringing her back.

Also by Leon Garfield and Michael Foreman
SHAKESPEARE STORIES

Twelfth Night
King Lear
The Tempest
The Merchant of Venice
The Taming of the Shrew
King Richard the Second
King Henry IV. Part One
Hamlet
Romeo and Juliet
Othello
A Midsummer Night's Dream
Macbeth